Ron Bouchard

Remembering the Kid from Fitchburg

Compiled and Edited by
BONES BOURCIER

COASTAL 181
PUBLISHER

CREDITS

Cover and Book Design: *Tammy Sneddon*

Photo Work: *Tammy Sneddon*

Editing: *Cary Stratton*

Front Cover: *Bouchard Family Collection*

Back Cover: #35, *Bouchard Family Collection*
#17, *Bouchard Family Collection*
#7, *Philip Hoyt Photo*
#47, *Herb Dodge Photo*

Every reasonable effort was made to locate and credit the original copyright holders and photographers of the photos included in this book. If your photo appears in this book and you are not properly credited, please contact the publisher.

ISBN 13: 978-0-9857735-8-8

For additional information or copies of this book, contact:
Coastal 181
29 Water Street
Newburyport, MA 01950 USA
(978) 462-2436, (877) 907-8181
www.coastal181.com

© Copyright 2016 by Coastal International Inc. All rights reserved.

No part of this book may be reproduced in any form, or by any means, without permission in writing from the copyright holder.

The author, publisher and copyright holder shall not be held liable for any incidental or consequential damages that might result from the content of this book.

First printing July 2016

Published by Coastal 181, Newburyport, MA, USA
www.coastal181.com

Printed in the United States of America

Table of Contents

Acknowledgements v
Foreword, *by Bones Bourcier* vii

PART ONE
The Kid from Fitchburg 1

Pete Salvatore 7
JoAnn Bouchard Bergeron 13
Dave Rossbach 19
Vic Kangas 25
George Summers 33

PART TWO
Purple Reign 39

Bob Johnson 47
Bugs Stevens 55
Jack Arute Jr. 61
Ken Bouchard 67
Gene Bouchard 73
Ed Flemke Jr. 79

PART THREE
"Just Good, Hard Racing" 85

Bob Judkins 93
Geoff Bodine 99
Clyde McLeod 107
Rob Bouchard 115
Rich Bonneau 121
Dick Williams 127

PART FOUR
Big League, Big Times 133

Bob Johnson 141
Paula Bouchard 147
Steve Bird 153
Ricky Rudd 159
David Ifft 165
Tracey Bouchard 171
Russ Conway 177
Mike Joy 185

PART FIVE
Second Life 191

Paula Bouchard 197
Chad Bouchard 203
Michelle Bouchard 207
George Summers 211

PART SIX
Checkered Flag 217

Paula Bouchard 221

Afterword 227
Index 229

Acknowledgements

This book could never have been produced without the support and active participation of many people. We owe a special thanks to the members of the Bouchard family who sat for chapter interviews, opening their homes and their hearts. Ron's wife, Paula; his children, Gene, Rob, Michelle, Tracey, and Chad; as well as his siblings, Ken and JoAnn, were more than gracious. Their memories paint a wonderful portrait of a husband, father, and brother, a man beyond the racer most of us saw.

Also sharing freely of their time for interviews were Jack Arute, Steve Bird, Geoff Bodine, Rich Bonneau, Russ Conway, Ed Flemke Jr., David Ifft, Bob Johnson, Mike Joy, Bob Judkins, Vic Kangas, Clyde McLeod, Dave Rossbach, Ricky Rudd, Pete Salvatore, Bugs Stevens, George Summers, and Dick Williams. Many of these also provided priceless photos from their personal collections.

We owe special gratitude to the RB Racing Museum and JoAnn Bouchard Bergeron for patiently dealing with our frequent "just one more, we promise" requests for photographs. Thanks also to Dick Berggren, the North East Motor Sports Museum, and Val LeSieur, all of whom opened their extensive photo collections for our use. Additionally, the family of George and Maggie Summers went above and beyond the call of friendship in a dozen different ways, all of which helped ease this project along.

We also thank the following for their invaluable contributions:

Mike Adaskaveg, Bob Bergman, Herb Dodge, Ed Duncan, Dave Dykes, Robin Hartford, Howie Hodge, Phil Hoyt, Dave LaCroix, Fran Lawlor, Buz McKim, Bryant McMurray, Tom Ormsby, Eddie Roche, David Rossbach Jr., R.A. Silvia, Phil Smith, Nick Teto, Gary Williams

Foreword

As much as any race driver I've ever known, Ron Bouchard was comfortable in his own skin, perpetually at ease. That allowed him to slip into any situation and look like he'd been born for it.

If you caught up to him before a race, he was focused but approachable, always, whether in the dramatic buildup to the Daytona 500 or during the intermission just prior to a 30-lap Modified feature at Thompson, Connecticut.

At any post-race gathering—and there were hundreds, in pit areas and speedway parking lots up and down the East Coast—he was there with a beer and a laugh, not needing to be the life of the party but certainly willing and able to go in any direction the party might veer.

In his post-driving days, nothing changed except his surroundings and his clothing. If you poked your head into the office at his string of automobile dealerships, he'd look up and wave you in with that big, warm smile. If you visited him and his wife, Paula, at their home, he wanted to cook you a meal, mix you a drink, listen to what you'd been up to, catch up on things.

Ronnie was so damned comfortable that I'm not sure I ever saw him *uncomfortable*.

He walked into the spotlight young, racking up track championships as a teenager and beating the best NASCAR Modified drivers in the Northeast in his early 20s. Today, teenybopper race drivers—even at advanced levels of the sport—are a dime a dozen, although even at that rate you'd be overpaying for most. Broadcaster Mike Joy, who saw a lot of Bouchard's early act, is quick to point out how exceptional Bouchard's accomplishments were 40-odd years ago, when this was a man's game.

"Don't forget," says Joy, "back then you couldn't start racing until you were 16. So at that age, if you were lucky, you started in an entry-level class at a Saturday-night track, and you worked your way up. Ronnie, on the other hand, was beating great drivers almost immediately."

He was immensely popular throughout the Northeast, partly because of his obvious talent and partly because he had terrific people skills. Bouchard once told me that his father, Bob, was to credit for that, but this was no genetic thing. Bob, who operated a moving and storage company, told all of his kids that when people moved from one place to the next, it was often because life had dealt them a bad hand, perhaps a divorce, a death in the family, or the loss of a job.

The moral was simple: Just be nice to people.

And in doing just that, Ron Bouchard put a whole city on the racing map. The first time many of us ever heard of Fitchburg, Massachusetts, it was being used at the end of an announcer's introduction:

"In car #17 …"—or #35, or #2X, or #7, or #3—"… ladies and gentlemen, the Kid from …"

But if Bouchard could be charming, he also often appeared charmed, touched by Dame Fortune.

"People always say that you make your own luck, and I'm sure that's true," says Paula Bouchard. "But I do believe that some people have more luck than others. Ronnie had a lot of instances throughout his life where he had a little bit of luck, and good timing."

The flip side of the argument is that good fortune glides past all of us at times, but only some are smart enough to recognize it, and grab it. And Bouchard sure did, every time, without flinching. Whenever a winning horse rode past with an empty saddle, he was on it in a flash, spurring it ahead. That was as true in business as it had ever been in the sport that made him somebody.

Maybe that's a confidence you have to be born with. Or maybe it comes from succeeding at just about everything you try. And, sure, maybe there's room in that equation for a little bit of luck. Whatever makes a man a winner, Ron Bouchard had it.

"Nothing he did ever amazed me," says Paula. "That was just Ronnie."

It sure was.

This is his story, told by some of the people who knew him best.

Bones Bourcier
Indianapolis, Indiana
2016

PART ONE

The Kid from Fitchburg

BOUCHARD FAMILY COLLECTION

Gosh, how differently everything might have gone, and how differently the history of New England racing might read, had a couple of people been in better health on that Sunday in 1963.

First, Bob Bouchard, who owned a tavern called the Strand in the French section of Fitchburg, Massachusetts, called Cleghorn, got news that his bartender for the day had phoned in sick. That was less than happy news for Bob, whose primary business, Red & White Movers, sponsored a stock car that would compete that afternoon at Brookline Speedway, just across the New Hampshire state line. Now, instead of watching his sharp #2, a 1948 Mercury coupe, in the capable hands of Pete Salvatore, one of the area's top drivers, Bob Bouchard would be sliding draft beers across the bar.

Then it turned out that Salvatore himself was indisposed, and wouldn't make it to Brookline, either. All these years later, the reasons are unclear. Ken Bouchard, Bob's younger son and a future race driver himself, recalls Pete having injured a leg; Salvatore believes it was an arm, but is less than 100 percent certain; the story told most often in all the old magazine stories is that Pete simply woke up sick, and that's how JoAnn Bouchard Bergeron, Bob's daughter, remembers it. At any rate, Salvatore telephoned the Bouchard race shop, located right there at Red & White, to report that he'd have to sit things out.

Answering the call was Ron Bouchard, the eldest of Bob and Lorraine Bouchard's three kids, and the person responsible for the events of that Sunday being turned into all those magazine stories. At 14, he was already part of the Salvatore crew; either tracks like Brookline had flexible rules about age requirements for pit passes, or young Ronnie was a nice enough kid that officials looked the other way. Both theories seem plausible.

Ron Bouchard put down the phone and told a crewman—it may have been Steve Hagwood, may have been Jimmy Hartman—that Salvatore wouldn't be racing that day, and then went right back to loading the truck for the 12-mile haul to Brookline.

"So who's going to drive the car?" asked his friend.

What Ronnie answered was, "Oh, we'll find somebody."

What he *meant* was, "I am."

He'd been waiting for an opportunity like this. He'd even rehearsed for it, as you will learn in the pages to come, although he surely figured his big chance was still a couple of years away. But now it was here, and he was going to make the most of it. So he and his associate pulled out of the Red & White complex on Lunenburg Street, and headed north on Route 13. Just a mile and a half after they crossed into the Granite State, there stood the giant Oilzum sign marking the entrance to Brookline Speedway, Sunday afternoon home of the Atlantic Racing Association.

Young Bouchard's illicit coming-out party did not begin well. He finished last in a seven-car Class A qualifying heat—"I ran most of the race sideways," he told writer Herb Dodge years later—and even managed to bend the front end. But from there, everything

2   Part One

went right. *Really* right. He and some helpers got the car repaired in time for Ronnie to run, and win, the very first feature race of his life.

If it sounds too good to be true, there are a few witnesses still around to verify things, including another Fitchburg resident who, at age 13, was selling popcorn in the Brookline grandstands. That vendor was Pete Fiandaca, who went on to race for 50 years and is today enshrined, as is Bouchard, in the New England Auto Racers Hall of Fame. Fiandaca remembers second place going to Mike Onners, from Shirley, Massachusetts, though this is disputed by area chassis guru Marty Harty, now aged 95; Marty recalls the runner-up being Lucky Thompson of Hancock, New Hampshire. Both Harty and Fiandaca agree that Homer Eggleston, who lived not far from the Bouchard shop, placed third.

Local lore has it that upon returning to Fitchburg, the crew carried Ronnie into the Strand on their shoulders and informed Bob Bouchard that his boy had won the feature. Bob's initial reaction was not quite as joyful as they'd expected. He hit the roof, furious that his son had pulled such a stunt.

But never mind all that, and consider this: Had Pete Salvatore not been dinged up, he'd have been in the Red & White Movers #2 that day, and Ronnie wouldn't have. And if that barkeep had reported for duty, as scheduled, Bob Bouchard would have been in the Brookline pits, and he'd have made damn sure that whoever drove his car, it wouldn't have been his 14-year-old son.

Maybe coincidence guides all our destinies. Something happens, and then something else happens, and that's your life.

But it sure seems in hindsight that a lot of things lined up just right for Ron Bouchard to become a race driver. For example, a couple of years before that fateful day at Brookline, he had talked his dad into bringing him to the Saturday-night races at Westboro Speedway, outside Worcester. Of all the bleacher seats they could have chosen—Westboro had a few thousand—they sat directly behind a woman who was clearly cheering for one car above all others, a red coupe. Making conversation, they learned that she was married to its driver, one Pete Salvatore.

"What do you do?" Mrs. Salvatore asked Mr. Bouchard.

"I have a moving company," he replied.

To which Mrs. Salvatore said something along the lines of, "Maybe you should sponsor my husband."

Pete Salvatore won that night, and later, in the pit area, Bob Bouchard and his son wandered over to say hello. It was the start of something big.

Until then, the Bouchard family's life was remarkably normal. They lived on the top floor of a three-decker in Fitchburg, the kind of blue-collar city that rewarded hard work and guile, and even as a boy Ronnie had more than enough of the latter.

JoAnn recalls, "My mother would say, 'Now, Ronnie, you have to take your sister outside to play,' but he could talk himself right out of that job. He'd say, 'Gee, Ma, it's cold out. Shouldn't she stay inside?' The truth was, he just wanted to take off and be with his friends." Normal.

But after those fortuitous events at Westboro and Brookline, nothing was ever normal again. There was a cooling-off period before Ronnie was old enough to compete by the rulebook, and in that stretch Salvatore did plenty of winning. But no one doubted that Ronnie would be back at the wheel once he turned 16, which happened on November 23, 1964. Narrow-framed, minimalist coupes called "cutdowns"—forerunners to today's Supermodifieds—had replaced full-sized coupes as Class A iron at Westboro and at Pines Speedway in Groveland, Massachusetts, so for '65 Bob Bouchard bought a flyweight cutdown from Haverhill's Sammy Sanborn. He painted a #2 on its primered flanks, and had someone letter his son's name on the door, misspelled as "Ronny."

"Ronnie got in the car for the first time," says Russ Conway, who has been a race promoter, a sportswriter of considerable repute, and a racing historian, "and won the feature at the Pines."

Now officially underway was a career that shot upward like a Roman candle. Aboard that cutdown, Bouchard won at New Hampshire's Hudson Speedway, later won three straight at Pines, and even managed to be spectacular when he wasn't winning. Take the night in '65 when he sailed the Deuce out of the ballpark at Pines and very nearly landed it in the Merrimack River.

Working the pit gate, with a very clear view of this, was teenaged Steve Bird, whose father, Amos, was the track steward. Sixteen years later, Steve, by then a respected mechanic, would ride to victory lane at Talladega on the hood of Bouchard's Buick.

"Between the track and the river was a road that led around to the pits," Steve Bird recalls. "Ronnie must have been 25 or 30 feet in the air when he went over that road. The car came down on its top, right beside the riverbank. Everybody ran over to help him out of the car. That was probably the first time I talked to him."

Bird grins. "By then, people already knew he was good. He won probably a half-dozen races [in '65] with that cutdown."

This burst of success got Bouchard pondering about what else the sport had to offer. Down in Seekonk, Massachusetts, just east of Providence, Rhode Island, promoter D. Anthony Venditti was paying rich purses for his own Class A division, whose cars resembled Late Model/Modified hybrids. Mostly semi-current Chevy IIs and "Tri-5" (1955–57) Chevy Bel Airs, Seekonk Speedway's Class A cars sported 13-inch tires, wider than standard Late Model issue. But you couldn't call them Modifieds, because the damn things had fenders, at least until they were knocked off by the frequent contact fostered by the tight quarter-mile confines.

Bouchard enlisted a few friends, chiefly a budding chassis man named Vic Kangas and local engine whiz Dave Rossbach, and headed to Seekonk in 1966. For the next six seasons he lit up Venditti's track, winning twice as a rookie and later earning four straight championships, 1968–71. It was Wally Saleeba, the track's colorful announcer—old-timers will recall the sew-on patches proclaiming one's membership in the Wally Saleeba Girl-Watchers Club—who dubbed Bouchard "The Kid from Fitchburg."

Seekonk was chock-full of tough-guy veterans, and a rivalry formed—at least in the eyes of rowdy fans—between young Ronnie and the '67 Seekonk champ, George Summers, his elder by 14 years. In truth, the pair had developed something of a father-son relationship, but that didn't lessen the fiery language raining down on Maggie Summers, George's wife, and their four children, sons George Jr. and Rick, and daughters Mary and Kathie.

"People would holler, 'You watch, Bouchard is going to put Summers in the wall,'" Maggie recalls. "Or they'd say, 'Keep an eye on this! Summers is going to park Bouchard when he tries to pass!' My kids didn't understand what was going on, because obviously they loved their father, but they also loved Ronnie. I remember Mary being upset and Kathie crying."

A more measured, objective view was taken by George's father, Bill Summers. Of course, measured objectivity had been a big part of Bill's life; he was a Major League Baseball umpire. When Ted Williams hit a Fenway Park home run with the final swing of his career, Bill was crouched behind home plate. Maggie Summers remembers her father-in-law watching Bouchard at Seekonk, and saying, "That kid, he's something special, isn't he?"

He sure was, on-track and off. A magazine profile by Herb Dodge mentioned "a rugged handsomeness that makes [Bouchard] the perfect image for a race driver and makes his legions of female fans swoon." Sister JoAnn recalls her exasperated father muttering, "Those girls! Too many girls!" Of course, never in history has there been a teenaged male who believed that there was such a thing as too many girls, but Ronnie settled things in 1967 when, at age 18, he married his first wife, Regi, who was three years his elder. Though the marriage did not go the distance, together they began the process of raising what ended up being four kids: sons Gene (whom Regi brought to the marriage, but who always considered Ron his Dad, "absolutely") and Rob (born in 1968), and daughters Michelle (1969) and Tracey (1970).

An amazing five-week run in the summer of '71 showed the racing world beyond Seekonk just how special this Kid from Fitchburg was. It started in the middle of July, when he hauled his Saturday-night Camaro to Connecticut for a midweek Modified event at the half-mile Stafford Motor Speedway. Powered by a peashooter Chevy small block, that car shouldn't have had a prayer against the big-block coupes, yet Bouchard trailed only former NASCAR champions Bugs Stevens and Ernie Gahan at the finish.

Then he accepted a tryout ride with flashy Massachusetts owner Dick Armstrong, and on August 8 arrived at Pennsylvania's Pocono Raceway for a rescheduled NASCAR Modified 200. Armstrong had purchased from North Carolinians Jack Tant and Clayton Mitchell the Flyin' #11 coupe driven to many victories by Richmond's Ray Hendrick; renumbered as an Armstrong #1, it had won that summer at Thompson, Connecticut, in the hands of Hop Harrington. But on the first weekend in August, when rain fell just after Pocono time trials, Harrington had missed the qualifying cut, so Armstrong rolled the dice and replaced him with this Bouchard youngster for the return trip. Ronnie breezed to victory in the non-qualifiers race, and lined up 41st in the big feature. He passed 20 cars in the first 20 laps, 17 more in the next 20—including a ballsy three-wide move between a lapped car and the great Hendrick, in a new Tant/Mitchell piece—and was lying fourth when he crashed out; we'll let Dave Rossbach and Vic Kangas explain all that.

Finally, on August 22, he was back in the Armstrong car for a 200-miler at New Jersey's Trenton International Speedway. Bouchard told Herb Dodge that upon seeing Trenton's long front straightaway, he had muttered to himself, "You've got to be shitting me." Today, Vic Kangas isn't sure if Bouchard was exaggerating to the writer, or if his friend was simply a good actor.

"Because if he had any fear that day," Kangas laughs, "he didn't show it."

Wife Regi, on the other hand, was justly nervous; the race was barely underway when she opted to go sit in the parking lot. As reported in *Stock Car Racing* magazine, curiosity ultimately got the better of her, and in the race's closing laps she wandered over and asked a gate attendant who was leading. He wasn't sure, he told her, because the announcer kept talking about the driver running second, somebody named Bouchard. That's where Ronnie finished, between winner Geoff Bodine and third-place man Richie Evans. Announcers would be talking about all three of them for years to come.

The Kid was all grown up. Timing, luck, and his own raw talent had shoved him into the spotlight.

BY PETE SALVATORE

"He watched me, yes, but then he took over, and look at everything he did"

The Bouchard family's first driver remembers its second

BOUCHARD FAMILY COLLECTION

Born in 1937, Pete Salvatore grew up in Worcester, but a repair shop in nearby Shrewsbury determined his future. Owned by the Garganigo family, Lovey's Garage was already deep into racing when teenaged Pete found work there. The job put him in the company of Mario "Fats" Caruso, a Shrewsbury legend whose career included victories from nearby Westboro Speedway to New Jersey's Trenton Fairgrounds. Inspired, Salvatore built his own car and won almost instantly. It was sheer chance that paired him with sponsor/owner Bob Bouchard, and the duo clicked; newspaper accounts describe the Bouchard #2 winning 40 features in two seasons, and Salvatore was being called "the All-American Boy." Soon, Pete helped steer—quite literally—the driving dreams of another Bouchard, Bob's son Ronnie. Salvatore eventually hung up his helmet to nurture his thriving towing business, but by then his place in regional racing history was secure.

Bob Bouchard was a nice man, easygoing, always laughing, always happy, especially when we did well, which was quite often. Geez, we won a lot of races together. In fact, at one point they put a bounty on us: "If anybody beats Salvatore," they told all the drivers, "there's a $25 bonus," and in those days that was good money.

I guess everybody's heard that famous story about Ronnie filling in for me one night at Brookline when he was just 14 years old. A lot of the things you read about that situation said I was sick, but actually I had hurt myself; I'd gotten my arm and shoulder banged up, and by that weekend it was still too sore for me to race. I couldn't have done a good job, and I knew that, so I called the shop and said I wouldn't be able to drive at Brookline. So Ronnie decided he'd just get into the car and sneak out there—because everyone knew he was underage—and, of course, he won the race.

Now, that sounds unbelievable, like a story somebody made up, because a 14-year-old kid shouldn't have been able to win the feature. But way before that day ever came around, Ronnie already had a pretty good idea what to do in a race car. See, when he was maybe 12 years old, he would ride with me during practice at Brookline. He would actually sit on my lap, and I'd put the seatbelt around both of us. Sometimes I'd work the throttle while he steered the car, and other times I'd steer while he worked the pedals, and I think he learned a lot from that. For instance, he'd step on the gas so hard that the rear tires would break loose, and I'd tell him, "Anytime you feel the car getting sideways like that, just let off the throttle a little bit."

It's crazy to think about it now, because we were turning some fast laps that way, with him riding on my lap. But in those days, we all got a kick out of it: me, Ronnie, and even Bob. And the way things worked out, I think all those laps he rode with me paid off. He knew that if the car jumped sideways coming off the corner, he didn't have to panic; everything would be okay if he just eased off the power. And he knew where to let off going into the turns, because he'd been through that, and we'd talked about it.

Yes, it's a lot different when you're out there by yourself, but he had a pretty good idea how things were supposed to feel.

The other thing you've got to understand is that Ronnie always paid attention. From the time he was just a young kid, he was wiping off the car, waxing it, keeping everything clean. He'd have the tires stacked up neatly, whether we were at the garage or at the races. At the track, he was a good little organizer. If we came in after a heat race and someone said, "We need to add gas for the feature," or "We need such-and-such a wrench," he'd have it ready to go, in a second. You couldn't have asked for a better helper.

And whenever I talked to the crew, Ronnie was right there, listening. I'm sure he watched every move I made—how I came from the back, where I passed cars—and every move the other good guys made, too. So he had a good understanding of what was *involved* in winning races, and you need that understanding just like you need natural talent and desire.

You know, I'd won right off the bat myself when I started driving because I had that same desire, and because I really worked hard at *understanding* racing. When

I was a kid pumping gas at Lovey's Garage, Fats Caruso was driving their race car. Fats was one of the top drivers of that era; he won all over the place, but he was really tough at Westboro, which was the closest track to us. All week long, when I wasn't busy pumping gas, I'd clean the cars and buff 'em up, just like Ronnie did with his dad's cars later on.

I can remember those guys at Lovey's loading the car every Saturday and taking off to go to Westboro. I'd stay behind at the garage until closing time, then I'd hurry down to the track myself. God, I used to love to watch Fats run that place.

Over time, I got more involved on the mechanical side of things. At night they'd have me grinding and polishing cylinder heads, or whatever was needed to get ready for the next race.

Well, the more work I did, the more I thought that maybe I'd like to build a race car of my own. So in 1958, I found a '47 Mercury and started turning that thing into a stock car. I'd had a '46 Ford sedan with a good, strong motor, so I took that motor and stuck it into the Mercury. But once I got that car ready, I realized that I had another problem: I had no way to get it to the race track. I found a guy who said he'd build me a simple, single-axle trailer, but the guy wanted $75 for the job, and to me that was a fortune. So we made a deal: I'd give him five bucks a week until I got the bill paid off.

Somehow I found out about a race up in Keene, New Hampshire, at the fairgrounds, so I loaded the Mercury on my new trailer, and off I went, with a couple of guys to help me. Well, it was quite a trip. Keene was only about 60 miles from home, but it was all two-lane roads, and I had to run really slow because that single-axle trailer wandered all over the road. Took us forever, maybe three hours.

Keene was a dirt track, and the only racing I'd ever seen had been asphalt. But I took to it pretty good; to go fast, you had to hang the back end out, and I liked that.

I don't recall much about that first race, other than the fact that the car bounced around a lot in the turns. I figured if I could torch the rear leaf springs and take out some of the arch, we'd get it lower and it would ride better, so I did that when I got home.

Now comes the next weekend, and we take another long, slow ride to Keene. We get into the pits, and the tech inspector is making his rounds, checking all the cars. He walks over to my Mercury and says it looks a little low in the back. Then he gets down on his hands and knees, looks underneath, and says, "Oh, you've torched the springs. We don't allow that. You're illegal. But I'll tell you what I'll do: If you figure out a way to heat those springs and get 'em back to stock height, you'll be okay to run."

So we find a guy with a torch, give him a few bucks, and start heating and bending the springs until the tech man comes back and said, "Close enough. You're legal."

Well, with the back of the car raised up again, I was worried that it'd be bouncing all over the place, just like the first week. So when the tech man walked away, I had my helpers stand on the back bumper, and I wrapped a chain around the chassis and the left side of the rear-end housing and stuck a bolt through the chain. Now I had the stock springs that the inspector wanted, but I had the car nice and low, the way *I* wanted.

I'm sure we must have run a heat race, but I don't remember that. In the feature, though, I had a hell of a time. I passed a bunch of cars, but then the engine started overheating and spraying water all over the windshield. On a pavement track that would have been no big deal, but Keene was dusty, and all that dust turned to mud on my windshield. I couldn't see a damn thing, so when a caution flag came out I came flying into the pits.

"Put some water in the radiator," I hollered to my guys. "And wipe the windshield. I can't see a thing!"

They said, "Well, you're going pretty good. You were running fifth!"

Geez, that got me all pumped up. I got back out there in time for the restart, and as soon as they dropped the green flag I started coming through traffic. Before too long the radiator started boiling over again, so now I was back to where I could barely see. But between me looking out the side windows and getting more and more used to sliding the car around, I was still passing cars.

Finally, as I'm coming off the fourth turn, I see a bunch of people walking toward the front straightaway, and some of them are waving at me, like, "Whoa, whoa! Slow down!" I figured there must have been a bad accident. So I'm idling down the track, and a guy stops me at the start-finish line.

He says, "The race is over. You won!"

I couldn't believe it. I had no idea that I was leading, and I never even saw the checkered flag.

I kept on driving my own cars for a while, running all over the place. One night after a feature at Westboro—I believe I won it—I was approached by a man who introduced himself as Bob Bouchard. He said he had a business, Red & White Movers, and that he'd like to help me out. Well, I'd heard that before. When you win races, people offer all kinds of things, and most of the time it doesn't work out. But I could see that this man was serious. He said that if I was interested, I could come up to Fitchburg and talk with him. And that's just what happened. I took a ride up there, we talked a while, and he started sponsoring me.

There's a funny story from those days. We'd been doing pretty well, winning races, and we decided to build a new car. I had a little one-bay garage here in Shrewsbury—it was actually an old fire station—and Mr. Bouchard was down one night helping me finish the car, putting in the gas tank and things like that. Well, we were underneath the car with torches, and some of the gas left in that tank spilled out. It doesn't take too much gas to start a pretty big fire, and the next thing we knew, the whole car was in flames. We managed to push it outside before anything else caught fire, but that car burned up before we ever even got it finished. Think about that: We started a fire inside a fire station!

We ended up putting together another car, and we raced it all over the place: Peabody, Westboro, Pines, Brookline. And along the way, Mr. Bouchard became the car owner instead of just the sponsor. I was working for Worcester Sand & Gravel, and at night I'd go up to Red & White and work on the cars. That was the arrangement we had at the time when I skipped that race, and Ronnie ended up winning it. After that, I got back into Bob's car, and we won a lot more races over the next couple of seasons.

Eventually Ronnie reached the age where he was okay to drive the car, and obviously that's what he wanted to do. I knew that day was coming, so it was okay with me. He started driving his dad's car, and I found a ride driving for Lovey's Garage, which was nice because I had started going to the races with them way back when. But I never really raced against Ronnie too much; most of the time we were either racing at different tracks, or in different classes. Then he moved on and started running Seekonk, and then Stafford and Thompson, and then all over the place. Pretty soon, he was winning everywhere. He went a long way in a short time, that's for sure.

I always paid attention to how Ronnie was doing, especially after he moved up to the Winston Cup stuff. I was proud of him, very proud of him. And, of course, when he won Talladega, I just couldn't believe it.

I stayed close to his family, especially his father. I used to go up to Fitchburg and see Bob sometimes, just to catch up. And his mother was a great lady, too, just a wonderful woman.

I've never been the type of person to brag, like, "I won this, and I won that." And the *last* thing I'd ever say is that I taught Ronnie Bouchard. He made it on his own. He watched me, yes, and he learned, but then he took over, and look at everything he did. He's one of the best we've ever had around here.

Still, Ronnie was nice enough to mention me in a lot of the stories people wrote about him, and that made me feel good. You bet it did. Because of him, my name became even bigger, more widely known, than it was when I raced.

He was such a good kid, and then such a good guy, very generous, always polite. I really looked up to him. That might sound funny, because I knew him when he was just a kid, but as I watched him go through his career and through his life, I really did look up to him.

You know, way back when, they used to call me "the All-American Boy." Well, Ronnie Bouchard really *was* the All-American Boy.

BY JoANN BOUCHARD BERGERON

"I knew the hottest young driver there, and it was my own brother!"

A sister reflects on the start of a family passion

DICK BERGGREN

JoAnn Bouchard Bergeron was the second child of three born to Bob and Lorraine Bouchard. A bit more than four years younger than Ron and two ahead of kid brother Ken, JoAnn was an eyewitness to a lot of racing history, from New England bullrings to Southern superspeedways. These days, she and her husband, Bob Bergeron— "Bergie," pictured here with JoAnn, has a long connection to the Bouchard clan —help run the RB Racing Museum, home to significant cars, trophies, and other artifacts from Ron's career. It sits on the grounds where once stood Red & White Movers and the family race shop. As she noted, much of her youth was spent on that piece of property on Lunenburg Street in Fitchburg, "and now I'm back here two Saturdays a month, showing people around." It was there, in the museum's office, that JoAnn spoke for this book.

Racing was part of our everyday lives, from when we were just kids. We grew up in it. We never went to the circus, or did anything else for fun. We went to the races. It started with my dad sponsoring Pete Salvatore, and it just went on from there.

That was all because of Ronnie, of course. He had gone to Westboro Speedway a couple of times with one of his friends and this kid's family, and he really liked it. Well, I guess one week the other guy's family didn't want to go, because I remember Ronnie bugging my father: "C'mon, Dad, let's go! It's really cool. We've got to go!" Finally my dad gave in and they went, and it was just a complete coincidence that they sat near Pete's wife, which is how my father ended up meeting and sponsoring Pete.

It's funny, the things that stay in your mind. I still remember sitting out on the front porch of our house, Kenny and I, waiting for my father to stop at home to pick us up to go to the races. The guys would load up everything here at the garage, then my dad and usually Ronnie would swing by the house with the truck, and we'd pile in. I remember a lot of trips to Westboro and Brookline in that truck, and sometimes an occasional trip to different tracks. But that feeling of waiting to go, that excitement, is something I've never forgotten.

I'm not sure if many of the other kids we knew—our friends from the neighborhood, or from school—ever figured out why we loved it so much. Racing wasn't very widely accepted back then, and even now it's not a sport you can just *explain* to someone. I think you have to go to the track a few times to understand it, and to really get into it.

Just recently, I happened to ride past where Brookline Speedway used to be, and a lot of the memories instantly came back. That was the coolest track, just a little quarter-mile that sat out in the woods with one small set of grandstands. My mother generally sat with Pete's wife and their two kids, so Kenny and I would hang out with them. Ronnie would be in the pits, helping the crew.

Of course, the day Ronnie won that first feature at 14 years old, Pete and his family weren't there, and neither was my father. But the rest of us—me and Kenny and our mother—were there, as usual. I have a vague memory of somebody coming up from the pits at some point, probably just before the heat race, and saying, "You know, Mrs. Bouchard, that's your son driving the car."

And my mother said, "No, that's not Ronnie. He told us he was going to find a driver."

Well, as we came to find out, it *was* Ronnie driving. In the heat race he hit everything but the flagstand, and he finished last. My mother said, "Well, he must be just warming it up. I'm sure they'll put a different driver in there for the feature."

But they didn't, and obviously Ronnie had figured things out a little bit better by then, because he ended up winning. I don't recall much about the race itself, but I do remember that by the time he got out of the car at the start/finish line, I was already standing right down in front of the grandstands; I can still feel my fingers gripping that fence. I said to myself, "This is the coolest thing *ever*."

And then, in the very next second, I thought, "My father is going to *kill* Ronnie."

My mother was livid, too. I mean, that's her *son* out there, just 14 years old! Later on she calmed down a little—even then, Ronnie was a charmer—but she was still upset that he'd driven the car without anyone's permission, and my dad was, too. I'm sure that deep down he was proud of Ronnie, but he certainly wasn't happy. So that was a really big day for the Bouchards, for a lot of reasons!

Then everything got back to normal for a couple of years, with Pete Salvatore driving the car and the rest of us watching. In a lot of ways, as kids we were a lot like Ronnie's own children were later on, always ready to go to the races. The only difference was, his kids went three or four nights a week, all over New England, and we mainly went to Westboro on Saturday nights and Brookline on Sundays. It's strange now, but back then even Westboro seemed like a long way from home. Brookline was close, only about half an hour from here, but it seemed to take forever to get to Westboro.

Once Ronnie was able to start driving the car legally, it became even more important to go to every race. We went to Brookline, Westboro, Pines, and I loved every minute of it. I mean, I knew the hottest young driver there, and it was my own brother! That was a big, big deal.

I remember paying attention to a few of the other drivers back then, like Bentley Warren and Tinker Progin, but the only one I really rooted for was Ronnie. I loved those cutdown cars from that era; it seemed like there was nothing to them, but they were really fast, and they looked so cool. But when I look at pictures of them now, it all looks so dangerous. It seemed like almost none of the drivers even wore firesuits back then.

I remember us sitting in the grandstands at Pines Speedway when Ronnie flipped over the bank and almost went into the river. The car landed on a trailer and he climbed right out, but it scared the heck out of my mother and me, mostly because we knew Ronnie couldn't swim.

As time went on, Ronnie kept telling my father about the purses they were paying down at Seekonk, and eventually he convinced him that that's where they needed to race. To me, it was like another adventure: It was even further away, so that meant a longer ride, and these were a different type of cars and a whole new bunch of drivers to learn about. But Ronnie was fast right away down there, and before long it felt like that was our home track. Ronnie seemed to fit in very quickly with the fans and the other racers at Seekonk—he had a magnetic personality even as a teenager—and it just became a nice place to go every week.

I don't know quite how to describe it, but I really liked the atmosphere at Seekonk in those days. After we'd been there only a little while, it seemed like we were always among friends; if it wasn't George Summers and his family, it was some other group. And anytime I walked through the grandstands and went past the tower, Wally Saleeba, the announcer, would say, "There goes my favorite Bouchard!"

It was also Wally who started calling Ronnie "The Kid from Fitchburg," and he played that up so big every week that it ended up sticking with him forever. By the time he went to race anywhere else, he was already known by that nickname, and it fit for a long time because he was still the new kid on the block. So people just kept on calling him that.

It was at Seekonk that Ronnie *really* started to build his reputation with people from our area, Fitchburg and all the towns around here, because he won all those championships in a row. As he started having success, I remember some of the guys who worked at Red & White Movers becoming really avid race fans. They'd argue about which one of them was going to drive the hauler down to Seekonk Speedway on Saturday afternoons. I'm sure it was a pretty big deal to pull into the track driving that Bouchard truck, because Ronnie was winning a lot. It was usually Louie Roy—we all called him "Bugsy"—who ended up driving the hauler, and he'd be all pumped up about that.

The first time my mother and I ever went to Stafford was when Ronnie went there with his Seekonk car, the Camaro. Again, it meant going farther away, traveling all the way down into Connecticut. And once we got there, it all seemed so scary to me. The other tracks we'd been to were so small—Seekonk was like a little donut—that you never worried very much about what might happen. But Stafford was a lot bigger, and those Modifieds just seemed so fast. And yet he seemed to take to it very quickly. It always felt like every time we went to a new track, he was competitive right away.

That never stopped, really, because in that same period he went to Pocono to drive for Dick Armstrong, and then they teamed up again at Trenton, and they did very well. That was amazing, to think that now he was racing in Pennsylvania and New Jersey. It seemed like it was all happening very quickly. I remember my father talking about that many years later, and saying that Ronnie's career took off faster and took him further than any of us ever thought it was going to, including Ronnie himself. In the beginning, racing was just something you did with your family and your friends on the weekends, and now you were looking at where the next big race was. It gave me butterflies, like all of a sudden I realized that Ronnie's racing was really going places.

A lot changed in a short period of time, because at that point we could see that he was probably going to be driving for other people from now on, meaning different car owners ad different teams. I'm sure it was strange for my father to get adjusted to in the beginning, not to be directly involved like he had been for so long. But once he saw that Ronnie was with good people, and driving good cars, he was fine with it. It actually made his life easier not to have to worry about maintaining a race car, and especially not to have to pay the bills anymore. And for the rest of us, I think the basic feeling was the same: We knew we were still going to go to the races, and we were still going to root for Ronnie no matter what car he was driving.

And, honestly, things around here didn't change too much, because almost as soon as Ronnie's stuff was gone from the race shop at Red & White, Kenny was just getting started with cars of his own.

It's crazy to think how much of my life has taken place right here on this property. First my father got the moving company going, and then part of the truck garage became a race shop, first for Pete Salvatore and then for both of my brothers. It seemed like I spent all my free time hanging out around those race cars. I was a little bit of a tomboy, so I'd do whatever I could to help: paint numbers, clean up after the guys, whatever it took.

Ronnie taught me how to drive a truck—I mean, a big rig—right outside this building. Later, Kenny showed me how to hook up a trailer, and how to back up a truck with a trailer on. I'm absolutely sure that right this minute, I could hook up a trailer, jump in the truck, and drive it away, because both of my brothers were good teachers.

A lot of this stuff happened when we were just teenagers, some of it before we were even able to drive on the streets. My father would be working in the office, and time after time the neighbors would call and say, "Uh, Mr. Bouchard, we don't know if you're aware of this, but your kids are outside driving in circles, going around the building with your trucks."

I even met Bobby, my husband, right here on this property, because he started working for my dad when he was 16, and naturally that led to him working on the race cars, first Ronnie's and then Kenny's.

So if I look like I'm right at home here, that's why.

You know, we did all of this as a family, and I think that's why we were always able to stay so close. We worked together all week at the moving company, we hung out in the race shop at night, and then on the weekends we went to the races together. Pretty much every race that Ronnie ran—and the same with Kenny later on—there was at least part of the family there. Where else in life can you maintain that kind of connection?

With so many families, even if they're together all week, the kids want to each go their separate ways on the weekends, and the parents are okay with that because they want to enjoy *their* free time, too. But with our family, it definitely seemed like everyone always wanted to be at the same place, whether it was the race shop, or Brookline and Seekonk in the early years, or later on at Stafford, Thompson, Westboro, Monadnock, or wherever.

It's amazing how many people we met in racing, and how many good friends we made just by being involved. And it all began with Ronnie.

BY DAVE ROSSBACH

"It didn't seem to matter where Ronnie started, he always got to the front"

Championship years, as reviewed by an old friend

For a guy who devoted a large chunk of his life to a very loud pursuit—building and tuning racing engines—Dave Rossbach is surprisingly quiet, to the point where it's sometimes easy to forget whether he was at this race or that race; that is, until you look at the old victory photos, and there he is, off to one side, smiling. Although he has worked with a number of drivers, Dave will always be most closely associated with the Bouchard family, having provided winning horsepower for both Ron and Ken. He even won "a couple of mechanic's races" at Monadnock in one of Kenny's cars. These relationships extended far beyond racing; Rossbach remembers playing co-driver for Ronnie on a few trucking jobs "way up into Canada." He turned 76 in December of 2015, just a few days after his old friend's passing.

ROSSBACH FAMILY COLLECTION

It was right around 1966 that I first got to know Ronnie. He was driving a '57 Chevy that Vic Kangas had built, and they had just started racing at Seekonk Speedway. I met the Bouchards through Calvin Blaisdell, who a lot of racing people in New England will remember by his nickname, Colonel Cal. He built one of Ronnie's very first racing engines. I knew Cal from hot-rodding and fooling around with street racing. I was always a motorhead, but I was really into drag racing; I used to run at Orange Dragway here in Massachusetts, at Sanford, Maine, and down at Connecticut Dragway in Colchester. Calvin was more of a hot-rodder. I'll bet he crashed more cars than the average three or people will ever own. Anyway, he had somehow gotten friendly with the Bouchards, and that's how I got to know them, too.

Up until then, I hadn't really been much of an oval-track guy. I had gone to Westboro and Peabody a few times in the early '60s. In fact, I guess you can even say I ran at Westboro. One Saturday night it had rained, and when the rain stopped they asked for volunteers to help dry the track. I had a '61 Ford Starliner, 375 horsepower, and I got right out there. They kept a pretty good eye on us, so I never got a chance to get out of control or anything like that. But you could say that was my only real oval-track experience until I got involved doing Ronnie's engines at Seekonk.

You could tell that people were already paying a lot of attention to him, because the next year Ronnie picked up a ride driving a Studebaker for Billy "Hooks" Ross. Hooks had good equipment, and it was kind of a big deal for a guy as young as Ronnie to be hired by a car owner. But I guess things just didn't click for whatever reason, and in '68 Ronnie was back driving for his father. Ronnie had gutted out a little Chevy II—it was actually a car he'd been driving on the street, but it had a bad oil leak—and we made it into a race car. I did the engine, and Vic built the chassis, probably from a frame we grabbed from the junkyard. And Ronnie did a lot of work on that thing, too. It ended up being a really good car. We won a few races at Westboro, and won a couple of championships at Seekonk.

That was a tough little circuit. At Seekonk you had Georgie Summers, Bobby Sprague, Red Barbeau, Eddie Hoyle, and the whole Astle family, it seemed like, because Deke, Freddie, and Jon Astle were all driving. All those guys ran hard, but the racing was usually pretty clean. There wasn't any real slam-bang stuff, as I recall. They'd rub a little bit, just because it was a tight little track, but for the most part everybody was fair about things.

Ronnie avoided a lot of that rubbing just by running the outside most of the time. He'd get out there three-wide if he had to, and work his way to the front. The fast guys started toward the back—I guess they handicapped the field by points—and the features were only 30 or 35 laps, so you had to go. But it didn't seem to matter *where* Ronnie started, he always managed to get to the front, running that high groove. Seekonk was almost a circle, and you'd swear he just about kissed the wall every lap with the right-rear tire at the start/finish line, right under the flagman.

I don't remember him ever being treated like an outcast or an outsider, even early on. That's probably because he was never a wild man on the track; he raced everybody cleanly, and in the pits he was always calm, easygoing, so he got along with not just the drivers, but the guys who worked on the cars, too. And, boy, there were some real characters at Seekonk. Tiny Levesque, who at that time built the engines for Sprague's team, was famous for doctoring up the fuel. Without even looking, you could tell when Sprague's car went by, because you could *smell* it. Tiny had some kind of banana-oil concoction that supposedly helped the gasoline to mix with whatever alcohol fuel he was slipping in there, and the exhaust gave off a *sweet* smell. He actually gave me the recipe later on, but, honestly, I never used that stuff. I *would* have, but I didn't know where to buy all the ingredients!

You could tell from the start that Ronnie was going to be one of the really good drivers. I've always thought about the fact that a lot of good race drivers, especially back then, were also involved with driving trucks. I don't know, maybe because they spent so much time behind the wheel, they were always comfortable driving; it's familiar to them. Well, that's true in Ronnie's case, because even as a teenager he and his father would drive up to Canada and haul back a load of Christmas trees. That's a lot of time sitting at the steering wheel.

He obviously had the raw talent for racing, but he also knew what he wanted from the car. He'd come in after practice or after the heat race and talk with Vic: "The car's doing *this*, the car's doing *that*." He had that real good seat-of-the-pants feel that people talk about the great ones having. So even if he wasn't necessarily a mechanic himself, and even if he didn't know what specific adjustments he wanted, he knew how he wanted the car to drive, and Vic was really good at getting it the way Ronnie wanted.

At the race track, Vic looked after the chassis and I took care of the engines, but we had other guys who helped, too. Mario Orsini from Fitchburg went just about every week, and Bugsy Roy used to drive the hauler, and Teddy Carlson, who worked at the International truck dealer in town and also helped maintain Bob Bouchard's moving trucks, would be there on Saturday nights. Everybody did his own job, and it was a good little team.

For our engines, we used to order our cylinder heads through Matthews Chevrolet right there in Fitchburg, complete with the valves and springs. Once in a while we might get a block from them, too, but normally we just had our old blocks machined at a shop that was run by a fellow named Dick Koivu in Townsend, just north of Fitchburg. Then we'd make sure we got a good set of connecting rods, and other than that, the engines weren't too fancy, just stock Chevrolet parts. We'd assemble everything right there at Red & White, and we'd run an engine for probably two seasons without really tearing it apart unless something went wrong.

In those days we even didn't do a whole lot as far as regular engine maintenance—just change the oil and run through the valves—so during the week I'd look after the bodies a little bit. Of course, that wasn't real serious, either! Just bang out the dents, and spray a little red paint sometimes. I was working at the

General Electric plant in Fitchburg, but every night I'd be at that garage, doing something.

After that Chevy II, we built a little Camaro that turned out to be a great Seekonk car. It kind of went together the same way the Chevy II did: Ronnie stripped the original car, Vic built the chassis from a junkyard frame, I put the engine together, and then Vic and I hung the body.

We worked hard, but we also enjoyed ourselves. Win or lose, we'd hang around in the pits or in the parking lot, partying half the night with guys from different teams. In fact, there was one stretch when Anthony Venditti got so sick of having to kick everybody out of his parking lot that he announced he was going to start penalizing the drivers if he caught them hanging around too long after the races were over. The following week, he came cruising through the parking lot a couple hours after the races, just kind of checking things out. I remember Ronnie running and jumping into the truck, hiding from Anthony so he wouldn't get in trouble.

That Camaro was the first car Ronnie ever raced anyplace bigger than a quarter-mile. We took it to Stafford for that open-comp Modified race in 1971, and all night long he ran with the best of 'em: Bugsy Stevens, Freddy DeSarro, Eddie Flemke, Hop Harrington, you name it. He finished third, and at the end of the race he had almost no brakes left. We used to run these big old Buick brakes that were fine at Seekonk, but they were just about gone after ten laps at Stafford, especially as hard as Ronnie was having to drive into the corners to keep up with those big-block cars.

I think Stafford and some of those other tracks—the NASCAR Modified circuit, basically—had been on Ronnie's mind for a while, because he and I had gone to Stafford a couple times before that race, just to watch. We also went to Norwood Arena once; I think Leo Cleary won that night, but I remember all the big NASCAR names being there. I think he went to those places because he'd heard about those Modified guys, and he wanted to see how they did things. And even though I never heard him talk about it, I'm sure that in the back of his mind he was thinking he wanted to join them, because they were supposed to be the very best. So I think running like he did at Stafford had to be a good feeling for him. Knowing how good those guys were, and then running right with them, that's got to do something for your ego.

It wasn't long after Stafford that Dick Armstrong called Ronnie to drive his coupe at Pocono. That was a famous car, because Ray Hendrick had had a lot of success with it, and then Hop Harrington had been driving it for Dick. I remember that weekend pretty well. For whatever reason, we needed to come up with a new motor for Seekonk, and Vic had a little 327, so I worked on that and got it ready. We won the feature on Saturday night, and then we all took off and drove to Pocono. I'm sure we must have had two or three carloads, heading out of Providence on I-95. That was quite a deal for us, because up until that point all we'd ever done was race at Seekonk and then go home, or maybe race at Westboro and then go home. Leaving one track and driving all night to get to another one was a big adventure for us.

To this day, I don't know exactly what had gone on between Armstrong and Hop, because when we got to Pocono, Hop was *there*, but he wasn't really in the picture. He was sitting in the pit stands with some of his friends, and when I was going through the valves before the feature I actually had to have somebody run over and ask Hop what the valve adjustments were.

Ronnie went really good in the race, but he ended up tangling with Denis Giroux, who was another very talented young guy. Ronnie hit the first-turn wall and broke some ribs. I can remember that on the ride home, he was kind of lying across the back seat of my car, moaning and groaning all the way. Oh, he was a hurtin' puppy.

Just a few weeks later he drove that Armstrong car again, at Trenton. Up until that day, I don't think any of us had seen a race track that big; I know I hadn't. The front straightaway looked like it went forever. I remember Vic adding pieces of sheetmetal here and there, little spoilers and trinkets, trying to make that coupe a bit more aerodynamic. Ronnie ended up finishing second to Geoff Bodine, so that was another big-deal race for him.

That season was pretty much the end of all of us working together, because in 1972 Ronnie went to run Stafford and the rest of the NASCAR tracks for Bob Johnson, and Bob already had his own group of guys. Other than one time at Thompson, when I fooled around with the carburetor and set the float levels, I don't think I ever worked on that car.

But, hey, that's part of racing. Drivers move up, and they find new rides, and it's something you just get used to if you're around for any length of time. And, obviously, that was a great opportunity for Ronnie. But pretty soon, along came Kenny, so I started working with him, and down the line I worked with a lot of other guys: Jerry Dostie, Tommy Bourget, Pete Fiandaca, and a bunch more. But nothing changed as far as Ronnie and I went, personally; we stayed as friendly as we ever were. In fact, I still saw him quite a bit in those years, because when I was working at GE it seemed like I always had a side job going—street car stuff, mostly—and Bob Bouchard used to let me use a garage bay right there at Red & White. If I needed to pull an engine or something, any kind of serious work, I'd do it there, and Ronnie would always pop in to see what I was up to. Naturally, we'd always end up talking about racing.

And if Bob happened to be shorthanded on a moving job, he'd put me to work. So I'd hop in the truck with Ronnie, and off we'd go. I can remember him saying, "Take a ride with me," and the two of us left on a trip to Canada. That's just the way things went with those Bouchards.

You know, at the time all this stuff was happening, we knew we were having fun. But it's only later, when you think back, that you see what a great time it really was. I mean, four track championships in a row, that was really the start of big things for Ronnie.

I can still see him at Seekonk, running that outside groove, lap after lap, almost clipping the starter's box.

BY VIC KANGAS

"I never, ever wished I'd had anyone else in the car"

Memories from a car builder, a teammate, and a pal

Vic Kangas has a solid and much-deserved reputation as a deep-thinking chassis man. A disciple of his innovative elder Marty Harty, Kangas had a hand in a number of Modifieds and Late Models that won throughout the Northeast, but he may be best remembered in the region for building the trio of Red & White Movers #35 cars that carried Ron Bouchard to his earliest fame—and four straight track championships—at Seekonk Speedway. Later, Kangas engineered IMSA road-race victories for Florida team owner Billy Dingman, and famously crew-chiefed Joe Nemechek to the 1992 NASCAR Busch Series championship, his crowning national achievement. Along the way he stood in victory lanes with George Summers, Gene Bergin, Ken Bouchard, and Bugs Stevens, but sentimental New England diehards will probably always connect Kangas to Ronnie Bouchard. And that's just fine with Vic. "We were friends," he smiles, "for 50 years."

BOUCHARD FAMILY COLLECTION

Back when Ronnie was just a teenager starting to drive moving trucks for his dad, I had a gas station in Lunenburg, which of course is right next door to Fitchburg. He used to stop there to fill up when he was going on a trip, and we'd always talk about racing because he knew that I'd been involved with building cars and working on them for a while. Honestly, by then we'd both been around racing for years already. I grew up in Lunenburg, but I used to ride my bicycle to Brookline Speedway on Sunday afternoons—it was probably 15 miles—or maybe hook a ride if I knew someone who was going. I'd sneak into the pits and help different people.

In 1964, Marty Harty and I built a car for a fellow who'd owned race cars for a while. I can't remember who had been driving for him, but the owner was ready to make a change, so we got Tinker Progin to drive this new car. Tinker was a good driver who'd won quite a few races around that area, and he had some strong runs with that thing, including a win in an open-competition race at Hudson Speedway. In '65 I had my own car, a Model A coupe, and we won the track championship at Hudson with Tinker driving. That same year, Ronnie had won a few races here and there with a car his dad had bought. So, like I said, we knew each other a little bit.

At the end of that season, I shut down my gas station and moved to Florida to take a temporary job with Pratt & Whitney in West Palm Beach. I was only down there for a few months, but I brought the race car with me. In fact, Tinker came down to run it a few times that winter, but then he had to go back home, so I hired a local guy to drive it. Well, don't you know, on the first corner of his first lap in my car, this guy crashed it. I mean, he flipped about as high as the light poles.

Calvin Blaisdell had come down to visit, and he was at the track with me. We watched this wreck take place, and when the car stopped Calvin said, "Vic, we don't need to run over there. I think he's dead."

The driver was fine, but the car was junk.

Early in '66 I moved back to Massachusetts, fixed the car, and had Tinker run it a few times. But it got wrecked again, and I decided enough was enough. That was the end of me owning race cars. By then, I'd already gotten more involved with Ronnie. He had made up his mind that he wanted to race at Seekonk, and he asked me if I could build him a car. Well, the cars that those guys were running at Seekonk were very much like the cars I'd seen Bobby Allison, Tiny Lund, and a few other people run in Florida. I knew what sort of suspension those guys ran, right down to the size of the sway bars, so that's what we built: a '57 Chevy just like the cars I'd seen in Florida. It had a big Lincoln sway bar that we got from a junkyard.

I didn't go to all the races with him in 1966—I had built a couple of cars for other guys, too, and that kept me pretty busy—but Ronnie took that car to Seekonk and won a couple or three races as a rookie. In '67 he drove for Billy Ross, but they didn't win any races, so for 1968 we built another car, a Chevy II, and I started going to all of the races with Ronnie. That turned out to be a really successful car. It was a '55 Chevy chassis, and the front end was very similar to our first Seekonk car, but the rear suspension was totally different; I used quarter-elliptic springs—it was actually the front spring from an International truck, cut in half—that came back from their mounting points and rode on little saddles under the rear axle, with a jacking bolt on each spring. It was something I just decided to try.

That '68 season was not the easiest for Ronnie and me. He was thinking more like a car owner than a race driver, so he didn't like to buy tires, and even back then new tires were faster than old ones. He'd have run the whole season on one set if it weren't for me saying over and over, "Look, sooner or later you're going to have to spring for some new tires." So every now and then, he'd buy a tire or two. Anyway, that Chevy II won races at both Seekonk and Westboro, and Ronnie won the track championship at Seekonk that year and the next.

For 1970 we built our third car together, a Camaro, out of a street car that had been in a fire. Now, that Camaro ended up being a fantastic car. It wasn't much different, chassis-wise, from the Chevy II, but I suppose you can say I had refined things a little bit based on what I'd learned. Ronnie won two more track championships with that thing.

By then it was clear to me that Ronnie was pretty special. He was a hard driver, but he was never rough, and it was so enjoyable to watch him get around Seekonk. Early in the feature you'd see him jump to the outside—out into the second groove if it was open, and the third groove if he needed it—and if he didn't get bottled up, he was going to the front. Some nights he won, and some nights he *would* have won if he hadn't run out of laps. One of those years with the Camaro, I think he finished second 12 times!

Geez, those Seekonk years were fun. All the guys that worked on Ronnie's car used to wear these welder's hats, red with white polka dots, and as things went along Ronnie had T-shirts and sweatshirts made, so it was almost like we were in uniform. And we all worked together really well; I never questioned what Dave Rossbach did with the engines, and he never questioned what I did with the chassis. Bob Bergeron was a bigger part of things than most people realize, too. Bergie's the kind of guy who likes to keep things looking good, so he'd always be adding some striping here and there to those cars. When you look at the old pictures, you can see a little bit of his handiwork. And Cal Blaisdell was around us quite a bit; he was more a part of the George Summers/Ken Curley team, building their engines, but he was still one of our good friends. Calvin *loved* the camaraderie and the competition of racing. He'd come over to our shop during the week and drive me crazy, just staring at our car to see what we were doing. Like I said, we had fun.

When you win that many races and championships, people tend to think everything must have gone your way. But nothing is ever as easy at it looks. One night Ronnie got into a tangle with the Camaro and it broke the gas tank bracket, so the tank was dangling. When he came into the pits, I took off my belt, hooked it around the frame and the tank bracket, and we sent him back out. He finished the race, and that meant a few more points. On another night there was a red flag and he was parked on the track. He had mostly missed the wreck, but you could see that the car had broken a ball joint. I walked out there with a spare ball joint, got the wrecker driver to pick up the front end, and changed the ball joint right there on the spot. But I think the incident that caused the most commotion was the night Ronnie slowed down to miss some kind of a tangle up ahead, and got hit from behind, which folded the rear of the frame downward. I had a come-along with me, and I figured that if I hooked one end of that come-along to the frame and other end to something good and sturdy, I could pull everything back into shape and get him going again. The sturdiest thing close by was one of the poles from the fence, so I hooked onto that. The next thing I knew, I was tearing down Anthony Venditti's fence. You can't win championships by giving up, and we never did.

Back then we were running these narrow M&H Racemaster tires. Ronnie kept saying that the right front would give up a little bit after 20 or 25 laps, and the car would start pushing. So we talked with Marvin Rifchin, who of course owned the M&H Tire Company, and he said he'd help us out. We actually loaded up the car and brought it to Marvin's place in Watertown. I brought along one of those old weight-jacker devices that were just starting to get popular with circle-track racers, the kind where you'd lift one wheel at a time with a lever. I don't think Marvin had ever seen one. Well, he got fooling around with that weight jacker, and you could just see the wheels turning in his mind. All of a sudden, we became his new project. He spent a lot of time with us that day, and he even came to Seekonk to help us out; I think he said it had been ten years since he'd been there.

Marvin really took a liking to Ronnie, and once he started helping us I'm not sure we—or any team Ronnie drove for—ever had to buy another M&H tire.

That Stafford race Ronnie ran in '71 with the Camaro, that midweek open-competition show, really got things going in the right direction for him. We'd been talking for a couple of weeks about running that race, but the car had gotten pretty badly bent up the previous Saturday night at Seekonk. Ronnie said, "If you guys think you can fix this thing in time, we'll go." We got it fixed, and off we went.

In the first practice down there, he was *really* getting through the turns, but it scared the heck out of me just watching him. See, we had brought our narrow Seekonk wheels and 13-inch tires, and it looked to me like the right-side tires were rolling off the rims. I told Ronnie, "Gee, this isn't looking too safe." I thought maybe a wider rim would help, but we didn't have any, and we didn't really know any of those NASCAR Modified car owners well enough to start borrowing wheels. Luckily, Bob Marvel, a friend of ours, happened to be with us, and he said he had some money with him, so we walked over to see Jimmy Bosco at the Commercial Tire truck. We bought two 15-inch wheels from Jimmy, and mounted our 13-inch tires on them. They had kind of a funny stance on those wheels, but in the next practice Ronnie was flying through the corners, and the whole situation looked a lot safer to me. He said it felt better, too, so we went racing.

You know, people still talk about the fact that he finished third that night, and, yes, that was great. But what was really incredible was how he did it: He passed 'em all in the turns, and all on the outside. Those guys had big blocks, so they'd kill him on horsepower, but he out-handled them. And, of course, he drove the wheels off of that car.

The guy who gave him the toughest time was Ernie Gahan, who was in his #29 coupe. For about the last 20 laps Ronnie would got alongside him, and almost past him, in almost every corner, but then Ernie would out-pull him on the straightaway.

While they were battling, Bugsy Stevens just jetted off with the lead, and that's how they finished: Bugsy first, then Ernie, and then us. But, *man*, that was really something, watching Ronnie dive into those corners to gain back all the ground he'd lost on the straightaways. You could just *see* how hard he was trying. He made a big impression on everybody there, because he was, what, 22 years old, and in those days that was really young to be going up against those top NASCAR Modified guys. Don't forget, both Bugsy and Ernie had been national champions. Those two guys had been everywhere.

Not long after that, we were working on the car one night and the phone rang. Ronnie went into the office to take the call. He walked back into the shop and said, "That was a guy named Dick Armstrong. He wants me to drive his car at Pocono."

I said, "Oh, yeah? What did you tell him?"

Ronnie said, "I told him no."

I said, "What you need to do is get on that phone and call him back. That might be the best Modified in the country."

See, I always had a lot of interest in what was happening elsewhere. If I wasn't busy getting ready for Seekonk, I'd be at Thompson or Stafford, checking out the top-running cars, seeing who was doing what. But Ronnie didn't pay much attention to what was going on outside of his own racing, so he didn't know anything about Dick Armstrong, and he probably hadn't heard of Jack Tant, or the Tant/Mitchell coupe, or even Ray Hendrick. All he really knew was *our* team, and he was really comfortable with us. If we told him to jump off the Brooklyn Bridge, I think he'd have given it a shot.

The Kid from Fitchburg

He said, "Okay, I'll do this, but I want you guys to come with me."

So that's what we did. Come that weekend, we won Seekonk on Saturday, and drove through the night to get to Pocono.

Now, that Pocono race had been rained out the previous week, after qualifying but before the non-qualifiers race. Hop Harrington had been Dick's driver—he also maintained the car—but Hop had missed the show. I guess that's when Dick decided he wanted to give Ronnie a shot; I'm sure he had seen Ronnie run that small-block Camaro at Stafford, and was as impressed as everybody else, and thought he'd give this kid a try.

But I knew something was strange, because when we got to Pocono the only person connected with that car who would talk to us was Dick Armstrong. Everybody else seemed to be mad at Dick, and because of that they were pissed off at us, too. We all showed up with our polka-dotted welder's hats, and I'm sure that to Hop and his guys it looked like this was some kind of an invasion. Pocono had a small grandstand behind pit road, and when Hop wandered over there and sat down, his guys went with him. I can understand that now, because Hop was their guy, and they were loyal to him. But, at the time, it kind of left the rest of us rookies all alone.

Dick just shrugged his shoulders and said to us, "I guess you guys can do whatever you want."

We worked on that coupe a little bit, and I made a few adjustments I thought might make things more comfortable for Ronnie, just based on the feeling I knew he liked. Then he went out to practice, and he was turning pretty good times. He pulled in and thought a minute, and then said, "It feels decent, but it's a little bit loose coming off the corners."

So we jacked up the car, and made a few more changes. Right then, Dick disappeared for a little while. He said later he walked behind the corner and threw up. "Too much stress," he said. I can understand that. Here he is with one of the fastest Modifieds anywhere, and all his regular guys are mad at him; now he's got a young driver and a bunch of guys he doesn't know, and we're changing everything around. Let's face it, Dick Armstrong was taking a heck of a big chance that day.

I made one chassis adjustment that I thought would correct that loose condition, but it didn't work, and Ronnie recognized that immediately. So we changed it back, and put on a slightly bigger left-rear tire to cut down the stagger and tighten up the car that way. The next practice began, and on his second lap Ronnie was under the track record. Suddenly, all those other guys who had worked on the car, including Hop, came wandering back. It was like they said, "Hey, this might be okay after all."

But that's the truth: Ronnie was as fast as anybody there. Now, you think about all that. This was by far the biggest track he had ever seen, a three-quarter-mile, and that big-block coupe was the first car he ever sat in that had serious, *serious* horsepower. But he'd always had a good instinctive feel for what any car could do, and as the day went along at Pocono it was really something to watch him make the most of this new situation.

He went out and won the non-qualifiers race, started deep in the pack in the big feature, and drove to the front like he was at Seekonk, passing cars on the outside. In fact, that's what got him in trouble. He was fourth, and just about to take third, when Denis Giroux ran him a little bit wide in the first turn. Not that Giroux did anything wrong; they were just racing hard for that position. Well, Ronnie got into the marbles, slid into the wall, and broke a few ribs on his right side.

He could barely breathe, could barely talk. He just made a noise like "*Ooooph*" every time he moved. But he raced the very next Saturday at Seekonk. He was favoring his ribs all night, but he was going well in the feature, duking it out with George Summers, as usual, and it all came down to a late restart. But because Ronnie was favoring those ribs—if you're sitting a little differently and it hurts every time you move, things just don't happen as naturally as they should—something went wrong. I can't remember if he missed a shift or maybe bumped the ignition switch, but something happened that made the car stumble, and George got away.

Armstrong asked Ronnie to drive his car again a few weeks later at Trenton. I went down to Dick's shop to help Hop rebuild it, and as we got to know each other, Hop and I became really good friends. I always knew he'd been a great driver, but he was also a great fabricator, and it was really enjoyable to work with him. But I did a couple things to the front end that I later wished I hadn't. See, I had a habit of running more caster in the left-front corner than in the right front; that was completely backwards from the way everybody else did things, but every bit of our success at Seekonk, all those wins and championships, had come with that setup. But at Trenton, with those long, high-banked corners and all the extra loads on the car, that was not the hot setup. Ronnie just couldn't steer the thing.

We finished second, right behind Geoff Bodine, and toward the end of the race Ronnie was running him down because, if I'm not mistaken, Geoff's clutch was slipping. So naturally everybody said, "Geez, if we'd only had a few more laps, we might have won this thing." But Ronnie pulled me aside said, "Vic, if that race was just a couple laps longer, I'd never have made it. My arms hurt so bad, they're about ready to fall off."

All those accomplishments he'd had by the end of 1971—the Seekonk stuff, plus what he showed he could do at Pocono and Trenton—had to build his confidence. But, you know, Ronnie had a lot of confidence anyway. I think he believed that he was as good a driver as anybody.

And you want to know something? I never, ever went anywhere with him and wished I'd had anyone else in that car.

BY GEORGE SUMMERS

"That kid had more damn talent than any kid I'd ever seen come along"

From "driving school" instructor to Saturday-night rival to friend

R.A.SILVIA COLLECTION

No less an authority than three-time NASCAR national champion Bugs Stevens calls George Summers "one of the most underrated guys in New England racing." A lot of this was because for years Summers raced just for fun, in the same way other men golf on the weekends. Instead of clubs, George packed a helmet bag and headed to Seekonk Speedway and its occasional sister track, Westboro Speedway, places which back then never grabbed the level of regional and national attention afforded to NASCAR tracks like Stafford, Thompson, or Norwood Arena. But don't think for a minute that racing "for fun" made Summers some kind of softie. Though always fair, he had the focused ferocity those bullrings demanded, as evidenced by his status as winningest driver in Seekonk history. Though they lived in Upton, Massachusetts, Seekonk was for years the Saturday-night address for George and Maggie Summers and their children.

Before Ronnie came to Seekonk as a teenager, I was completely unaware of him. I'd be willing to say that I'd probably never even heard his name. Obviously, I learned later on that he'd already done some winning in the cutdown cars, up around Pines Speedway and Hudson Speedway and those places, but that was an entirely different circuit.

You've got to understand, Seekonk Speedway was the only place I really paid any attention to at that point, except for some years when I'd also race at Westboro. Racing at Seekonk was my hobby, the thing I did every Saturday night, and I was doing very well there. It was where I wanted to be, and I just didn't ever look around to see who was doing what at any of these other tracks. And, don't forget, there was no local racing paper then. *New England Speedway Scene* hadn't come along yet, so you didn't read about the guys who were winning elsewhere, or see any pictures of the cars they were running.

When Ronnie showed up at Seekonk in 1966, I'd already been there a long time. I think it was in 1958 or '59 that I'd first raced there, and pretty soon I was one of the guys to beat, along with Deke Astle, Joe Rosenfield, Dave Dias, Red Barbeau, Eddie Hoyle, and a few more guys. I just loved Seekonk; don't ask me why, but I loved everything about that race track. Things just seemed to click there for me.

In the period we're talking about, I was driving Ken Curley's #31. Ken was the head mechanic as well as the car owner, and Calvin Blaisdell built the engines, and that was a really good combination of two smart guys. Then here came Ronnie with his #35, and he had some smart people around him, too, with Vic Kangas working on the chassis and Dave Rossbach doing his engines. Both of our teams, I think, were the cream of the crop for that era at Seekonk, just in terms of having the right combinations of people.

The way Ronnie always told it, when he first got there he went to Anthony Venditti and asked him, "Tell me, who's the hot dog down here?"

And I guess Mr. Venditti said, "Son, do you see that #31 car over there? When you can beat that guy, you'll be winning races."

I didn't know any of this, of course. But pretty soon it was time for me to climb into the car and strap in for warm-ups, so that's what I did. Well, Ronnie was already sitting in his car, ready to go. He followed me out of the pits, and from the minute they waved the green flag, he stayed right on my bumper. Wherever I went, he went.

For the next few weeks it went the same way. I'd pull onto the track for warm-ups, and there was Bouchard and that #35, in my mirror. By now I had talked to Ronnie a little bit, and I liked him right off the bat. And, you know, I suppose I kind of took it as a compliment that he was looking at me as the guy he wanted to learn from.

Naturally, though, as we got more and more comfortable with each other, we started getting racy, even in the warm-ups. I'd let him get to my outside, and we'd run like that for a few laps, and then maybe we'd swap positions for a few more laps, with me on the outside and him down low. It got to the point where Ken Curley pulled me aside one night and said to me, in this really serious voice, "Hey, George, listen, we're not running a driving school here. You don't have to show that kid *everything*."

Well, that kid had more damn talent than any kid I'd ever seen come along, and that's what I told Ken.

Ronnie won a couple of features at Seekonk that first year, but the biggest thing he had going for him is that he was consistent. He always finished up near the front, just as I did. So, because of the handicapping system, the two of us always started toward the back of the pack with the rest of the fast guys. That meant I saw an awful lot of that #35, and he saw an awful lot of my #31, because we'd start deep in the pack together, we'd race through traffic together, and it seemed like we'd always get to the front together. And that's pretty much how it went for the next several years.

At Seekonk you had to be aggressive, because the regular Saturday-night features were so short. But you also had to be smart; you couldn't just hammer your way to the front, or you'd end up in a wreck. You had to have that balance, somewhere between aggressive and overaggressive. I think I had it, and so did Ronnie, and so did guys like Rosenfield and Bugsy Stevens, who had won track championships at Seekonk just before we did.

Ronnie was one of the first guys I remember who would put himself on the outside, three-wide, *on purpose*. Sometimes guys got shoved up there and went backwards, but Ronnie used that third lane to go forward. Seekonk was narrower back then than it is today, but even then it was famous for producing side-by-side racing; the layout and the banking were perfect for that. Well, if you're starting eight or nine rows back and the whole field can stay side by side, you don't have to be too smart to see that it's going to be hard to get to the front. So early on, Ronnie started jumping up into that third lane—maybe because he just didn't know any better at first—and you'd see him make his way to the front, passing two cars at a time. That got my attention.

I said to myself, "Well, Summers, if this kid can do that, so can you." So every week I'd follow him out there in that third lane, or, if I happened to start ahead of him, he'd follow me. Many, many nights it seemed like I spent almost the whole feature out there, with two cars to my inside, Bouchard either right ahead of me or right behind me. Both of us would be scraping the outside wall coming off the corners, not hard, but just enough to throw sparks. Finally, with a few laps to go, we'd break out of that mess and then the two of us would fight for the win with whoever else was up there in the lead.

I'll tell you, on a small track like Seekonk, things happen fast. When you're running three-wide, and you're scraping that wall and dealing with the two guys alongside you, you usually don't have time to do anything but look ahead. But once I made it through the worst of it and I finally had a chance to look in the mirror, it never failed: There was Ronnie. I'd say to myself, "Okay, it looks like it's going to be between you and Bouchard."

And I'm sure he had the same thing happen to him on a lot of Saturday nights, when he'd look up and see that I'd followed him all the way to the front, and it was down to the two of us.

I can remember Ronnie and I both half-heartedly bitching to Anthony Venditti, saying, "Geez, how come we have to start so far back every single week? Why can't you change the handicapping system just a little bit, and move us up a couple of rows?"

And Mr. Venditti would point up at the grandstands, which on most Saturday nights were pretty full. He'd say, very calmly, "Do you see all those people sitting there? They came here tonight to see if you guys can make it from the back to the front, just like you did last week and the week before. Some of them are hoping you can, and some of them are hoping you can't. But that's why they're here, to watch and find out."

We couldn't argue with that. So we'd just climb into those cars, line up in the back, and try it all over again.

We had so many nights when we'd be fighting for the lead, and anytime I happened to catch a glimpse of the crowd—maybe when I looked up at the flagman, or something like that—I could see the fans going crazy. My wife, Maggie, used to tell me that she'd hear the people sitting around her saying, "Hey, watch this battle! Summers and Bouchard *hate* each other!" Well, I'm sure that was good for Seekonk and Anthony Venditti, because the fans turned it into this big rivalry, but Ronnie and I were already good friends by then. Most Saturday nights we'd get out of our cars smiling and laughing, whether he won or I won or somebody else won.

Here's how close we were: I can remember Ronnie and his first wife stopping at our house on a motorcycle on a Sunday afternoon. It was a beautiful day, and I guess they'd been out for a ride, so they just stopped in. I'm sure we had probably raced hard together the previous night, and maybe one of us had beaten the other to win the feature, but that didn't matter. We were already dear friends, to the point where he felt comfortable just showing up at our home.

Our youngest daughter, Kathie, was born in 1965. She was always a feisty kid, right from the beginning. At some point during the '67 season, it looked like the Seekonk track championship was going to come down to Ronnie and me. So one night at the track, she marched over to Ronnie, and this feisty little girl said, "You're *not* going to beat my father. He's going to win the championship this year."

Ronnie thought that was great. But just to fire her up, he said, "I'll tell you what. If your father wins the championship, I'm going to buy you a lobster dinner."

Well, the season rolled along, and I did end up winning the Seekonk championship. And I'll be damned if one night he didn't show up at the house with this great big five-pound lobster.

He wanted to know, "Where's Kathie?"

Maggie and I said, "She's already in bed."

No problem. Ronnie came in, marched right upstairs, and put that lobster in her bed. He said, "Here's that lobster dinner I promised you!"

The next year, 1968, he had the last laugh, because he won the championship himself, and he also won the next three in a row after that.

What won Ronnie those championships was the fact that he *always* seemed to finish. He won his share of races in that period, but he wasn't like he was *the* dominant driver at Seekonk. When they inducted us both into what they call their Wall of Fame in 2013, it kind of surprised me that Ronnie had only 29 wins there. Yes, he really only ran there regularly for a handful of years, but because of all those championships I just figured he had won more than he did. So what helped him, like I said, was that he always finished, and he seemed to win the *big* races, the double-point nights and so on.

You know, Ronnie had such a great personality. He came into Seekonk so young and beat all of us veterans, but nobody held that against him, or seemed to be upset about it. I think everybody liked him.

I've said this before, but I mean it: Within a couple of years, he was better than I was. I remember telling him, "Listen, Ronnie, Seekonk is great, and we're having a good time, but you've got the capability to do much bigger things. You're wasting your time here."

I might have laughed a little and added, "Plus, you're taking all my gravy."

He told me that he was interested in advancing, and seeing what else he could do, and I told him that he really needed to look hard at doing that. I think maybe that opened his eyes a little bit, and made him think more about what else was out there.

Dick Armstrong had seen Ronnie race, and had heard a little bit about him, and, like everybody else, Dick really took to Ronnie right away. He offered him the ride in his coupe for those big races at Pocono and Trenton, and Ronnie said yes. And, of course, he really made the most of that opportunity, because he turned a lot of heads at those two races. Looking back, that was obviously a big turning point for him, and it probably helped Ronnie decide for himself that it was time to move on.

I'll tell you a funny story: It was me who first introduced Ronnie to Bugsy Stevens. Bugsy, of course, had been a Seekonk guy, and then he'd gone on to be a NASCAR Modified champion. We were good friends, and we still are. Anyway, right after they met Bugsy said to me, "George, send that kid over to Stafford. We'll cool his heels a little bit."

Except it didn't work out that way. Ronnie won a few features in his first season at Stafford, which was just about unheard of, and the next year he won the track championship. And he beat Bugsy to win it!

But, hey, the way I looked it, that was Bugsy's problem. At least that kid wasn't stealing my gravy anymore!

PART TWO

Purple Reign

MIKE ADASKAVEG

Nobody goes straight to Broadway, or straight to Fenway Park, or straight to what was then the major short-track league in New England, the NASCAR Modified circuit, without some training. What minor-league stints with the Raleigh Capitals and Minneapolis Millers did for a Red Sox prospect named Carl Yastrzemski, six seasons at Seekonk Speedway had done for Ron Bouchard. They sharpened him, toughened him, showed him that he had what it took. And it was time to move on.

It took some coaxing from rivals past and future, like George Summers and Bugs Stevens, but Bouchard made his move in the winter of 1971–72. It's curious, the way the great ones know not to move too fast. He weighed all options, considered every angle.

Dick Armstrong, for whom Bouchard had driven with such panache at Pocono and Trenton, kept calling with updates on the new car Hop Harrington was building him, reminding Ronnie that the seat was his if he wanted it. But the gang at Red & White in Fitchburg was also putting together something new, a NASCAR-legal #35. And a man named Bob Johnson rang to say that he, too, was building a new car, and that he was shopping for a driver.

Put yourself in the shoes of 23-year-old Ron Bouchard, and think about the offers on the table.

The smart bet, on paper, was that Armstrong ride. Here you had a wealthy owner—Dick's Nu-Style Jewelry operation in Franklin, Massachusetts, was doing well—willing to spend what it took to win. On top of that, in Harrington he had an excellent chassis man who could also be a fine coach for an up-and-coming driver visiting a lot of unfamiliar tracks.

On the other hand, human nature tends to steer us toward the safe bet, which is to go with what you know, with what is familiar. In Bouchard's case that would have meant hunkering down in the shop on Lunenburg Street, alongside Vic Kangas, Dave Rossbach, kid brother Kenny and the rest of the crew, and completing the car that would mark their jump from Seekonk to Modifieds.

The bet with the longest odds looked to be this Johnson fellow, way down in Westbrook, Connecticut, a sleepy town along Long Island Sound. There is nothing to indicate that Bouchard knew Bob Johnson's name any more than he'd known Dick Armstrong's the previous summer. And while Johnson's coupe had put in a few good runs with drivers like Rene Charland and Jerry Dostie, it was hardly one of New England's marquee rides.

But Bouchard agreed to drive down and see what Johnson had going on. It was two hours down and two hours back, but in between he got to got to know Johnson and his wife, Gussie, and he checked out Bob's new Pinto, and something about the events of the day took root. Ronnie Bouchard ended up going with the long shot, telling Johnson a short time later that he'd drive for him in 1972. It turned out to be one of the best bets of his life.

And a pretty good bet for Johnson, too. His Pinto—painted a deep purple, with a white #17 on its doors—was a match for anything the era had, and so was its young driver.

Which was saying something for both of them, because it wasn't as if Bouchard and Johnson caught Modified racing during one of those weak periods every division sees from time to time. Their main focus would be Saturday nights at Stafford—owned by construction-company boss and Modified enthusiast Jack Arute, the track was the heartbeat of NASCAR racing in New England—where the talent on display was astounding. Wherever you looked, there stood another top-shelf driver, another estimable mechanic.

Bugs Stevens was riding a wave of popularity the likes of which Modified racing had never seen. He'd won three NASCAR national championships, 1967–69, driving for a Massachusetts eccentric named Len Boehler. Lenny's act was 100 percent poor boy—he was always in a work shirt with someone else's name on it, and wasted no time on paint and polish—but he was a genius mechanic. When the pair split in '71, Stevens took a ride with Rhode Islander Sonny Koszela, who owned a lumberyard and a speed shop. Koszela's Modifieds, built by quiet Dave Tourigny, were as neat as Boehler's were battered, and just as fast.

When Bugsy jumped ship, Boehler did the convenient thing and hired Koszela's former driver, Fred DeSarro, who'd won the national NASCAR title in 1970. It was like trading Mickey Mantle for Willie Mays. In 1971, DeSarro won at Stafford, Thompson, and New York's Utica-Rome Speedway, among other places; in '72, Fred and Boehler's Ol' Blue coupe won the inaugural Spring Sizzler at Stafford, and went on to take the track championship.

And then there was Ed Flemke. A Connecticut native, Flemke spent the early '60s carrying trophies out of tracks in Virginia and North Carolina; on the way down and back, he'd pick up more in New Jersey and Maryland. In 1967 he jumped into a coupe owned by another Nutmeg Stater, Bob Judkins, and they closed the decade winning at New England's NASCAR tracks—Stafford, Thompson, and Norwood Arena, outside Boston—and making lucrative raids into upstate New York. Early in '71, Judkins saw a Pinto pull into his service station and thought Ford's new subcompact would make a dandy Modified. But NASCAR rules allowed only coupes and sedans and more recent compacts like Falcons, Camaros, and Mustangs, most of which looked awkward. Judkins built his Pinto anyway, and Stafford's Arute lobbied hard to get it legalized. NASCAR relented, and Gene Bergin drove the Judkins #2X to victories in an August 50-lapper and the Labor Day 200. The Pinto Revolution, which also welcomed Chevrolet's Vega and the AMC Gremlin, was underway. Come the close of '71, Judkins sold that first Pinto, started building a second, and in '72 both were winning with Flemke in the saddle and Bobby on the wrenches.

Bergin, meanwhile, took the Armstrong ride Bouchard turned down. He was on his way to winning March's Dogwood 500 at Martinsville, Virginia, when his engine blew. But he rebounded nicely, winning a pair of Stafford features in 1972. Gene's natural ability wowed even his most accomplished rivals. Pete Hamilton, who had graduated from Modifieds to winning the 1970 Daytona 500—and who had raced door-to-door with A.J. Foyt, Richard Petty, David Pearson, and Cale Yarborough—called Bergin "one of the greatest drivers I've ever known. Not just one of the greatest Modified drivers, or one of the greatest New England drivers, but one of the very best drivers I've ever seen."

In other corners of the Stafford pit area you had Bob Santos climbing into Art Barry's coupe, rugged Leo Cleary chatting with car owner Bob Garbarino, Fred Schulz leaning on the car he'd be steering for Joe Brady, and a smiling young guy named Ray Miller, just a few years older than Bouchard; Ray would also score at Stafford in that summer of '72.

It's worth pointing out that every one of the drivers and owners and mechanics listed above has been inducted into the New England Auto Racers (NEAR) Hall of Fame. This was the tough weekly arena into which Bouchard and Johnson stepped.

And when they took their act on the road, the talent pool only got deeper. New Yorkers Geoff Bodine and Richie Evans, who had finished on either side of Bouchard in his 1971 runner-up finish at Trenton, were still on the ascendant. Jerry Cook, who like Evans raced out of the city of Rome, had just sewn up the first of his six NASCAR championships. Maynard Troyer, a Rochester open-comp ace who'd also done a Winston Cup stint, was now hauling his beautiful Modifieds to more NASCAR-sanctioned events. And Montreal's Denis Giroux was in the best days of a star-crossed career; he would suffer career-ending injuries at the 1974 Spring Sizzler, but in '72 Denis won the Labor Day 200 at Stafford.

Every trip south introduced Ronnie and Bob to new foes, from veterans like Paul Radford and Harry Gant to young Satch Worley, who was the same age as Bouchard and generating a similar buzz.

So, you ask, how did they do? How did Bouchard and Johnson do in this thrill-a-minute era, against such formidable competition?

Well, they did fine, for better than four full seasons.

1972: At Bouchard's request, the Johnson #17 debuted at the first Spring Sizzler with no name above its door. Perhaps he was hedging his long-shot bet. That day ended when oil from his own blown engine spun him into the wall, but the car was a bullet, vaulting from a sixth-row start into the top five in just a few laps. Two weeks later, upon winning Stafford's regular-season opener, Bouchard greeted Johnson with the words, "You can paint my name on the car now!" … Ron won twice more at Stafford, and one of his conquests was the Permatex 150. He was, no surprise, the track's Rookie of the Year … Bouchard also took top rookie honors at New York's Albany-Saratoga Speedway. Though winless at the Friday facility, he consistently ran in the top five … One of Bouchard's biggest days did not involve a victory. In a Pocono event named for an oil additive called Flight 216, he was in the hunt, but chaos reigned. Chuck Fierson of the *Pocono Record* described "a five-way race between [Maynard] Troyer, Ron Bouchard, defending champion Bryan Osgood, [Richie] Evans, and Ray Hendrick." But Hendrick, Troyer, and Evans pitted under green, which would have put all three a lap down, at least until Bouchard and Osgood came in under green. Then a caution flag waved. Fierson continued: "Bouchard, who had assumed the lead, pitted under a yellow. Suddenly Evans was declared the leader and Hendrick second. Nobody could figure out where they came from. Timing and scoring officials explained that the pair had passed the pace car under the yellow flag. A preliminary ruling said the pair would be penalized, but the ruling was later reversed and Evans and Hendrick continued to run one-two [until] Troyer gained second place when he passed Hendrick on the 188th lap." At which point a cloudburst ended everything, and officials lost the plot. Someone decided the $3,800 winner's payout should go to Evans, and Richie, in those days an unsponsored gas-station owner trying to make ends meet, was smart enough to take it. Troyer was placed second, Hendrick third, and Osgood fourth. Bouchard, who had pitted under yellow, while leading, was somehow adjudged to have lost two laps. But on neutral turf, against the biggest names in Modified racing, he had turned plenty of heads. Again.

1973: The signature season of the Bouchard/Johnson partnership, highlighted by the weekend of June 2-3. On Saturday at Stafford, Ronnie and the #17 blazed to a track record in qualifying for an extra-points 100. In the feature, he and Evans lapped the field, no small feat given that Stevens and Flemke finished third and fourth. The next day at Pocono, in the Parodi Cigar 150, Bouchard avenged the previous summer's robbery by defeating Cook, Flemke, and everybody else … That Stafford 100 was one of ten Bouchard victories there, including three straight in the spring and then five in a row in the heat of summer. He clinched the track championship with weeks to spare … Another big score on the road came on Independence Day weekend, when Bouchard beat Giroux in a 100-lapper at New York's Oswego Speedway … In October's prestigious Race of Champions at Trenton, Ronnie was in contention for the win, but ultimately sheared a wheel … Bouchard's last victory of 1973 came in early August, and the autumn months tested Johnson, who was the temperamental type. There were some fiery outbursts around car #17, usually directed at no one in particular, with language as purple as the Pinto. Vic Kangas, Ronnie's old Seekonk ally, was among those looking on from a safe distance. Today, Vic says, "Anybody who ever observed Bob at the race track knows he didn't worry too much about the care and feeding of his drivers. Warm and fuzzy was not part of his program." No matter. Johnson and Bouchard were by now one of the best teams in all of Modified racing.

1974: Stafford was now what Seekonk had once been to Ron Bouchard—the centerpiece of his racing, the place his weekends revolved around—and he had another great season at Arute's track, winning four straight in June and a 100-lapper in August. But track champion Bugs Stevens won eleven times, including the Spring Sizzler, a 100-lapper in September, and an 80-lapper in October ... Elsewhere, there was real momentum behind the small-block Modified movement, from the fast five-eighths-miler at Thompson to quarter-mile bullrings like Westboro, where Ronnie had first discovered racing, and New Hampshire's Monadnock Speedway. Johnson prepped a second car, a Vega, for the small-block wars, and he and Bouchard won immediately ... Come October, two huge Sundays cemented the Bouchard legend in the minds of race fans both local and far-flung. First came an open-comp twinbill at Thompson, with the track's regular small-block Modifieds and their big-block cousins each running 50-lap features. Ronnie won both. His small-block ride was the Manchester Sand & Gravel Pinto owned by Connecticut's Bill Thornton. In the big-block main, Stevens had the lead until Bouchard pinned him behind a lapped car. Dr. Dick Berggren, writing in *Stock Car Racing* magazine, called it "a very neat move." Berggren also noted the underdog third-place finish of 19-year-old Ken Bouchard in the big-block event. "It was, without a doubt, the day of the Bouchard family," wrote Dr. Dick. Two weeks later came more acclaim when Ronnie beat Richie Evans to win the Modified portion of the Cardinal 500 at Martinsville. The Late Model Sportsman half went to Ray Hendrick. Martinsville's trusty PR man, Dick Thompson, made sure the traditional post-race photograph of the two winners was distributed to every racing outlet, as well as to the wire services. Monday-morning newspapers from Virginia's *Danville Bee* to California's *San Bernardino County Sun* carried the race report, many illustrating their stories with the photo of Hendrick, at 44 one of American short-track kings, shaking hands with 26-year-old Bouchard, one of its princes.

1975: Here, there, and everywhere, that was Ron Bouchard as the decade reached its halfway point. He and Johnson expanded their horizons, dabbling with a Late Model Sportsman Chevelle owned by Montreal's Paul Boyer. With Johnson building the engines and handling crew-chief responsibilities, Bouchard finished tenth in February's Permatex 300 at Daytona. While there, he ran a road-course event for NASCAR Modifieds aboard brother Kenny's Vega, powered by a small block. Oiling issues knocked them out, but Ronnie's speed through the twisty infield section amazed his old pal Dave Rossbach: "The guys with the big blocks would get away from him down the long straightaways, but through all those corners in the infield he'd catch right back up" ... In the Dogwood 500, Bouchard looked set for a second straight Martinsville win until a throttle spring failed 13 laps from the end; he coaxed the #17 home second ... Back home, the New England scene was in disorder. Stafford experimented with narrow, 13-inch tires for its Saturday-night NASCAR program, but by the end of May the rule was dropped. Bouchard won the first feature back on standard Modified tires, running M&H Racemasters supplied by his friend and patron, Marvin Rifchin. It was his only win of a weird Stafford season; ten different drivers won, and the track title went to newcomer Geoff Bodine, who had taken a job driving and helping maintain Dick Armstrong's Modifieds. Jack Arute also tried a series of Sunday-night small-block shows, a contentious move given that Thompson, not 45 miles away, had an established Sunday small-block program. Stafford dangled a fatter purse and drew more cars—50 on average—but fan support was abysmal. Thompson rocked on with a loyal fan base and a field that included Bouchard and the #17, which won four times ... The small-block events presented Ronnie some other neat opportunities. With Johnson's Vega he won at Monadnock, and copped five more and a cherished track championship at Westboro ... Like Evans, Cook, Stevens, and a few other Modified travelers, Bouchard occasionally shuttled from one track to the next via private aircraft, in his case a plane owned by old friend Wes Sleeper ... In their big-block travels, Bouchard and Johnson had a fine year by most standards, but not their own. Martinsville's spring and fall classics gave Ronnie a second and a sixth; he finished fourth in an Oswego 75; and in a one-time visit to New York's Shangri-La Speedway he ran third to Evans and a rising star named George Kent.

1976: Not everything lasts forever, in racing or in life. When he left the comfortable cocoon of weekly racing at Seekonk for the busier world of regional racing, Ron Bouchard was a married father of four. By the second half of the decade, he and his wife had split, and Bouchard was juggling fatherhood with his job at Red & White Movers and an ever-increasing race schedule. The Modified division was the busiest it had been in years, and, as always, great drivers were in demand, so he was now racing three or four nights a week. His kids, who were with him on the weekends, were almost always at the track, shepherded by Ron's mother and his sister, JoAnn. And Ronnie was often in the company of a new partner, Paula Flemke, daughter of one of his biggest rivals, Ed Flemke. This was not met with instant approval on Eddie's part. Wise to the ways of the world, and also to the ways of some of his less chivalrous peers, Flemke was just looking after his daughter. He needn't have worried. This, all soon realized, was a relationship built to last ... On the other hand, Bouchard's first real relationship with a car owner was coming apart. Few saw it coming. He and Bob Johnson and Paul Boyer gave Daytona another whirl in February, finishing ninth this time. Back in the Modified, things had a lukewarm start: a DNF at Martinsville; third behind Flemke and Bodine in Thompson's chilly Icebreaker; seventh—a good seventh, behind Troyer, Evans, Bodine, Stevens, DeSarro, and Cook—in a Stafford small-block event called The Race, run on the Saturday of Spring Sizzler weekend, before the Sizzler itself rained out; and second to Flemke in a Thompson small-block show. Then came the start of Stafford's regular season, and the pairing of Bouchard and Johnson just ... *dissolved*. No ugly blow-up, no loud spat; only, as Bob Johnson puts it, differences on "a few small things." Again: Not everything lasts forever, in racing or in life. But, Lord, what a mark they made together. Just try picturing Modified racing in the first half of the '70s without Ronnie and that purple #17.

BY BOB JOHNSON

"If I told Ronnie that we were good to go, he'd just climb in and go wide open"

One half of a great Modified duo discusses the other

MIKE ADASKAVEG

Bob Johnson's purple #17 remains one of the iconic Modifieds of the '70s. If you are of a certain age, it's probably also the car you picture when someone mentions Ron Bouchard. It certainly helped gain Ron his first real fame; photos of his Martinsville and Pocono victories made the national racing magazines. Today, folks still smile about the pairing of the easygoing Bouchard and the volcanic Johnson, but theirs was clearly a case of opposites attracting. Though he later became a winning NASCAR Cup series crew chief, in his Modified days Bob was a thoroughly old-school car owner, building and wrenching his own iron, wife Gussie always by his side. When he first teamed with Bouchard, Johnson worked for his hometown of Westbrook, Connecticut, doing road maintenance. Before long, though, "all I did was race. We could make enough money to do that."

Pocono in '71. That's where I first got a real good look at Ronnie. I'll tell you who first put me onto him: It was Jimmy Bosco, the fellow who owned and ran Commercial Tire. I'd been running my coupe, and I was thinking about different drivers for the following year, 1972, and Jimmy said, "You know, there's a kid who runs at Seekonk …"

He told me a little bit about Ronnie, and he said, "I'm telling you, this kid will get the job done."

So I go and run the Pocono race, and, sure enough, this Bouchard kid shows up there with Dick Armstrong's coupe, and he really looks good. I called him up sometime later—I don't know where I'd have gotten his phone number—and he came down to see me. By then I was putting together my first Pinto, which I designed and built myself, and he looked everything over while we talked. We were getting to know each other, you might say. I think we kind of hit it off right from the get-go; Ronnie was a friendly guy, anyway.

One thing I recall is that you could just *tell* that he wanted to do well. He wasn't one of those guys who was going to take a ride just so he could go to Stafford and ride around. He wanted to be sure that he'd be competitive. That impression has stayed with me.

But when he left, he still sounded really undecided about what he wanted to do. And I understood that; he didn't know me at all, and Armstrong was talking with him at the same time. So he said, "Let me think about this a little bit." And yet it seems to me now that it was within just a day or two that we talked again. This all happened a long time ago, so I can't recall if I called him, or he called me, but as I remember it was all pretty quick. And he said, "Well, hell, let's give it a whirl, and see what happens."

I finished up the Pinto, and we brought it to the first Spring Sizzler at Stafford. We were running good, running *great*, but the motor blew and he backed that thing into the wall in turn one. So now I've got a brand new car all wadded up, and the regular Stafford season starts in two weeks. I remember Ronnie asking me how long I thought it would take to fix it, and I said, "Oh, we'll be ready for opening night."

Well, we *were* ready, and he won the feature. Was I happy? Oh, *man*. I had won a few races here and there before Ronnie showed up, but to go that good right away with a new driver at a place like Stafford—and then to win a couple more there that same season—that was a pretty big deal.

Running with Ronnie, that was also the first time I really had any success on the road, meaning in the big Modified races that you had to travel to. We went to Pocono in 1972 for the Flight 216 race, and ran great all day. In fact, I still think we won that thing. But somehow the scoring got all messed up, and then the race got shortened by rain, and they gave the win to Richie Evans. Now, there were a bunch of guys standing around who figured that they won that race. In my mind, either Ronnie and I won it, or Bryan Osgood won it, but Richie definitely *didn't* win it. In fact, that fall we were standing around at Martinsville, and Richie and I were talking about that Pocono race, and he admitted it. He laughed and said, "I know I didn't win it, but they couldn't make up their minds, and I needed the money."

Sometime later, at an auto show they used to have in the winter in New London, I ran into one of the NASCAR officials who'd been in charge that day.

He told me, "You know, Bob, it turns out you were right about Pocono. We eventually did find that mistake, but it was long after we could have done anything about it."

But my point is, in our first season together Ronnie and I were running good against the top guys, whether it was at Stafford or someplace else in those big shows. And the next year, '73, we went back to Pocono and won it outright. I mean, there was no doubt about it this time. That same NASCAR official was standing there, and I said, "It's pretty damn bad when you have to win a race *twice* to get paid for winning it once!"

That 1973 season was incredible for us. Until I read something not long ago, it had slipped my mind that the night before Pocono, we had won a 100-lapper at Stafford, a big race with everybody there. I think about things like that, and about the people we were beating, and it's really something. A few weeks later we went to a special show at Oswego, and we won that, too. I remember Ronnie passing Maynard Troyer, and in those years Maynard was the man up there.

We won something like ten races that season at Stafford, and got the track championship, and Stafford was really *the* hot place in Modified racing at that time. I'll tell you how good we were there: We had been running Albany-Saratoga sometimes on Fridays, and I guess one night we had a bad race there. I must have looked kind of dejected, because Leo Cleary said, "Don't worry, tomorrow night you get to go to Stafford and pick up your regular paycheck."

But, boy, Stafford was such a tough track. It's different on both ends, so you had to have the car set up just right, and the driver really had to know how to get around that place. Ronnie was so good there; he was never afraid to jump to the outside and start going to the front, and that outside lane won him a lot of races.

You know, speaking of Stafford, the Arutes absolutely revived Modified racing in New England, and the entire Northeast, really. Things had gotten a little bit stagnant in the late '60s, but then Jack Arute bought that place and he really cleaned it up. He moved the pits, and he just made the whole place nicer. He also got NASCAR to allow the Pintos and Vegas and the newer-type cars. I don't think some people today realize how much Jack did for the sport in those years. But I'm the first to admit, I didn't always see eye-to-eye with Jack and his son Jackie. They wanted everything prim and proper, including the appearance of the cars. That certainly wasn't wrong, but there were a lot of times when that was the last thing I worried about. Lenny Boehler and I were almost like rednecks that way; neither one of us had a lot of money, and going fast was more important to us than looking good. So it took a while for my relationship with the Arutes to jell.

One night there was a race with infield pitting, and something went wrong, and I guess I was swearing out loud. I wasn't swearing at an *official*, or anything like that. I was just madder than hell about something, and swearing at the whole situation. As a result, Stafford suspended me for two weeks. Well, they didn't know it, but both weeks I was in the pits anyway. I just slid under the fence—saved myself a few bucks—and kind of hid from the officials. The first week, Ronnie won, so that was great. The second week, there was a hell of a crash during the Modified feature; a car got hung up in the front-straightaway catch fence, and they had to throw a red flag. Ronnie had *just* taken the lead from Bugsy Stevens in turn one, and he was a car-length ahead coming out of turn two. The fence was all torn up right at the starter's stand, and when Jack Arute and the officials looked it over, they decided there was no way they could repair it that night. That was fine with me, because I figured they'd just finish the race the following week. But it was past the halfway point, so they called it a complete race, reverted to the previous lap, and announced Bugsy as the winner.

Well, I went bullshit. I charged out of the pits and up into the grandstands, and I was heading straight for the official's booth, running. Jackie was up there announcing, and at the last minute he saw me coming up the aisle and tried to lock the door. He actually had his hand on the knob when I whipped that thing open, and out he came, still holding onto the doorknob. Naturally, we had a few words, with me hollering and him hollering. Finally—and I can't help laughing when I remember this—Jackie said, "Hey, wait a minute! You're not even supposed to *be* here!"

But the biggest blowup between me and the Arutes, the thing a lot of people still talk about, was the Governor's Cup fiasco. Every year, Stafford would designate a certain race as the Governor's Cup event; the winning owner and driver got a nice plaque in victory lane that night, and the winner's name would be engraved on this beautiful trophy, the Governor's Cup, which was kept at the track. The really cool part of the deal was that if you won that race three years in a row, you actually got to keep that cup. We won it in 1972, won it again in '73, and now we're into 1974, and I really wanted to win that thing. Remember, Ronnie and I were racing three nights a week, sometimes four, so I didn't really think much about anything outside of the next race. But one day it dawned on me: "When is that Governor's Cup race? We haven't run it yet."

Then we got busy again, and I forgot all about it. So the season ends, and we go to the banquet. Bugsy and Sonny Koszela won the track championship, and Ronnie and I were second in the points. At some point during the night, I see the plaque for that Governor's Cup race sitting with all the trophies. I *knew* they hadn't run that race, and so I say to my wife, Gussie, "You watch, they're going to give Bugsy that plaque." That was the easiest thing for them to do, since he'd be up there getting all kinds of other awards anyway. Now, you've got to understand, I had nothing at all against Bugsy Stevens. I've always thought the world of that guy; in fact, we actually won the one race we ever ran together, at Waterford. But, anyway, as I was sitting there, I could see this coming.

Surer than hell, ten minutes later here they are, presenting that plaque to Bugsy for winning the Governor's Cup race. I'm steaming. I knew enough not to say anything to the Arutes right then, because, believe me, that wouldn't have been pretty. But Gussie went over and talked to Jackie. He told her that the race had originally been rained out, so they ran it on such-and-such night, but she knew that didn't sound right. And as they were talking, Jackie said something like, "Hey, that's the way the cookie crumbles."

Well, Gussie came back to where we were sitting, and she probably shouldn't have told me what Jackie said, but she did. Now I'm *really* mad. In the middle of my table, right in front of me, is my trophy for finishing second in the car-owner points. I stood up, grabbed that trophy, and I *smashed* that thing on the floor. Jack Arute came right over, and we got into it big-time. He said, "I've got people from Winston here, and people from NASCAR..."

I said, "I don't give a damn *who* you've got here. What's right is right, and what's wrong is wrong. And this was wrong, Jack." And then, naturally, Gussie and I left.

Two or three days later, I'd been gone someplace, and when I pulled into my driveway there was a package on the front doorstep. I looked at the return address: "Stafford Motor Speedway." For a minute I kind of thought maybe it was a bomb. I shook it a little bit, and it rattled. Those guys had actually packaged up all the little pieces of that trophy I'd smashed, and they sent it to me. I was still mad, but I had to admit, that was pretty good.

So we go to Stafford in the spring of 1975—it must have been the Spring Sizzler—and I'm in the pits, working on my car. At this point, I still haven't spoken to Jack or Jackie since the banquet. Jack used to have a small motorcycle that he'd ride in the pits, checking things out. He rides by me once, and doesn't stop. He rides by again, slows down, but doesn't stop. On his third time by, he stops behind my car and motions for me to come over. So I walk over there.

He looks at me, real serious, and he says, "Bob, do you think we can ever be friends?"

I look at him, and I say, "Jack, I never thought we *weren't* friends."

Well, from that day on, we were good. I still got mad sometimes, and I still might have run my mouth a little bit, but I never, ever had anything against the

Arutes. And I think maybe they had started to understand that as much as they cared about their track, I cared just as much about my racing. The only reason I ever got upset at a race track is that I cared so much about what I was doing.

I'll show you what I mean: Once we were at Westboro, and we had one of those nights when you lose a race you think you should have won. That almost never happened with Ronnie driving, but on this night he'd been leading with four or five laps to go, and he finished *second*. I was madder than a sonofabitch when he got back to the pits, and I don't think I even talked to him. I climbed into that car, fired it up, and drove it up onto my ramp truck so fast that I put the front bumper right through the back window of the truck. Then I got the hell out of there and drove home, still mad. The next day I'm looking at the car, and I see that the motor mount on the left side is all torn apart. That's when I figured it out: Whenever Ronnie ran down into the corner and lifted, the engine would roll because of that broken motor mount, and the accelerator wouldn't come back like it should. So it wasn't his fault that we hadn't won; we'd actually been lucky to finish second.

But before I knew all that, when we were on that ride home from Westboro, Gussie said to me, "What's wrong with you?"

I said, "What do you mean?"

She said, "You can't win every race!"

I said, "Why the hell *can't* I?"

Part of that was just being young. I understand these things better today. But, you know, once we had started winning a lot, I really did want to win *everything*. Take Martinsville; we won there in the fall of 1974, but instead of being happy all winter long, I kept telling myself, "Damn it, I hope we can run that good again when we go back down there in the spring." That's just the way I thought. And, don't you know, in the spring of '75 we're leading the race, and the laps are winding down, and a throttle-return spring breaks. I didn't have a toe-strap on the pedal for Ronnie to pull it back, but luckily he didn't crash, and he was able somehow to limp it home and finish second. But Bugsy got by us, and he won the race, and I wanted to win them all.

Man, I loved racing with Ronnie, no matter where we went. We won at Stafford, won at Thompson, won a ton at Monadnock, won a track championship at Westboro. We ran the Pinto in the big-block races, and in the small-block shows we ran a Vega that Bobby Turner built for me.

The key thing was, Ronnie and I had a *lot* of confidence in each other. One Friday night the Vega got really torn up at either Monadnock or Westboro, and of course on Saturday we ran the Pinto at Stafford. In between all that, I fixed the

Very early on, race cars were Ron Bouchard's playgrounds, just as race tracks would be in the years ahead. (Bouchard Family Collection)

(Above) In its day, Bob Bouchard's Red & White racing team was one spiffy outfit. (Bouchard Family Collection)

(Right) Another feature win for a hot combination at the dawn of the '60s, Pete Salvatore and car owner Bob Bouchard. (Balser/Bouchard Family Collection)

(Right) History in the making: Ronnie's first "legal age" victory, in a lightweight cutdown at Pines Speedway. (Bouchard Family Collection)

(Above) Dashing from the beginning, Ronnie (and not "Ronny," as the lettering indicates) strikes a pose. (Bouchard Family Collection)

(Left) Ready for anything, Bouchard lines up alongside one of the era's stars, Tinker Progin. (Dave Dykes Collection)

(Left) Starter Earl Grant congratulates Seekonk Speedway winner Ron Bouchard, by now known as the Kid from Fitchburg. (North East Motor Sports Museum)

(Above) This clean Chevy II carried Bouchard to Seekonk track titles in 1968 and '69. (North East Motor Sports Museum)

(Right) A pair of aces: George Summers in the Curley #31 leads Bouchard's #35 through the weekly Seekonk traffic jam. (R.A. Silvia Collection)

From left: crewman Louie "Bugsy" Roy, driver Bouchard, engine whiz Dave Rossbach, and chassis guru Vic Kangas. (Rossbach Family Collection)

Ronnie flashes that winning smile as son Robbie joins him after another Seekonk score. (R.A. Silvia Collection)

1971: On a day that changed the course of his career, Bouchard gets set to tackle Pocono aboard Dick Armstrong's coupe. (R.A. Silvia)

Looking comfortable in Bob Johnson's purple Pinto, which carried Ronnie to victory on Stafford's opening night in 1972. (Bouchard Family Collection)

Feedback at dusk: Just visible through the window net, Bob Johnson listens to his driver. (Dick Berggren)

In the middle of his red-hot 1973 season, Bouchard copped an Independence Day weekend 100-lapper at Oswego, NY. (North East Motor Sports Museum)

(Top) Bugs Stevens low, Ron Bouchard high in a classic Stafford Motor Speedway standoff. (Mike Adaskaveg)

(Left) Here's Ronnie just a car length in front of another Modified legend, Steady Eddie Flemke in the Judkins #2X. (Mike Adaskaveg)

June 3, 1973, Pocono: Another big on-the-road score for Ron and the Johnson #17, here passing New York icon Maynard Troyer. (Rick Huff/Tom Ormsby Collection)

(Right) The '74 season closed with Bouchard and Ray Hendrick sharing the honors in Martinsville's Cardinal 500. (Sonny Richards Collection)

(Below) With New England's small-block Modified scene taking off, Bouchard was a frequent winner (this time at Monadnock) in Bob Johnson's new Vega. (Dave Dykes Collection)

(Right) In the '70s, two of Modified racing's most popular men were Fred DeSarro and Ron Bouchard. (Bouchard Family Collection)

Vega to get it ready for Thompson on Sunday. I remember Ronnie showing up late at Thompson, for some reason—maybe he had a moving job or something—and because he was late we completely missed warm-ups.

He said, "Is this thing ready to go?"

I said, "Hell, yeah."

He went out and won the heat race *and* the feature. That's how we were: If I told Ronnie that we were good to go, he'd just climb in and go wide open. That's a big thing for a mechanic and a driver, having that complete faith in each other. In 1975, Stafford went to a narrow, 13-inch tire for the Modifieds, and for several weeks everybody had trouble getting their cars hooked up with those things. On Memorial Day they had a 150-lapper, and I told everybody I was going to bring my small-block car, the Vega. People said I was nuts, because Stafford was a horsepower track, but Ronnie said, "If you want to try it, let's try it." Well, we finished second to Moose Hewitt, and Ronnie damn near got by him at the end. He believed we would run good because I said we would, and he went out and did the job. Then Stafford switched back to the big tires, so we went back to running the Pinto.

Ronnie and I ended up splitting early in 1976. We didn't have any kind of a big fight or anything, but we disagreed on a few small things. If I was a little older and a little smarter, maybe I'd have done things differently, but in those days once I made up my mind about something, it was made up. So I told him, "Listen, maybe it's better for both of us if we do something else."

It wasn't anything I'd *planned*, and, again, if I was ten years older at that point, I might not have handled things that way. And I'll bet if we could ask Ronnie right now, he'd probably agree that he'd have handled things differently, too. Hindsight is always perfect, right? But things happened the way they did, and that was that. He went off and drove for Bobby Judkins, and I put Don LaJoie in my car for a while, and then Satch Worley.

But, you know, we didn't split up under *bad* terms. It might have hurt Ronnie's feelings a little bit, but not to the point where we didn't talk to each other. And, of course, down the road we were back together again, with the Winston Cup car.

When I look back today at that period, 1972 right on up into '76, yeah, it was a major part of my life, and I know Ronnie felt that same way.

Maybe it's human nature, but you don't always think about things and appreciate them while they're happening. Just recently—not long before he passed away—it occurred to me how young we both were back then. Ronnie was 23 when he first got in my car; I was just two years older. Imagine that? I'd never thought about it, but that's pretty incredible. He was up against all these great drivers, and

I was up against some great car owners and mechanics, and look at everything we won in that short period of time together. I'd almost bet you couldn't find another driver/ owner combination that won so much at such young ages.

And I'm not bragging in any way when I say that. I'm just amazed by it all.

I mentioned that to Ronnie just a few months before he died. We were talking on the phone, and I said, "You know, Bouchard, when we whipped the asses of all those guys, we were just kids."

We both laughed, and he said, "I guess you're right."

BY BUGS STEVENS

"He was one of the better drivers I ever ran against, and that's saying something"

Reflections on a great rival who was also "a great kid"

Carl Berghman, who in the 1950s adopted the name "Bugs Stevens" to go racing while AWOL from Air Force duty, was the king of the NASCAR Modified hill when Ron Bouchard arrived. In many ways, Stevens took over where George Summers had left off, becoming Bouchard's benchmark and also a pal. But while the Summers/Bouchard show had been confined to Seekonk, Bugs and Ronnie took theirs on the road. In 1972 Stevens won at Pocono, so Bouchard did the same in '73; in 1974 at Martinsville, Bugsy won the spring Dogwood 500, Ronnie the fall Cardinal 500. Stafford, however, was New England's red-hot Modified hub, and Bouchard later recalled the "many nights" when he spent entire features there—"whether it was 30 laps or 100, coming through traffic"—within a foot or two of Stevens. The memory made Ronnie smile. Today, it makes everybody smile.

MIKE ADASKAVEG/COASTAL 181 COLLECTION

I t's true that it was George Summers and me who talked Ronnie into going to Stafford. I think he had worn out his welcome at Seekonk. I don't mean that in any kind of a bad way, but he'd won four track championships in a row, and it was time to do something else. So he came to Stafford, and Thompson, and pretty soon everyplace else.

People have asked me if I followed what he was doing in his early years at Seekonk, probably because that place is just down the road from my house, and because I had raced there. Well, the answer is no, because I was never home! Don't forget, at the point when Ronnie was winning those Seekonk championships, I was running all over hell and back with Lenny Boehler, chasing NASCAR points all over the East Coast.

Christ, we were on the road four or five nights a week, racing everywhere we could. Even on a normal week, things were hectic: Thursday nights at Catamount Stadium up in Milton, Vermont; Fridays at Stafford, or Albany-Saratoga; Saturdays at either Norwood Arena or maybe Plattsburgh, New York; and then Sunday afternoons at Thompson. Many times we'd load up as soon as the Thompson feature ended, then jump in the truck and go like hell out the Massachusetts Turnpike and the New York Thruway, something like 250 miles, to race at Utica-Rome on Sunday night. If there was an extra-points show somewhere down South on a given weekend, we might be in Connecticut on Friday, Virginia or North Carolina on Saturday, and New York on Sunday. And when we weren't running the NASCAR races, there was always something coming up in the middle of the week, like an All Star League race on a Tuesday night.

So I might have heard about this Bouchard kid who was going really good at Seekonk, but I didn't have time to think much about any of that stuff. I do recall him coming to Stafford with his Seekonk car in 1971, but only vaguely. And yes, I remember him running Dick Armstrong's coupe in a couple of races, but, again, they aren't strong memories. I always joke that maybe it's because I've hit a lot of walls, but a lot of things from that period are foggy to me. My own life, my own racing, was so crazy back then.

Now, I do remember Ronnie coming to Stafford with Bob Johnson in 1972, and winning races right away. That was pretty impressive, because there was a tough group of guys at that place. You had Freddy DeSarro, Eddie Flemke, Gene Bergin, Leo Cleary, Bobby Santos, just a whole bunch of good guys. By then I was driving for Sonny Koszela, and we were running awfully good, too. So Ronnie winning there definitely got everybody's attention, including mine. Although, to be honest, I would have looked at him the same way I used to look at *every* driver: as just another guy I had to try to beat. That was how I operated in those days. I think it came from my background in football and baseball. I just did my best, and didn't stop to think who I was up against.

It's hard to say how Ronnie might have looked at the rest of us when he first came in. I had been in that same position myself back in the '60s, when Boehler and I were just starting to travel. I was the new kid on the block at Norwood, Thompson, Utica, every one of those NASCAR tracks. But, you know, we all think differently. Some new guys get intimidated, and some don't. Ronnie was a racer—he'd been brought up around it—so I don't think he was ever intimidated.

But I'm sure that walking into Stafford in 1972 and looking at the competition there, he'd have been very busy, mentally. Everything is new, and you're taking it all in, and you can't help but be excited.

But the good ones get over that in a hurry. If you're going to operate a vehicle in those conditions, at the level it takes to win, you need to focus, and that focus knocks everything else out of your mind. And Ronnie, he got dialed in pretty quickly.

You know, over the years I got to know his father, and Bob Bouchard was a tough man. Not just strong, but *tough*, determined. Ronnie had a lot of that in him, too. It wasn't an obvious thing, but he definitely had that same determination, and you could see that once you got to know him. I'm sure that helped him every time he took another step up the ladder.

Once he started winning, the management at Stafford played the two of us up as big rivals, which was understandable. I had won a few national championships, and Ronnie was the young guy coming in, and we were both running up front. So Jack Arute and his son, Jackie, and Pete Zanardi, who was the PR man there for quite a while, really worked that angle. And we went right along with it; we played the game. I'd been through that before, because different promoters had made rivals out of me and Ray Hendrick, me and Eddie Flemke, me and Fred DeSarro. Hell, Freddy and I were the best of friends, and for most of our careers probably half the people in the grandstands figured we were bitter enemies! Now it was me and Ronnie. Different people, same game. Heroes and villains, that's what sells tickets. That's what puts the fans in the stands.

See, I realized early on that we were showmen. Pleasing the fans, in the long run, was good for us. Anthony Venditti had preached that to me at Seekonk Speedway, and once I got to Stafford, Thompson, and those places, Eddie Flemke really drilled it into me. Eddie was the brain behind some of the great heat races we used to put on, where once we got ourselves into qualified spots we'd basically concentrate on giving the fans a good show, running side by side, swapping positions. The feature was lined up by the handicap system anyway, so where you finished in the heat race didn't mean a damn thing. There were a few of us who played that game, and it didn't take long for Ronnie to become part of that little group, because we trusted him.

In fact, later on, in 1977, he and I were part of one of the best heat races anybody ever saw at Stafford, or anyplace. Bill France Jr. was there, and that was a big deal for Jack Arute, having the president of NASCAR at his track. Well, it ended up that Ronnie and I were in the same heat, along with his brother, Kenny. So once the three of us got to the front, we didn't even bother with the two-abreast stuff. We got ourselves *three*-wide, and we ran that way lap after lap: me on the inside, Kenny on the outside, and Ronnie right there in the middle. Of course, that was something we worked out before the race, but France didn't know anything about that. He was watching from the press box, and the people up there told me later that he was going crazy watching us. So were the fans, and that was the idea.

Ronnie and I, we never let any of that "rivalry" stuff get in the way of our relationship. We were friends, good friends, right from the start. I don't believe we ever once had an argument, or even a disagreement. He was a likable guy, and above all he was *real*. See, when you go through periods when you're on top, like I was when he came along, some people get jealous, and they play their little games with you, either sucking up or trying to get an edge on you. I could pick that out right away in most people. But I never saw any of that stuff in Ronnie; we became friends naturally, week by week, and I don't think the fact that I was winning had a damn thing to do with it.

Don't forget, he was doing a lot of winning himself. He and that Bob Johnson car got to the point where they could win just about anywhere they went: Pocono, Martinsville, you name it.

He and Bob were obviously a great pair. Bob was a hard worker and a fantastic mechanic, all business. He did have quite a temper, which is something everybody remembers, but I got along with him very well. I had a lot of respect for Johnson. I'm not sure we'd have gotten along as a team, though. He'd get emotional if things went wrong; he'd yell and scream at the driver. He loved Ronnie, but Bob was just a high-strung guy. To listen to all that hollering, you'd think there was no way in the world those two could ever win a damn thing together. I know I wouldn't have dealt with it very well; if a car owner or a mechanic ever yelled at me the way Bob yelled at Ronnie, that would have been the end. But Ronnie was smart; didn't take it personally. He understood Bob Johnson. He'd just walk away and let Bob cool off.

And the biggest thing they had going for them was that they believed in each other. Ronnie knew Bob would give him a good car, and Bob knew Ronnie would always drive the wheels off it. And because of that, they accomplished a lot together. I know that first-hand, because there were a lot of races where I ran second to Bouchard and that #17.

I'll tell you, Ronnie was a good shoe. A *really* good shoe. Bullrings, fast tracks, it didn't matter, and you couldn't say that about everybody. There were guys who might go like hell at the quarter-mile tracks, but once you got to the fast tracks they were over their heads; on the flip side of that, there were guys who were fast and smooth and might give you a run for your money at a place like Thompson, but they weren't big threats on the little bullrings, because those small tracks require a whole different set of skills. But Ronnie, he was good everywhere, and he proved it over and over. Anywhere you went, you knew he was going to be in the picture. Honestly, he was one of the better drivers I ever ran against, and that's saying something.

He was smart, and he was steady, and I always trusted him. I've said this many times: You could bet your life on Ronnie not trying anything stupid, anything crazy. Looking back, I think he felt that way about me, too. He must have, because the two of us had some incredible races. No matter where we were, or what teams we were with, we seemed to end up battling, and it was always a clean battle.

Anytime we ever bumped, believe me, it was an accident. In fact, I used to joke with him that he never, ever spun me out—which was true—but I *did* spin him out once. We were at Monadnock, and I was chasing him off the fourth turn, and his car hesitated. He might have been loose, or maybe he just slipped; believe it or not, even the best drivers out there have a brain-fart once in a while. Anyway, I was already on the gas, and, bang, I hit him square in the back bumper, and around he went, into the infield. Boy, Bob Johnson was pissed off at me about that. But you know something? I don't think Bouchard and I even discussed it that day, because he obviously knew I hadn't done it on purpose. I'm sure he had as much trust in me as I had in him.

When you find yourself running wheel to wheel with a guy you're really comfortable with, that's the best part of racing. Yes, I've won a lot of races by running away because I had a fast car, and *any* victory is nice, because winning is the name of the game. But those wins when you have to try really hard to out-drive the next guy, and out-think him, those are the best, and I had an awful lot of nights like that against Ronnie. In fact, I probably ran as many laps beside him, fighting for a spot, as I did with any other driver in my career. You name a track—Stafford, Thompson, Seekonk, Westboro, Monadnock, Waterford, Martinsville—and I guarantee you we went wheel-to-wheel there, multiple times. Sometimes he won, and sometimes I did, but most of the time we got out of our cars smiling.

Ronnie and I stayed friends through his whole Modified career, his whole Winston Cup career, and his whole business career, too. The way I've lived my life is that if you're a friend of mine and you do well, I'm happy. Good for you. And he worked hard for everything he had.

We had a lot of fun together, I can tell you that. A lot of laughs. People always talk about me and Richie Evans being the big party guys, and Richie and I definitely did our share of hell-raising, but I remember Ronnie being right there with me on a lot of nights. We'd hang out in the Stafford parking lot, the Seekonk parking lot, the Thompson parking lot. Ronnie was a big part of that scene. He was a good beer drinker; I was pretty good, but I promise you, he was better. One night down at Daytona, he and George Summers kidnapped me out of one bar and brought me to another bar, when the only place I should have gone was straight to bed. *Jesus.*

You know, when I say that some of my old memories are foggy, I mean it. But sometimes, it all comes right back like it was yesterday. Ronnie, he was just a great kid.

BY JACK ARUTE JR.

"They did their best to rattle him, the way veterans do, but Ronnie never blinked"

Thoughts on a rising star, as seen from the announcer's booth

Jack Arute Jr., known to longtime friends as Jackie, was working at Stafford Motor Speedway even before his father bought the place in 1970. "I was the assistant flagman," he points out, "working right behind Earl Grant." Once papa Jack was in control, Jackie's role changed. One night he "made the mistake" of complaining about one of the announcers, and his father fired back, "If you think you can do better, get your ass up there." Thus was born a career on the microphone that eventually carried the younger Arute to radio and television roles at venues like Indianapolis, Daytona, and Charlotte. At Stafford, where he also served as general manager, he was part of a fondly remembered announcing team that included gentlemanly Bill Welch and another broadcast icon in the making, Mike Joy, who is quick to say, "Jackie helped make Ronnie Bouchard a star."

BOUCHARD FAMILY COLLECTION

Way back when, there was a night when I nicknamed Ronnie "The Wasa Wasa Kid." Many people called him that through the rest of his career, and to this day I get asked what it meant. The truth is, it didn't mean anything. He came to Stafford in an era when a lot of drivers had nicknames. You had Leo "the Lion" Cleary and Steady Eddie Flemke; hell, even Bugsy Stevens was the nickname, or at least the racing name, of Carl Berghman. I don't think I was consciously trying to give Ronnie a nickname, but up there in the announcer's booth it came out: "In row seven, from Fitchburg, Massachusetts, the Wasa Wasa Kid, Ron Bouchard." It just spilled out, and it stuck.

Honestly, if Ronnie was anything, he was the Great White Hope. In that period, 1971–72, Stafford was the exclusive territory of Freddy DeSarro and Bugsy Stevens. The odds were that one or the other was going to win the feature. Yes, you had Eddie Flemke and Leo Cleary and Gene Bergin winning occasionally, and for the NASCAR national races you'd have a few outsiders capable of knocking on the door, but Stafford had become Freddy's and Bugsy's house. Then along comes this Bouchard kid, and I think everybody saw the potential: Here was a guy who might be able to unseat those two. And, of course, that's exactly what happened.

Ronnie won the opening feature of our '72 season, and he did it by going where no one else dared to go, by hanging his ass in that outside groove. That became his signature style at Stafford; people said you couldn't make time up there on the high side, but Ronnie didn't quite understand why he couldn't *try*. So through all his years in the Bob Johnson #17, when everyone else was lined up on the bottom, that's where you'd find him: upstairs.

He was perfectly comfortable up there, and he was not going to be intimidated. Sure, people *tried* to intimidate him, but you could almost hear Ronnie saying, "Oh, so you want to take me up a little high in the corner? That's okay. I'm fine." He'd just leave it there, and eventually he'd get that position.

You know, a lot of things were changing in the early '70s, in society and in racing. For one thing, in the Modified division you had the Pinto Revolution versus the coupes, and the sport suddenly looking more modern. Well, Ronnie was one more change. Compared to some of the gray-haired veterans, he was a matinee idol, a big, tall, good-looking young guy.

Think about this: When we opened that 1972 season, Cleary was 43 years old; Flemke was 41; Bergin was just about to turn 40; Bugsy was 38; DeSarro and Bobby Santos were the young pups of the group that had come along in the '60s, but they were both 34. Ron Bouchard was 23. *Twenty-three*. This was long before the days of teenaged drivers at this level, and 23 was very young. You could draw a direct comparison between Ronnie's impact on Modified racing in New England and Jeff Gordon's impact on the Cup series in 1993 and '94. It had that same feel.

Ronnie won twice more at Stafford that year, and the following season he was the track champion. All that early success was a validation for Bob Johnson, who had taken a real shot on Ronnie. Bob and Gussie Johnson didn't have a lot of money; they went racing the hard way. Bob put everything he had into building that new Pinto, and he hired this young kid to drive it, and it all worked out.

I have to say, I've never been around a more intense human being in my life than Bob Johnson. He had a level of passion that would sometimes push him over the edge. There's a night I will never forget, from when Jerry Dostie was driving for Bob in the coupe days. Jerry had a bad restart that spoiled what might have been a feature win, and when he got back to the pits Bob picked up a big wrench—the one he'd use to change weight with the jacking bolts in the front end – and pounded the shit out of the hood of his brand new Ford truck. And although that night might have been an extreme example of Bob's passion, it was not exactly uncommon.

But somehow, Ronnie provided the balance to that. It was a yin-and-yang situation. On one hand you had Bob, the Mr. Excitement of the pit area, the man with the short fuse, and on the other hand you had this gentle giant, this big kid named Ron Bouchard who everybody loved. And Ronnie knew exactly how to handle Bob; I was subjected to Johnson's wrath more than once, and one of the wonderful things I learned from Ronnie was to just count to ten and then walk away for a while. Before long, Bob would cool off, and everything was good again, because when Bob Johnson was calm, he was the nicest guy in the world.

The drive from Stafford to Westbrook, where Bob and Gussie lived, would take an hour and a half if you were hauling a race car. Well, I can't count the number of times when Bob left Stafford right after telling me what I should do to myself *and* the horse I rode in on, and then, 90 minutes later, I'd pick up the phone in the track office and hear that quiet voice that you didn't always hear from Bob Johnson: "Hey, Jackie, I'm sorry ..."

Not everyone understood Bob. I'd like to think that I did. It was me who sent him the pieces of that trophy he smashed at our banquet in 1974. It wasn't a game of trying to gain the upper hand in that situation, but more an unspoken way of showing respect. Each of us, meaning those of us at the track and Bob as a car owner, recognized the importance of the other.

I will add this about Bob Johnson: People remember him for that temper, but he was as smart with a race car as anybody. Bob was not a conventional thinker; he went his own way on things, and he thought things out.

And, really, Ronnie did the same thing behind the wheel. Eddie Flemke used to preach about the importance of "building the notebook." Richie Evans talked about having a filing cabinet in his head. I think Ronnie was that way, too, constantly acquiring information, studying how to make moves, studying other drivers.

Look how quickly Ronnie fit in with all those older drivers we talked about. That's because early on, they did their best to rattle him, the way veterans do, but they saw that he never blinked. More importantly, when they did something to test him, he never retaliated. He treated those guys with respect, so they treated him with respect. That was part of their code.

When it came to having an iron code, those New England Modified racers were tougher than the Mafia. They would race the hell out of each other, and sometimes somebody might get wrecked, but then they'd drink a beer and help that guy fix his car so they could all get to the next track and do it again.

Racing in those days was a lot like a morality play. Some guys wore white hats—and you'd have to put Ronnie in that group—and some guys wore black hats, and some people were politically incorrect, but they were all so damn *real*. Nobody had an image that was fashioned by a marketing person. You simply promoted those characters as they were.

The day-to-day operation at Stafford consisted of myself and Bill Slater, who was the race director, and Pete Zanardi, who helped so much with public relations. Pete was not working there full-time, but he was around to make sure that I didn't screw things up. And when it came to public relations, a lot of our work was easy. With Ronnie coming in the way he did, we instantly had a couple of great storylines. Number one, I think we did a great job of presenting the saga of Ron Bouchard and Bob Johnson. They truly were an underdog team; Bob's car didn't have much sponsorship, other than maybe a few cases of Wynn's Friction Proofing they'd gotten from Wally Saleeba. But here they were in 1973 and '74, swapping wins and track championships with Bugsy Stevens and Sonny Koszela, and that Koszela #15 was a pretty well-financed operation. Ronnie had his own fans, but because of that underdog dynamic there were a lot of people who pulled for him after *their* guy dropped out, and that included many of Bugsy's fans.

The other obvious thing to promote was the story of the young guy against these older guys, the kid against the veterans, be it Bugsy, Freddy, Eddie, or whoever. You can try to build up fake rivalries, but that usually doesn't work. In this case, it was simply a matter of talking about this kid who was taking on all these champions. And, by the way, those other drivers were all smart enough to buy into that. They went along with it because, again, it was real, and because they understood that it helped the show, and they were part of that show.

All these guys we've talked about, Ronnie included, said to me on different occasions, "Gee, the crowd didn't look that good tonight." They paid attention to that stuff, because they felt like they had a stake in it. And I think they appreciated what my dad was trying to do at Stafford. By 1972, which was our third year there, we were starting to make major infrastructural improvements, as opposed to just cosmetic changes. Although, I must say, there were still some cosmetic changes going on. That spring we went to Martinsville for the Dogwood 500, and my father looked at all the shrubs Clay Earles had planted outside the turns. He liked what that did for the appearance of the place. Now, my old man had a little bit of larceny in his heart, as Eddie Flemke used to say. He was still involved in the family construction company, and they had a huge shipment of evergreens that were designated for use in the highway medians. Somehow, a bunch of the leftover evergreens got "lost" and ended up at Stafford. Today, when you see the giant evergreens outside turns three and four, those were from that load. They are a legacy of that commitment he made to make the place more professional.

At the same time, my dad used to say, "You can have the prettiest hardware store in the world, but if you don't have the right product on the shelves, nobody's going to shop there." Of course, the drivers and the car owners were that product. So we did things no one else was doing. No other track asked—or in some cases *forced*—the car owner to join the driver in victory lane. No other track interviewed the first-, second-, and third-place drivers. Sometimes it felt like we had more announcers than support-division cars. But it added to the professionalism.

Years later, when Ronnie was in Winston Cup and I was working for the Motor Racing Network, he used to laugh and say, "I never used to understand why at Stafford, you were always sticking a microphone in my face. Now I get it." Meaning that by then, he was comfortable with it.

One of the things that I think helped bring out the best in Ronnie was his interaction with Seymour the Clown, who was part of the show at Stafford for several years. Butch Farone, who dressed as Seymour, never got enough credit for the role he played in allowing the personalities of the drivers to show. He did that with Bugsy, who would be the jokester, and with Flemke, who would chase Seymour around with his race car. And he did it with Ronnie, who always smiled and went along with any little stunt Butch was trying to pull.

I think that was a comfortable way for Ronnie to learn that he could be himself in front of the crowd. It allowed Ronnie to just be Ronnie, and people liked what they saw. And I'll bet that if you ask someone who was a kid back then what they remember about Ron Bouchard at Stafford, they'd talk about the way he had fun with Seymour the Clown.

If you were a race fan, you had to appreciate his style. He was always *trying*, never afraid to probe for the opening, and, again, never afraid to go to the high side. And if you were an announcer, you were glad to have Ronnie in the starting field because, on a lot of nights, he was the whole show. On some nights it was Bugsy, and on other nights it was DeSarro, or Bergin, or Flemke, or later on Geoff Bodine. But on an awful lot of nights, Ronnie was the guy.

Those nights always had that special moment to them. You had all those guys coming from the back, and you saw Ronnie back in 14th, then tenth, and then eighth, moving up. Then there would be a caution flag, and you'd catch your breath, and you'd start calculating where everybody was going to be on the restart.

And suddenly, it hit you: You said to yourself, "Hey, we're only at halfway, and Ronnie's going to restart in sixth. He's on the outside, right where he wants to be. Oh, boy, he's going to make something happen now!"

BY KEN BOUCHARD

"We never had that kind of rivalry where we hid things from each other"

Sibling rivalry and brother love, running side by side

VAL LESIEUR COLLECTION

Ken Bouchard, Ron's younger brother by six and a half years, put together one of the Northeast's most accomplished and interesting racing careers. Often finding himself in situations where his primary car owner was dedicated to a specific track, Kenny simply went on the hunt and chased down rides for the other tracks. As a result, he kept a busy schedule driving for an astonishing number of Modified teams, and won with most, scoring feature victories at Stafford, Thompson, Westboro, Monadnock, Waterford, Plainville, Seekonk, Riverside Park, and a few more tracks along the way. Later, Kenny followed his big brother up the NASCAR ladder, first competing in what was then the Busch Series before jumping to Winston Cup in 1988. To this date, the Bouchards remain the only brothers to have won the NASCAR Winston Cup Rookie of the Year award.

It was fun to compete with Ronnie, and sit there knowing it's your brother in that other car beside you. But he was a hard guy to race against, for me. I had learned so much by watching him, and because of that it seemed like he always knew everything I was about to do. If I thought I might be able to go around him, on that lap he'd run the outside. If I thought I could shoot under him—like using that crossover pass that worked so good in turn one at Stafford—he'd have the bottom protected, and all I could do was follow him. He had every move figured out even before I started to make it. It was like trying to outguess *myself*.

The first time I ever drove a race car, it was back when Ronnie still had his cutdown. He'd go to Hudson Speedway sometimes to practice—not on a race day—and when they were all through he'd throw me his helmet and say, "Go ahead, make some laps. Just be careful."

It's hard to believe it now, but I was ten years old.

I'd been going to the races since I was a little kid, watching Pete Salvatore drive my dad's car. You know how people still talk about Ronnie *always* running the outside? I'm sure he got that style from watching Pete Salvatore. Pete wasn't scared to jump to the outside at Westboro or Brookline and march to the front. I saw him win a lot of races that way.

I would beg to go down to the garage after school, so I could help out. All I could do at that age was sweep the floor and maybe wipe off the car, but that was fine with me. Ronnie was older, so he'd be changing the rear end on my dad's coupe, because you needed a different gear at Brookline than you did at Westboro. I'd be his little go-fer, getting the wrenches. Once Ronnie started driving, I'd be at the garage all the time, helping Vic Kangas and Dave Rossbach. Dave and I would usually stay late, and then he'd give me a ride home; in those years, he was almost like a second father to me.

I used to sneak into the pits at Seekonk to help those guys. It was like a game: I'd sneak in, the officials would throw me out, I'd sneak back in, and they'd throw me out again. After a while, they just ignored me. I think Anthony Venditti may have had something to do with that, too. Anthony and his wife, Irene, were great people; they were good to our whole family. In fact, Anthony let me start racing there when I was still a little bit underage. In most cases like that, the driver has to lie to the promoter, but here the promoter was telling me, "If anybody asks, tell them you're 16."

Early on, I didn't really have any intention of driving race cars myself. I was happy just working on Ronnie's stuff. But one night at Seekonk a good friend of ours, Al Becker, walked over to Ronnie's pit and said, "Hey, I just bought a car and a ramp truck." It was a B-division car that had been wrecked that night. The front snout had been ripped off, so the guy loaded it backwards onto his ramp truck and Al bought the whole operation. I rode home with him, and I'll never forget that trip. It was a short-wheelbase Dodge truck, and you'd swear it kept picking the front wheels off the road all the way from Seekonk to Fitchburg. We blew three tires, and we only had two spares. By the time we got home, the sun was up.

Al and I became 50/50 partners. He was the driver, and I was the crew chief. I must have been 13 or 14. We kept the car at Red & White, and I put a new frame under it. Dave and Vic were there if I needed them, but they made me do the work myself. We raced on Friday nights at Westboro, and Saturday nights at Seekonk. At Westboro we had to work on the car in the parking lot, just outside the pit gate, because Harvey Tattersall Jr., who was the promoter then, said there was no way I could get into the pits. When it came time for the heats or the feature, I'd run up into the grandstands and watch. Al Becker was a good driver, and he won quite a few races in that car. And along the way, I started thinking I was going to drive myself.

When I was 15, that's when Anthony Venditti said, "Okay, kid, go ahead." I was big for my age anyway; my father started using me on moving jobs when I was in eighth grade. Plus, I'd been around the pits so long that I'm sure everybody else just figured I was legal, because no one said a word. So that was the start of my own driving career.

At that stage, Ronnie was still racing at Seekonk every week; he was right at the end of that period. He was really good about giving me advice, and, believe me, I needed it. The first practice I ever ran, I bounced off the wall in every corner except turn one. We patched the car up so I could go back out and hit the wall there, too. Poor Bob Bergeron; Bergie had painted and lettered that thing up really nice, and now he had to do it all over again. That was a good lesson for us: Anytime you've got a new car or a new driver, always practice in primer first! If everything goes well, *now* you can paint it.

Then we went a year and a half or so when Ronnie and I raced at different places. On Saturdays I'd be at Westboro, and he'd be at Stafford with Bob Johnson's Modified; on a Sunday I might be up at Oxford Plains running one of those Getty Opens for Late Models, and Ronnie would be at Thompson. I think that was probably tougher on our parents than it was on us, because each of them had to choose who they were going to watch. Usually my father came with me, mostly because he wanted to keep an eye on things, and my mother would take Ronnie's kids and go watch him.

On Monday morning we'd all be at Red & White, comparing notes. Nothing happened until we had talked about how we had done and where we finished. The employees there used to tell Ronnie and me, "Please win this weekend. When you guys have good races, your father is in a much better mood on Mondays."

I started having good results pretty early; we won a couple of those Getty Opens at Oxford, and those races were a big deal for the Late Model guys. But it didn't make me more hungry, or anything like that. If you're a competitive person, that hunger is just in you. Ronnie and I were both that way; if we were unloading a truck, we had to make it into a contest.

The first time I ever drove a Modified, it was at Stafford in 1973. John Lukasavage asked me to drive his Pinto, the #1C, and that was a big step. Everything about it felt different. The NASCAR Modifieds in those days had big blocks, and one of John's drag-racing friends built his engine, so that car had plenty of power. Getting it around the corner wasn't always easy, but, boy, that thing sure went down the straightaway.

Ronnie was a big help, but he did it the right way. He'd never push it. He'd sit back and watch, but unless I was really doing something wrong he'd leave me alone to figure it out for myself. If he really thought he needed to say something, he'd come sit on my nerf bar and talk to me. I remember him telling me, "Sometimes you need to slow down to go faster," and that was definitely true with those big-block cars.

And, you know, he never stopped being there for advice, even as I got better and became competitive. Anytime I asked him a question, he would always give me a straight answer. In fact, once I got going good there were times at different tracks when he'd ask me what *we* were doing. We never had that kind of rivalry where we hid things from each other.

He was really fast at that time, driving Johnson's car. He and Bob were a great combination. Ronnie could make that #17 run on the outside wherever he went, especially at Stafford. If he caught a bunch of cars and they had the bottom blocked, he'd just drive right around 'em all on the top.

The competition back then was so good. Freddy DeSarro, Bugsy, Eddie Flemke, Ronnie, and a few more, those guys really were great, great drivers. Just when you'd get to where you could run with them sometimes, and you'd start thinking, "Okay, I'm *there* now," they'd knock you off your pedestal. You always had to work hard against that bunch. But, you know, you could race close with every one of them.

In my opinion, Modified racing right then—the middle '70s—was the best you could ever see. We were just lucky enough to live in that time. You had the first Spring Sizzlers, the first Thompson 300s. You had big-block shows, small-block shows, the Yankee All-Star League, all kinds of open shows. You could run three nights a week all season, and four in the summer.

Ronnie was lucky, because Johnson had his big-block Pinto and his small-block Vega, so he could run all those races with the same car owner. I usually had to scramble to find different rides. But I think that paid off for me down the road, because I was always driving a car that didn't handle anything like the one I'd driven the night before. It made me a better driver, because I didn't get locked into any one *feel*. Today you have guys that drive a Troyer car for several years, and when they get into a car built by somebody else, they're lost for a while. I drove Lukasavage's car, Bob Ramstrom's car, and I had my own Vega that I raced at a bunch of places, even Trenton for the Race of Champions.

My Vega had actually started out as Ronnie's Seekonk Camaro. Bob Johnson bought it and ran it as the #17 Camaro, and then I bought it from Johnson and we put a Vega body on it. Ronnie ran it in one of the road-course races at Daytona, and I drove it several times. That car was five or six years old—had a '55 Chevy frame—but it still handled like a dream.

Bob Ramstrom's car, the white McFee & Newton #35 Vega, was a really good ride for me. Jean Michaud built that car, and Dave Rossbach did the motors. Dave was working the overnight shift at General Electric, so when he got out of work at 7:00 a.m. he'd run down to Worcester and work at Ramstrom's until the early afternoon, then go home and sleep. With that car we won the 1975 Yankee All-Star League championship, beat Richie Evans to win a race at Westboro, and just had lots of really good runs.

Things started to take off for me pretty good after that. In the next few years I drove for Angie Cerease, Billy Corazzo, Ralph Solhem, and Sonny Koszela, and later for Teddy Marsh, Lenny Boehler, Bob Stearns, Bill Flynn, Joe Brady, and so many more that I can't remember them all. I think that among the car owners, I had established myself as a driver, and not just Ronnie's younger brother. I had come out of his shadow a little bit.

But I knew that to a lot of other people, I was *still* Ronnie's younger brother. I'm sure there were people who looked at me that way through my whole career, and I had no problem with that. You know, Ronnie was a great driver *and* my brother, so I never minded being associated with him that way.

He and I had some really good battles over the years, and if I had to finish second, I'd rather finish second to Ronnie than anybody else. We raced hard, but he was always fair, and I think I was, too. We gave each other the room we needed, but never any *more* room.

The only time we ever had trouble was one night at Westboro. I was leading the feature, but Ronnie was right on me. We had probably half a lap over whoever was running third. Well, he tried to sneak under me in turn three, but he got into my left-rear corner. It was an easy tap, but at that point you're right on the edge of control anyway. My car did a long, slow slide. I hung onto it, sideways, all the way through turn four, but I just couldn't catch it. Ronnie almost came to a stop behind me, because he didn't want to pass me that way. But finally my car spun, and he had to go on by. I was looking at him, and he was looking at me, and he took both hands off the wheel and shrugged.

But that was the only incident when he and I ever tangled, and we're talking about running thousands of laps together. We rubbed and banged here and there, because that's going to happen sometimes. But we never had a problem other than that one.

I got a flat tire out of that deal, but I restarted at the back and still got a top-five finish, as I remember. I was disappointed that I'd lost out on a shot to win, but I was basically okay with it. Those kinds of bumps are just part of the deal at a small track like Westboro. Now, my dad, he was *not* okay with it. Oh, man, he was hot. He had gone from having a perfect night, with his sons probably finishing first and second, to watching the two of us get together and one of us spin out. I saw him coming, and he was red in the face. He got to my pit stall first, hollered for a while, and then walked off to find Ronnie.

I remember Dave Rossbach saying, "Hurry up, let's load up and get the hell out of here before your old man comes back!"

And that's just what we did.

That whole week at work, I don't think my dad talked to either one of us.

BY GENE BOUCHARD

"All I cared about was the weekend, when we'd all head to the races"

Growing up with a New England legend in the making

Gene Bouchard is the oldest of the race-going Bouchard kids, and as such his memory reaches further back than those of his siblings. As you'll read, Gene has some entertaining speedway remembrances, but there are also many that took place far from any track. One starts out as a typical father/son memory, but ends with a twist that isn't at all surprising: "My dad taught me how to drive," he says, then adds with a laugh, "and, let me tell you, he was a tough teacher. I mean, the toughest. He'd throw out these comments, and it made me so nervous." These days Gene is an accountant, a role he unknowingly began training for while working in the parts department at his father's car dealership, "stocking, reordering, and watching inventory levels." Gene and his wife, Annette Lussier, live in Gardner, outside Fitchburg, with their children Joshua and Katie.

BOUCHARD FAMILY COLLECTION

There were trophies all over the house. That's what I remember when I think of my childhood. In fact, I have a very vivid memory of my dad bringing home a grandfather clock when he won at Martinsville in 1974. That was pretty neat.

I do have a few older recollections, like going to Stafford when he first raced there with his Seekonk car, the #35. When was that, 1971? I was awestruck by the size of the track. My only reference at the time would have been Seekonk, so when I saw Stafford I thought, "This place is too big! My dad should not *be* here." Obviously, my fears were unfounded. I also remember him going away to race Dick Armstrong's car at Pocono, and coming home with broken ribs. My mother was freaked out about that, and I think that's probably why I still have the memory.

The period when my memories start to become a bit more clear began when he was driving for Bob Johnson. I remember a Stafford banquet when I had an ear infection; actually, I believe it was a *double* ear infection. I think it was in 1973, when my dad won the track championship, but I was miserable the whole night.

I remember Bob Johnson being tall, and over the years I've heard stories about him being intimidating. Maybe he could be that way in the pits, but I don't remember ever feeling afraid of him, or anything like that. What I do remember is going to visit Bob and Gussie at their place in Connecticut, and eating a steak dinner. But when you're young, you don't understand certain things; like, I never really understood how my dad got together with this car owner from way down in Connecticut. And then, from there, how did they become as good as they were? It was like it all just *happened*.

Part of the problem was that, with my family dynamics being as they were, there was a lot going on. Maybe if you're in a nice little nuclear family, where the mother and father and the kids gather every day, you hear more conversation, so you have a pretty good idea what everybody's doing. But in my case, it was hard to get a true picture of everything that was going on. It was like having two or three families at the same time.

I do have some nice memories from when my parents were still married, just simple little things. For example, for some reason my dad used to love the Minnesota Vikings, so we'd sit and watch football together, and he'd end up falling asleep. I also remember that for a while, my time on the weekends was divided between being with my grandfather—Grandpa John, from my mother's side—and going to the races. I remember being at Grandpa John's house and waiting for updates of how my dad had done that night, wherever he was racing.

As I got older, I began to feel a bit left out, because my siblings—Robbie, Michelle, and Tracey—were *always* going to the races, and I wasn't. So I pushed to be more included, because I really enjoyed going. I had made friends at the tracks, Stafford in particular, a core group of kids I'd hang out with.

And, of course, those kids at the track looked up to my dad. They were fans of his, and he was winning a lot, and because of that they looked at *me* differently. In school I was just another kid, because just about all of my school friends were indifferent to racing. But at the track, I was kind of riding on my dad's coattails. I'm sure that was part of our enjoyment of going to the track: being Ron Bouchard's kids. It was like having local-celebrity status. It was an environment we could feel comfortable in. You didn't have to get to know people; it was like these people already knew us.

It got to the point where, as soon as Monday morning came along, all I cared about was the weekend, when we'd all pack into the car and head to the races. The weekdays seemed to take *so* long. That was true even up through high school.

To me, the most exciting part of every weekend was when it came time for the feature at Stafford. The Modifieds would be on their pace laps, and over the speakers you'd hear the "Theme from *Shaft*." It always gave me chills. And Stafford was my favorite track, anyway. I liked Thompson, too, but it didn't have quite the same effect on me in those days. Westboro was fun, but as a kid it felt like it was a step down from Stafford, maybe just because everything was smaller. And there were places I only went a few times, like Waterford, because a lot of my dad's races there were midweek events.

We usually rode to the races with Aunt JoAnn and Nana, my grandmother on the Bouchard side. My dad and Uncle Kenny had to be there early so they could be ready for warm-ups, so the rest of us went down later. Looking back, it must have been hectic getting all of that figured out. It *had* to be. If you told me right now that I had to do something two or three nights a week and get all of these people organized, I couldn't find the time. But as a kid, it never felt like it took any effort. That was our life.

We hung around the Kangas family a lot, I remember that. Aside from them, Robbie and I had our friends at the track, and my sisters had their group. Sometimes we'd come across one another, but usually each group kind of did its own thing. For the most part, we were all good kids. We never crossed any boundaries, never did anything we weren't supposed to. At the track, we were pretty much on our best behavior. Which was a good thing, because although we didn't know it at the time, there must have been a lot of people watching us, since everything we did got back to Nana and JoAnn. Everybody knew the Bouchard kids, I guess. I think the biggest problem my grandmother and my aunt ever had was keeping track of where we all were.

At Stafford, Robbie and I would watch the Modified heats, and then head to the clubhouse while everything else ran. We weren't as interested in the other divisions. I do remember watching Seymour the Clown and his antics, but mostly we just paid attention to the Modifieds and ignored everything else. We'd play pinball in the clubhouse until five minutes before the Modified feature, then we'd head for our seats and root for my dad.

It's funny to think about it today, but for a long time the Modified drivers I liked the least were Bugsy Stevens and, later on, Geoff Bodine. See, I wanted my dad to win every race, and Bugsy and Geoff were usually the guys he had to beat. I look back now and it was just stupid kid stuff. I still don't know too much about Geoff, but everything I've ever heard about Bugsy tells me he's a great guy, yet in those days they were the enemies. I'll admit, I was just a little bit biased.

Now, in Robbie's case, Maynard Troyer was absolutely his favorite driver. Maynard only came to New England for the biggest races, but whenever Robbie knew Maynard was coming, that's all he could talk about. I think if a race came down to a battle between Maynard Troyer and my dad, Robbie would *grudgingly* root for Dad.

One thing that was difficult about being at the track was that even after the races, we got very little of our dad's attention. We had to share him with other people, whether it was the guys who worked on the car or the fans who wanted to talk to him, especially if he happened to win. I understand that now, but as kids I think it was hard to know why it was like that.

You know, when he started going to race at all those far-off places, that was really cool. Like when he won at Martinsville; somehow I knew Martinsville was special, either from reading about it or just from listening to people. I knew it was a place where the Grand National guys raced, and I was a big fan of the Allisons, Bobby and Donnie, so it seemed like a big deal that my dad won at a track where they also raced. But, honestly, the biggest thing was that grandfather clock!

I also have a memory of me, my dad, and somebody else, maybe Calvin Blaisdell, flying up to Oxford, Maine, in Wes Sleeper's plane, so my dad could race a Late Model at Oxford Plains. I remember there being a huge thunderstorm, and us flying through it. The race might have gotten rained out, because I have no recollection of it; I don't even remember what car my dad was supposed to drive. But maybe that's because I have such a vivid memory of that storm.

As far as regular, everyday things, I remember spending a lot of time around Red & White. When I was 12, I was already working there, doing odds and ends around the garage, which was fun because at that time Kenny had a car there. I even went on some moving jobs with my grandfather, who was always Pepe to me. He'd let me carry little things, when all I wanted to do was help the adults move the bigger things. My favorite moving jobs were always with my dad and Uncle Kenny, because sometimes I'd be with Bergie or Pepe, and those two guys were *serious*.

My dad not only moved furniture, but he also did a lot of freight deliveries, so he was away quite a bit, driving the truck. So I didn't see him a lot, because between the races and the freight jobs he'd be gone so much. At that age, I didn't have any idea about all the work he had to do; I just wanted to see him more. But now I can see that he was working all the time.

I think your work ethic is something that gets passed along. What I mean is, I may have gotten mine from my dad, but I think it all came from *his* dad, my grandfather. I don't think I've ever met anybody who worked as hard as Pepe did. He was a tough man; to look at him you wouldn't know it, but he was powerful.

I went to a trade school, and for a long time my true desire had been to take up carpentry. My Grandpa John was a jack of all trades, and among other things he was a really good carpenter. He built houses, and things like that. I looked up to him a lot, and there are days even today when I wish I had pursued that, and maybe been a contractor, with my own company.

I thought a lot about racing, too, right up until the time I graduated high school and went into the Air Force. I always wanted to race a car myself, and to this day I regret never pushing to at least try it. But you make choices, and you live with the choices you make, and my choice at the time was to go into the service. I had friends who were signing up in that same period, and I remember thinking, "Hey, this could be my opportunity to get some training that I can use later on." That didn't necessarily turn out to be the case, but I was thinking along those lines.

Plus, I was at that stage a lot of kids reach, where you want to get away and see what's out there. You want to get *out*. I just felt like I needed something else in my life at that point. I wanted to be independent. I think it's different today; kids seem to want to live with their parents until their mom and dad kick them out, maybe because they have so much at home to keep them occupied.

Anyway, I joined the Air Force and went to Texas. I did my basic training at Lackland Air Force Base in San Antonio, and then went to tech school in Wichita Falls, where I learned to work on teletype equipment. My first duty assignment was at Goodfellow Air Force Base in San Angelo. After all that, I couldn't wait to get *out* of Texas, so I volunteered for a remote tour and ended up at Shemya Air Force Base in Alaska, out in the Aleutian Islands. I spent a year there, and the wind blew the whole time.

When I got home, I ended up working for my dad, and then I started down the path that led toward me being an accountant. And that was probably for the best, because the things I'd dreamed of doing when I was younger—either racing or being a carpenter and a contractor—can wear you out early. As an accountant, I can work until I'm in my 70s, if I have to.

You know, there are clearly ways in which my dad influenced me. I already mentioned the work ethic, but being dedicated to your family and your kids, that's another big one. I'd do anything for my kids, and I just have to assume that comes from my dad. I'm sure that later in life he wished that he'd have been able to spend more time with all of us when we were young, but he couldn't. That wasn't his fault; he certainly did the best he could. But what my wife and I do, as parents, is try to give our children as much of ourselves as we can.

He's someone I'll always look up to. *Always*. A lot of the life lessons I learned, I learned from my dad. And the person I am, I am because of him.

BY ED FLEMKE JR.

"He never rubbed anybody wrong, never banged and crashed his way to the front"

Ruminations on a special era, and the part Ron played

As his name makes clear, Ed Flemke Jr. is the son of the late Steady Eddie Flemke, one of the great legends of the Modified division and, indeed, of American short-track racing. But don't discount the younger Flemke's own career; "Little Eddie" was a 17-time winner on NASCAR's Modified Tour, was twice runner-up in series points, and in 2002 was voted the tour's Most Popular Driver. He is also a respected fabricator, building cars under the RaceWorks banner, a brand he launched alongside his father in the late '70s. Eddie Jr. had a long and multi-dimensional view of Ron Bouchard: In the early '70s he watched his father battle Bouchard; in the early days of his own career, he and Ronnie often shared the track; and their friendship deepened in the course of the long relationship between Ron and Eddie's sister, Paula, who ultimately became Paula Flemke Bouchard.

VAL LESIEUR COLLECTION

There's a memory I have from when Ronnie really started making an impression on my world. He was driving for Bob Johnson, and they were winning not just at Stafford, but at a bunch of different places. I can't remember the actual words he used, but one day my father said something like, "What do you think they're doing?"

He didn't mean cheating, or anything like that that. It was more like he was just wondering out loud what that team was doing, and why they were so fast. That was rare, because my father wasn't the type to look over his shoulder or show any concern. I realized that this was his way of acknowledging that Ronnie was for real. It wasn't just because Ronnie and Bob had won some races; it went deeper than that. I think talented people have a way of understanding talent, of picking out other talented people, and that's what was happening.

So to me, the message was, "I'd better watch this guy."

The very first time I had ever heard Ron Bouchard's name was when he came to that midweek show at Stafford in 1971. He had his Camaro, with the little wing on the back of it. He didn't kick everybody's ass that night, but he definitely made everybody take notice. Seekonk was kind of its own little island in those days, so we just didn't follow what went on there. We all learned later that Ronnie had already won a few championships at Seekonk, but I'm sure a lot of people who were at Stafford that night didn't know that. Up until that time, if you raced a NASCAR Modified, of if you were a fan of NASCAR Modifieds, the Saturday night track you paid attention to was Norwood Arena.

But all of a sudden here came this kid we didn't know, driving what to us was a silly-looking car with a body that was, like, *half* a Camaro, like a Late Model that had been wrecked. You just didn't take it seriously ... until you saw what Ronnie did with it.

In that period, Stafford was just getting to be a big, big deal. To me, it was the first time you felt that racing was real, that racing people *mattered* outside of our own small circle. You've got to understand, I had once had the parents of a good friend tell me that racing was "seedy." I actually had to find a dictionary and look up what that word meant, and it certainly wasn't very nice. But by the early '70s, the sport started to come out of that era when the image of a racer was the grease-monkey guy with the cigarette pack rolled up in his sleeve. A little at a time, it was becoming respectable, and you could especially feel that at Stafford. Pretty soon Thompson began to get more polished, too, but Stafford was first. You could actually say to your friends that you were involved in racing, and it meant more than it had, say, ten years earlier.

Even among the guys who raced at other tracks, there was that feeling; they looked up to Stafford. When I first started running there in 1974, that attitude had existed for a couple of years. I shared space in a Quonset hut in Southington with a bunch of other racers: Stan Greger, Ron Vanesse, Joe Bubbico, and a couple more. One Saturday, I just missed qualifying for the feature at Stafford, and that same night Stanley won at Plainville Stadium. Well, his guys said, "Geez, we heard you were only one spot away from qualifying. That's awesome!" And I was like, "Wait a minute. You *won*." The difference was, I was racing at Stafford, and that was special.

So that was the atmosphere at the time when Ronnie came in and started making his mark, and his timing was perfect.

Don't get me wrong, I hated seeing this guy come in with this oddball Seekonk car and this little motor, and run so well against some of the best Modified teams. That should *not* have happened. You didn't just come in there as an outsider and do that. Most guys from those little tracks just stayed in their own pond. You didn't see guys from Waterford bring their regular Speedbowl cars to Stafford and run that good; you didn't see Riverside Park guys with their little engines even bother to show up at Stafford. They'd never even think of that. But Ronnie *did*.

Then he came back and started running Modifieds on a regular basis with Bob Johnson's car, and they won a lot of races. Looking back on it now, I think Ronnie and Bob both had that burning desire to be on top, and each of them made the other one better. What they did, putting all those ingredients together just right and being that successful right away, was almost unthinkable, especially against that level of competition.

It's funny, but for a year or two Bob had a bigger impact on me than Ronnie did. I think that's because Bob built his own cars, and I was just starting to race my own stuff. And Bob was the kind of guy who, if he saw you struggling, he would try to help you. Don't get me wrong, if you reached out to Ronnie, as a driver, he'd take the time to give you whatever advice you needed. But as someone who had a race car, I kind of looked toward Bob. He was a hard worker, and he was smart; in my eyes he was like Bobby Judkins and Beebe Zalenski, guys who got everything they could out of what they had.

And Bob was one of those guys who would pay it forward, as people say today. When Marvin Rifchin from M&H Racemaster was helping that team out so much, Bob would quietly say to me, "Hey, kid, come down to my shop sometime. I've got some take-off tires you might be able to use." He was really good to me that way.

In a way, Ronnie snuck in under the radar. Don't get me wrong, he made a big splash, winning against the guys he was beating. He made a lot of headlines, but not because of any controversy. He never rubbed anybody the wrong way, never banged and crashed his way to the front. He didn't take anything; he *earned* it. And when he had success, he didn't rub anybody's nose in it. He didn't make waves, the way some other guys did. He was the real deal. He did everything the right way, so he was accepted without any fuss.

My first real racing interaction with him came one night at Stafford, when the two of us were in the same heat race. We were both starting on the front row, which would have been kind of unusual because of the handicapped starts, so maybe it was early in the season, before the handicapping kicked in. He walked over, put his arm around me—got me in that Bouchard headlock—and said, "Hey, Eddie, let's remember to put a show on."

That was a pretty big honor. I'd watched my father and the rest of those guys do that, so just to be invited to be a part of it was something else for me.

Ronnie said, "Whichever one of us gets to the first turn first can lead for a while, but then let's mix it up a little."

I said to myself, "What does he mean, whoever gets to the first turn first? This is Ron Bouchard! *He's* going to get to the first turn first."

But they threw the green, and between him playing and me having the best start of my life up to that point, I led into turn one. So we ran a couple of laps like that, then he passed me in typical Ronnie fashion, on the outside, and led me down the straightaway and into the next corner. Well, he drove in there a little easy, still playing, but I went in with everything I had, trying to keep up. I ran right in the back of him. Damn near spun him out.

That ended the playing. He let me stay close, but we didn't do any more of the back-and-forth stuff.

After the heat race he came right over and said, "Eddie, what the hell was that all about? We were out there putting on a show!"

The truth was, I just didn't know how to play the game yet. I didn't know how to race at 90 percent; I was out there running at 100 percent, just hoping to stay with him.

The first time I spent any real time with Ronnie away from a race track, I suppose he and Paula were on kind of a date, but I didn't know that. We were out someplace in Daytona—maybe the old Mac's Famous Bar—and Ronnie was there, too. I figured he had stopped in to have a drink with some friends, but maybe I was just naïve. It wasn't until months later that I found out there was any real interest between him and my sister. That was just before my father found out, which is a story in itself.

Somebody mentioned that they were seeing each other, which was news to me, and then soon afterward I heard it again from somebody else, so I figured maybe there was something to this. Paula and I were both working at Burnside Motors in East Hartford, and one day as we were riding home I said, "Uh, I've heard something from a couple of sources, so this is something people are aware of. And, just so you know, Dad is going to *kill* you."

Part of that was because Ronnie was older, and he had been married, and this was my father's little girl. But the biggest thing was that my father was very strict about wanting to hear anything important directly from *us*. He never wanted to hear anything second-hand. He always said, "Come to me first."

I said, "Paula, either you're going to tell him, or I am."

She said, "Okay, okay, I will."

But she didn't do it fast enough. That same evening I went to my shop in Southington. This was long before cell phones, but when I got there one of the guys said, "Hey, your father is trying to get in touch with you. He wants you to call him at home."

I figured he wanted me to pick up a pizza or something. So I called him, and the first thing he said was, "What's this I hear about your sister and Ronnie?"

I said, "I'll be right home."

He was upset—understandably, because this went against everything he'd said about wanting to hear things from us—and it was not the most comfortable conversation we'd ever had. Obviously, he was worried about his daughter, and he was protective of her. I'm sure he was concerned that this was just some kind of a fling. But, to make a long story short, look how wrong that turned out to be. Those two grew into *such* a great pair.

But, getting back to the racing, Ronnie had a way of connecting with people, and making his fans feel close to him. A good friend of mine, Rick Drezek from New Britain, told me a story once about something that happened way back then. Rick had a young son who'd been diagnosed with cancer at ten years old. Ten. So, of course, he tried to do as much as he could with his son, and one of the things they did together was go to the races at Stafford. They sat in the grandstands and picked which drivers they were going to root for, and for whatever reason his son picked Ronnie. At some point they walked over to the pit fence, and the son saw Ronnie and called his name. Now, that happens a lot to drivers at Stafford, because Jack Arute's best move was to relocate the pits directly behind the grandstands, where the fans can really get close to what's going on. But sometimes drivers are busy, and sometimes they don't have a minute to go and see the kids at the fence. But Ronnie always made time for that, and on this night he came over, knelt down, signed something Rick and his son had—maybe a program—then rolled it up and slipped it back through the fence. And he stayed there a minute and *talked* with this kid, not knowing anything about his situation or anything like that. I know Rick never, ever forgot that.

And Ronnie was a good guy to be a fan of. He raced hard, but he was a clean driver, like all the top guys from that era were. I've said this many times, but those drivers believed that the front bumper was there to protect the radiator. It wasn't a weapon. It wasn't there to knock your opponent out of the way. They were serious racers, but they had so much respect for each other, and for what they were all a part of.

Looking back on those years, the sad thing, to me, is that I know so many of us took that era for granted. I'm sure we knew that we were in a great period, a special period, but we were not really aware of *how* special it really was. It's like surfing; you paddle out and catch a wave, and while you're riding it you don't quite know how big it's going to get. You don't realize until it's over that you were on the ride of your life. That's what we all had going on, and Ronnie Bouchard was right there in the middle of it.

PART THREE

"Just Good, Hard Racing"

PAUL BONNEAU

Every form of racing has its Golden Ages—plural—and if you ask a dozen fans of that discipline to name one, you're likely to get a half-dozen different answers. But if you followed asphalt Modified racing in the Northeast, and specifically New England, there's no denying that the short, sweet stretch from 1976–80 was indeed a gilded epoch.

It started, ironically, with some bad news. Jack Arute, entering his seventh year of Stafford Motor Speedway ownership, had been as pleased as punch with its on-track action, but not so thrilled with its gate receipts. It seems almost inconceivable that a track that regularly pitted beloved old lions like Flemke, Stevens, and DeSarro against hungry pups named Bouchard, Bodine, and John Rosati could ever struggle, but Stafford was up against a lot of competition. In addition to movie theaters, the beach, and other activities enjoyed by Mr. and Mrs. John Doe and their kids, there was Saturday-night racing to be found at Riverside Park (20 miles away by car), Plainville Stadium (43 miles), Waterford Speedbowl (48 miles), Seekonk Speedway (65 miles) and the Danbury Racearena (90 miles). The fact that each of those tracks had its own rules and its own local heroes kept drivers and fans close to home, which did Stafford no favors. Arute's joint may have served up the best hardcore racing in the Northeast, but if there weren't enough hardcore fans dragging their wives and kids through the turnstiles, what did that matter?

The track opened its regular season on Saturday, May 8, 1976—by coincidence, the same night Ron Bouchard and Bob Johnson ended their partnership—under the heavy weight of an ominous Arute declaration: that if crowds didn't pick up in the next few weeks, he'd have to rethink Stafford's future.

Then, from an odd direction, came a tailwind: Jackie Arute, Jack's son as well as Stafford's energetic general manager and lead announcer, showed such promise in the latter role that NASCAR's Motor Racing Network—on the recommendation of Vermont's own broadcast legend in the making, Ken Squier—offered him a full-time gig. Jackie accepted, and went on to radio and TV fame. Back home at Stafford, papa Jack filled the GM vacancy by sliding ex-driver and chief steward Ed Yerrington behind Jackie's old desk. Depending on his mood, Ed could be charming, prickly, or somewhere in between, but he combined a no-nonsense attitude with a racer's natural inclination to take risks. And history credits Yerrington with the gamble that not only turned around Arute's facility, but also electrified New England racing through the rest of that decade: Stafford's 1977 switch to Friday nights.

That was one beautiful maneuver. Fans from all those other tracks could now visit Stafford without missing a race at home. The fact that many became Stafford regulars showed on nights like July 4, 1980, when a whopper of an offering—a fireworks display paired with the Ferrara 100, one of the speedway's marquee events—drew more than

12,000 people, so many that columnist Phil Smith reported "ticket booths and admission gates were closed at 8:30 p.m., with people lined up out to the road."

Far beyond Jack Arute's property line, the move had similar results. Many of Stafford's top NASCAR names headed elsewhere on Saturday nights, adding star power to those tracks and returning Ron Bouchard to Seekonk, where he had known such glory. And Thompson's ongoing Sunday program meant that Modified racing in New England was a three-nights-per-weekend affair, boosting the win totals—and the daily sports-page profiles—of the handful of drivers who consistently ran up front, like our man Bouchard.

Ronnie was on fire anyway. In 1976 he'd driven for frugal Bob Judkins and flashy Bill Hood, and won with both. From 1977–79, he had the best of both worlds, driving an ex-Hood car—now owned by Marvin Rifchin—wrenched by Judkins, and the trophies kept coming. In 1980, backed by Rifchin, Bouchard was in Len Boehler's famous #3 and moonlighting for Dick Armstrong in selected events; he parked both their cars in the winner's circle.

And, as in his early years at Seekonk, it was the way Bouchard won that grabbed your eye. He *always* seemed to be passing somebody. New England's Modified tracks still started their fastest cars and drivers toward the rear of the field, using money-won handicapping systems, and it was a rare night that Ronnie started fewer than eight rows back. So if in a given season you saw him win 15 features from the 15th starting position, you'd watched him pass 225 cars. That doesn't take into account the nights he finished second, third, or fourth, and doesn't include all the cars he'd passed in his qualifying heats. What's more, he did it with style, overtaking with an artistry his old-school up-bringing demanded. Rarely was there a clash, a clang, a thump. Bouchard made the pass cleanly, or he didn't make it at all.

Years later, Ron said, "I think that's what people came to see: hard, clean racing. I always wanted to win, but I was also the kind of guy who figured if the best I could do was second, that wasn't too bad; if the best I could do was third, that wasn't too bad, either. As long as I knew I'd done everything I could, I was happy.

"And the better the race, the more fun I had. It was really exciting to us in the cars, and I know it was to the people in the grandstands, because at some of these places you could actually see 'em jumping up and down."

Ron Bouchard made an awful lot of people jump up and down, and never more than in those golden, glorious late '70s.

1976: You wouldn't have expected it to take long for Bouchard to find a seat once he and Bob Johnson split, and it didn't. Within days he accepted a ride with Bob Judkins. That was met with great enthusiasm in Meriden, Connecticut, where the fabled Judkins #2X was tended by Bob, his right-hand man Chuck Grime, and the odd volunteer, one of whom was teenaged Steve Kalkowski. Having landed on the team when it was running a casual, now-and-then schedule with veteran Gene Bergin, Kalkowski noticed a sudden jump in the collective pulse. "It was really interesting," Steve remembers, "to see how excited Bob and Chuck were to have Ronnie on board." ... Judkins had two Modifieds, but both had some age on them. His Stafford car was the same one that started the "Pinto Revolution" in 1971. Bouchard put his spurs to the old horse and was rewarded with a fifth in his debut, a scrappy seventh in the postponed Spring Sizzler, and a great pair of seconds in June. But he was outmatched by modern pieces like Geoff Bodine's latest Armstrong #1, a low-slung beauty with coil-over suspension. Nor was the small-block #2X fresh, having been constructed in 1972. But in the right hands it could still dance, particularly on a driver's track like Monadnock, where in mid-June Bouchard grabbed the Yankee 100, his first win for Judkins ... In the middle of July, Bouchard and Judkins separated—temporarily, as we shall see—on friendly terms, with Ronnie leaving Bob's low-dollar operation for one with a much larger budget. The "Big Bucks" slogan emblazoned across the rear of the Hood Enterprises #7 did not endear owner Bill Hood to Modified diehards already boiling over the era's influx of money, but the car, a Vega built by renowned Midget constructor Rollie Lindblad, put Bouchard back in the game, particularly at high-speed tracks like Stafford and Thompson. At Stafford he immediately racked up two runner-up finishes in NASCAR events, and later, in a three-race September series for small blocks, he notched two wins and a second. But it was at Thompson that the car really flew. That track was a favorite of JoAnn Bouchard Bergeron, watching from its old wooden stands alongside her mother and Ronnie's kids. "I loved the way some guys would go high on those banked turns, then cross over and pass on the inside," JoAnn recalls. "Ronnie was so good at that. I'd say, 'Watch, Ma, on this next lap he's going to get him.'" And Bouchard got a bunch of them, bagging three Thompson wins in the Hood #7 ... Just for kicks, Bouchard paid a surprise first visit to Connecticut's Plainville Stadium, and drove Billy Corazzo's Sherri-Cup coupe to victory in an open-comp 100-lapper.

1977: At first glance, '77 doesn't stand out as one of Bouchard's great seasons. Historians mark it more for the popular Stafford comeback of Bugs Stevens, who won eight times there, and for the sixth and final NASCAR title of Jerry Cook's career. But Ronnie won more features overall than either of those guys. Before the campaign even started, Rifchin had purchased Hood's #7, replaced its obnoxious "Big Bucks" message with M&H Racemaster lettering, and entrusted the Vega to Judkins, with whom Bouchard had formed a solid bond. "Bob could fabricate anything," says Steve Kalkowski. "Give him some scrap metal, and he could make something out of it." Together they won here, there, everywhere: April's Blast-Off 100 at the Waterford Speedbowl; four Friday-night features at Stafford; a Memorial Day weekend show at Seekonk, where Bouchard, Stevens, and DeSarro were helping pack the joint on Saturday nights; five Sunday races at Thompson; Wednesday-night events at Westboro and at New Hampshire's Star Speedway, which boosted Ronnie to the Yankee All-Star League championship; and, in October, a 250-lap NASCAR special at Tennessee's Kingsport Speedway, another track Bouchard had never seen ... New England's busiest Modified schedule in years intensified both rivalries and friendships; post-race revelry soared. "It was nothing to see five or six haulers parked outside the pits, and a bunch of people enjoying themselves," Bouchard once said. "Somebody was going to cook some clams and lobsters, and we were going to drink some beer, and we were all going to laugh." Kalkowski recalled a Sunday night at Thompson, probably after one of those five victories: "We're hanging around—Bob, Chuck, Ronnie, Paula, and a few others—and pretty soon, it's pitch dark. Well, out of the darkness, here comes a bottle rocket: *Ssshooo, bang!* It's Bugsy, firing at us from across the parking lot."

1978: For several years, the World Series of Asphalt Stock Car Racing at Florida's New Smyrna Speedway had been a satellite to the February goings-on at Daytona International Speedway, a dozen miles up the road. But it was only in 1976 that Modifieds were added to the World Series, with five events the first year and six the second. Legendary ex-driver Bill Slater, who'd helped Jack Arute revive Stafford and was now chief steward at Thompson, ran the Modified portion, and nobody could marshal the troops like Wild Bill; he'd help arrange hotel rooms, slip a few pit passes to struggling teams, whatever it took. By 1978, when the World Series ballooned to nine nights, the entry list included names like Evans, Stevens, Bodine, Flemke, DeSarro, Cook, Worley, Charlie Jarzombek, Junior Hanley, and even Bobby Allison. New Smyrna was now a genuine happening, and its Modified champion was Bouchard, driving a new Judkins #2X built on a Hop Harrington chassis. Evans and Bodine each won three times, but they lacked Bouchard's blend of speed and consistency. Ronnie had one victory, two seconds, a third, two fourths, a fifth, a seventh, and one DNF ... Though the '78 season belonged to Geoff Bodine, who won a startling 55 times, Bouchard—dividing his time between the #2X and the M&H #7, both backed by Rifchin—also had a fabulous year. There were three straight wins at Waterford, including a second consecutive Blast-Off 100, a Stafford victory, and eight wins apiece at Thompson and Seekonk, including streaks of four in a row at each place. Kalkowski says, "With Ronnie, we never went to a track where we said, 'Maybe we can get out of here with a top-five finish.' Every race we went to, we knew we had a shot to win." ... Come autumn he won his first Thompson track championship and his fifth at Seekonk, where, Kalkowski recalls, "those people just loved him." Truth be told, Bouchard was loved just about everywhere. Barbara Savitsky, who'd first seen him race when both of them were Seekonk Speedway teenagers, steered the Ron Bouchard Fan Club and oversaw busy displays at all three of his weekly tracks. "Wow, those days were so much fun," Barbara muses all these years later ... There were those who wondered if Bouchard's 1978 win production might have been higher were it not for his team's allegiance to the M&H Tire Company. Lest you sense some disrespect here, those doubters included Racemaster boss Marvin Rifchin. In 1977–78, Goodyear's Modified tires, winning left and right with Stevens and especially Bodine, were so good that even Firestone loyalists Evans and Cook switched brands, and by the summer of '78 Firestone left the division entirely. Though Rifchin relished the "mad scientist" aspect of the tire business, fiddling with new rubber compounds, by the summer of '78 he was exasperated. Bouchard's old pal Vic Kangas says, "I was standing right there at Stafford when Marvin told Judkins and Ronnie, 'Look, guys, I don't have anything that's going to win the race for you. Put on a set of Goodyears.'" Ed Flemke Jr., also on the scene, recalls, "Everybody said, 'Marvin, you're going to buy somebody *else's* tires?' And Marvin said, 'Why not? We've got to beat these sonsabitches.'" Meaning, of course, Bodine, Stevens, or anybody who stood between Bouchard and victory lane ... For a second straight year, Ronnie capped his season with a Tennessee waltz to victory in the Kingsport 250 ... But everybody's 1978 went to hell when Fred DeSarro died on November 1 from head injuries sustained three weeks earlier in a Thompson crash. Few knew it, but Len Boehler, Fred's car owner and friend, was already battling lymphoma. Even Golden Ages have their blue periods.

1979: Sad winter, heavy spring. Some of Boehler's crewmen banded together to launch the annual Fred DeSarro Award, given to the top performer in Stafford's Spring Sizzler, a race whose inaugural edition Freddy had captured in 1972. Bouchard won the award for his inspired pursuit of winner Maynard Troyer. Clearly moved, he accepted the $500 prize, then turned the money over to Linda DeSarro, Fred's widow, and their sons, Gary and Bryan ... For a second straight year, Bouchard, Judkins, Rifchin and company easily cleared the 20-win mark. A Stafford track title, Ronnie's second, was probably the highlight, especially given the way he clinched it. In each of the final three features of the regular season, Bouchard—wheeling Rifchin's new Troyer car—beat Richie Evans to the checkered flag, and in the final reckoning his margin over Evans in the title fight was a scant two points ... At Seekonk, Ronnie won seven features, four of them in a row, but it was at Thompson that he was most dominant, scoring nine times. Reacting to rising engine costs, promoter Don Hoenig instituted a rule calling for "stock" cylinder heads. That led to weekly Sunday-morning engine swaps for the Judkins team, either outside Seekonk's Esquire Motel or at the Blackstone, Massachusetts, shop of Bouchard's old pal Calvin Blaisdell, now Rifchin's engine builder of choice ... Even with that cylinder-head rule, the gap between the haves and the have-nots, best reflected in the closing rates between fast cars and backmarkers, shone more vividly at Thompson than at any other New England track. That played straight into Bouchard's hands. "A lot of drivers don't look any farther ahead than their radiator caps," says Chuck Grime. "Ronnie always seemed to be laps ahead of whatever situation he was coming up on: 'Can I trust this guy? Where should I make the pass?' He was a smart, smart driver." … Elsewhere in 1979, they won another New Smyrna feature and a pair of Westboro 50-lappers … As strong at Bouchard was that year, the relationship between Rifchin and Judkins was fraying. After Ronnie fell out of Stafford's twice-postponed Fall Final, they did not field a car for the Cardinal 500 at Martinsville. Instead, Bouchard finished third in a back-up Evans #61, renumbered #81 for the occasion. No one knew it at the time, but they'd seen the last of one of the decade's great driver/mechanic pairings. Though Ron Bouchard and Bob Judkins remained friends, they never ran another race together. You can liken it to the Bouchard/Johnson divorce that brought Ronnie to the Judkins team in the first place, by shrugging and reminding yourself that nothing lasts forever.

1980: One of the finest seasons of Bouchard's career began in complete disarray. At some point over the winter of 1979–80, it became clear that Ronnie had a ride waiting with Dick Armstrong—who had lost Geoff Bodine to Winston Cup and Late Model Sportsman racing in 1979—but only for the major events; Armstrong had lost his zeal for weekly action. That left some big holes in Bouchard's schedule, and for a while he had no clear way to fill them. He drove for Lee Allard at New Smyrna, but their abbreviated World Series was a mechanical disaster. (Interestingly, Ronnie also reunited with Bob Johnson for Daytona's 200-mile superspeedway Modified race, finishing seventh. He'd looked like a sure bet to place anywhere from third to fifth before a black flag triggered by an eagle-eyed NASCAR official who observed Bouchard's arm holding up a window net that had managed to unlatch itself.) Come April he ran the Spring Sizzler for Armstrong, and then, still in the #1, spent a hectic late-April Saturday finishing second to Evans in Martinsville's Azalea 150 in the afternoon, and second to Cook that night at North Carolina's Caraway Speedway … It looked for a while as if Bouchard, using Rifchin's Troyer #7, might run his own team in weekly events, and briefly he did, but "it got to be too much," he told a *Speedway Scene* columnist. Behind the scenes, Rifchin put together a deal pairing Bouchard with a recovering Len Boehler, who, though frail, had wrenched Leo Cleary to the '79 Seekonk championship. By late May, Bouchard was in the Boehler #3—at Stafford it was re-badged as the #7, to maintain Bouchard's points status—and off to a torrid summer: six wins at Stafford, four at Thompson, and five at Westboro, which had become a Saturday-night Modified hotspot after Seekonk dropped the division. Westboro's promoter was nice-guy Dick Williams, who'd also taken the reins at Monadnock and moved the latter track's race night to Thursdays. Some of 1980's hottest action was between the Bouchard brothers at that woodsy New Hampshire bullring, where both had multiple wins ... "Ronnie always drove for friendly people," says JoAnn Bouchard Bergeron. "After the Johnsons it was Judkins and his guys, then Boehler and his crew, and they were all nice to us. I guess they figured that if you got Ronnie, you got the whole Bouchard family!'" ... Sixteen times that season, Bouchard won with Boehler's blue Chevettes, but his brightest moment in 1980 came aboard Armstrong's red Pinto. That was on September 19, when he won the Thompson 300. The race finished under yellow after rain fell in the closing stages, but there was no doubt as to who was the day's dominant driver. A *Speedway Scene* report noted that Bouchard "led 233 laps, and was in second place on almost every lap he didn't lead." ... A week later Ron and the Armstrong #1 were at Pocono, chasing Richie Evans and Geoff Bodine to the end in the Race of Champions, and at Martinsville in October the order was only slightly altered: Evans, Bouchard, Bodine. There were years when Ronnie B. had won more races, but there are those who believe that in 1980 he was at the top of his Modified art. He was 31, and he had as much speed and savvy as anybody in the game.

BY BOB JUDKINS

"Everybody goes out to win, but with Ronnie you knew you could do it"

A Hall of Fame car owner on his Hall of Fame driver

Some car owners have a transitory impact on their chosen divisions. They're here, they win for a while, and then they're gone, replaced by the next fat wallet. Then there are men like Bob Judkins, whose name will be relevant as long as Modifieds race. Though he fielded cars from the early 1960s into the '90s, employing star drivers like Tony Mordino, Fats Caruso, Stan Greger, and Jerry Marquis, the Judkins legend revolves around three key periods: 1967–69, when Ed Flemke steered Bob's coupe to scores of victories across New England and New York; 1971–75, when Flemke and Gene Bergin took turns wheeling a pair of Judkins Pintos, including the first NASCAR-legal version of that body style; and 1976–79, when Bob turned wrenches on both his own #2X Pintos and Marvin Rifchin's M&H Racemaster #7 cars, all of which were big winners in the hands of Ron Bouchard.

STEVE KENNEDY

Before I got together with Ronnie in 1976, we had raced against each other quite a bit. Depending on the year, I had either Eddie Flemke or Gene Bergin in my car, and Ronnie was driving for Bob Johnson. I knew both of them pretty well, and I was friendly with Ronnie and Bob. It makes me laugh a little bit now, but sometimes I would pit right beside those guys, especially at Stafford, and Bob would lose his temper quite a bit. He'd be hollering, throwing things. I could never understand how he could be so calm one minute, then fly off the handle, and then calm right back down again in the next minute. I always thought they were a strange fit, because Ronnie was so easygoing.

No matter where we went in those days, Ronnie was one of the men to beat, and sometimes *the* man to beat. With both Gene and Eddie driving my car, we had a lot of good races with him. It was always hard, clean racing, and then after the races we'd hang around and have a beer. Back then it always seemed like all the guys he was racing against were a lot older than Ronnie, but he fit right in. He was a likable guy.

I always said Ronnie was a natural-born race driver. He was just so good, no matter who he was driving for. Eddie had been the same way; it seemed like whatever car he got into, he'd manage to get it up front. You don't see that in very many guys, but Ronnie definitely had that ability.

I never really knew what happened between him and Johnson, and why they went their separate ways. It was none of my business. But when I heard they had split up, I called Ronnie about driving for me, and I was awfully glad to get him. Our first big race was the Spring Sizzler in '76 with my #2X, my first Pinto, but we must not have done too good because I don't remember much about it. Then we went to Monadnock and won an open show, which I guess was our first victory together. That was with my second Pinto, which was smaller all around than the first one. I remember Ronnie complaining that it was too tight inside for him; he said he could see how it was a good car for Eddie, because Eddie was small, but Ronnie was all cramped up in there.

That summer Ronnie ran a few races for Billy Hood, who had been a car owner for a while with George Summers. Rollie Lindblad had built a Vega for Hood, and Ronnie really liked that car. He won a few races with it, but that team didn't stay together long. I guess Billy Hood decided to get out of racing, so Marvin Rifchin ended up buying all of Hood's equipment, including that Vega. Ronnie and I had been running well, and we both enjoyed working together, so Marvin had all that stuff sent to my shop, and I started taking care of that car, too. We kept the paint and the number the same—it was a black #7—and it just went from being the Hood Enterprises Vega to being the M&H Racemaster Vega.

I had a shop down below my gas station on the Berlin Turnpike, basically two bays and a little bit of extra space. It would have been perfect for one car, but I usually had two, and it was really jammed with all my stuff in there and Marvin's stuff, too. But I was used to that, because back in the '60s I had built my first coupe in a little hole-in-the-wall garage in Meriden. That place was so small that I actually had to walk sideways to fit between the car and the wall. Compared to that, the shop at my gas station was roomy.

Having the race shop at the gas station was both good and bad. I'd work all day upstairs, pumping gas and working on cars for my customers, and at closing time

I could just walk around the building and down the hill and start working on the race cars. So it was convenient that way, which I loved. But if you're not careful, you start feeling like you're spending your whole life in one place. Most days, as long as I was basically caught up with everything, I'd go home to eat dinner, relax a little bit, and then go back and work on the race cars until ten o'clock or midnight. That's still a long day—I don't know how I ever did it—but at least I had a little break if I went home for supper.

Ronnie and I clicked really well, right from the start. I think that's probably because we were both pretty laid-back. He used to tell me, "Judkins, you're going to live forever, because nothing ever bothers you." But he was the same way, even at the races. He was really easy to work with. He'd go out and practice, then come in and tell me what the car was doing. He wasn't a chassis guy himself, and he didn't try to be. He'd just describe what it was doing, and leave it up to me.

I was always big on watching my cars closely, anyway, and I could usually tell how good or bad it was handling, whether it was pushing or loose or just right. I got better at that when I had Bergin driving, because Gene didn't know a thing about the chassis. He just climbed in and drove, and it was up to me to set up the car. In fact, one time Gene said, "It feels like the front end is trying to push the back end." That sounded a little mixed up to me, so I just nodded, did what I thought was best, and crossed my fingers.

Ronnie's feedback was a lot more detailed than that. We didn't get into talking about springs and shocks, but he could tell you exactly what he was feeling. After we talked about that for a while, he'd laugh and say, "Just fix it." Then he might wander off until it was time to go back out and run again.

At first we mostly focused on Stafford and Thompson, because in those days Stafford still ran on Saturday nights. When they switched to Fridays in 1977, that kind of opened it up for everybody to run wherever they wanted on Saturdays. We started racing at Seekonk, and so did a lot of guys; Bugsy Stevens and Fred DeSarro went there, and Geoff Bodine ran there quite a bit, and so did Kenny Bouchard.

I don't remember exactly how we decided on Seekonk, but I'm sure that would have been Ronnie's first choice because he'd had so much success there in his early days. Marvin liked Seekonk, too. I had never really run there too much, but Eddie Flemke and I had won there. And the money was good at Seekonk; Anthony Venditti always paid good purses.

That gave us a nice three-night circuit. We'd run Stafford on Friday nights, then I'd go home. On Saturdays we'd drive over to Seekonk, and when we got done racing there we'd usually stay over at the Esquire Motel right down the street. Then on Sunday afternoons we'd drive from Seekonk to Thompson, which wasn't too far.

Sometimes we'd go to Calvin Blaisdell's shop on the way, and change motors if we had to.

Those Saturday nights at Seekonk were really something. It seemed like we always ran first, second, or third, and once we got everything packed away and loaded we'd hang around in the parking lot for hours. The motel was only a mile or two away, so there was no hurry to get on the road. It always seemed like there were a dozen cars with their trunks open; people had coolers full of beer, and food, and it was just a great time. In that way, I probably had more fun with Ronnie than with any other driver. He always had a lot of good people around him.

That's once thing I notice when I go to the races today: Nobody seems to get together and hang around like we did. Instead, everyone huddles with their own groups. Back then, we'd laugh and joke and raise hell for half the night with Bugsy, Joe Brady, Lenny Boehler, all kinds of guys from different teams. Everybody got along.

All of that racing kept us pretty busy, but I didn't mind because we were running good and winning a lot at those three tracks. That was one thing about Ronnie: Anywhere you brought him, he was going to be fast. He loved the big tracks, but he was also good at little places like Seekonk. And anytime we went to a new track, he adapted really quickly. I remember going to Kingsport Speedway in Tennessee twice, and he won both times, against some really good competition: Harry Gant, Satch Worley, Paul Radford, and the rest of the best Southern cars, plus Richie Evans, Jerry Cook, Geoff Bodine, and some good Northern cars.

And there were a lot of places closer to home that we didn't run every week, but we did really well when we went there. We won at Waterford, Monadnock, Star; we won the World Series championship in '78 at New Smyrna.

The best thing about having a driver that adapts so well is that no matter where you're going, you know you've got a shot. Everybody goes out to win, but with Ronnie you *knew* you could do it. We had so many wins that I don't remember most of them, but I do remember riding home from all those places happy because we had won, or *almost* won.

Marvin and Ronnie had a relationship that was like father and son. Ronnie really liked Marvin, and in Marvin's eyes Ronnie could do no wrong. Marvin helped out a lot of racers over the years, but I think Ronnie was his number-one guy. They had been together before Ronnie and I hooked up, and I really liked working with Marvin.

Of course, there were times when that arrangement didn't work out in our favor. Marvin *loved* to try new things, and when you experiment with tires it doesn't always go your way, because there are so many things that go into building a racing tire. We had one compound he came up with that was fast, but it only lasted about 20 laps, and the features were 30! I'd watch Ronnie drive straight to the front, but then with ten laps to go he'd start sliding back and we'd end up third or fourth. Ronnie didn't like that, and neither did I, but we both had the attitude that Marvin paid the bills, and he was trying to come up with better, faster tires, so we lived with it.

One night after the races, I saw Marvin looking over one of those tires. I said, "Well, Marvin, what do you think is the matter?"

He just smiled and said, "Too much salt and pepper."

I never did figure out what he meant, but that was Marvin.

And, don't forget, there were also many, many nights when his tires helped us do well. Ronnie won a lot of races on those M&Hs.

Marvin was a very competitive person, and not just as a tire manufacturer. He was that way as a car owner, too. I remember a stretch when Goodyear had a really good tire; they had Geoff Bodine, Richie Evans, and a lot of guys on them. For a few weeks, nothing Marvin tried was working, and I think he got tired of Ronnie getting beat. Finally he just said, "Let's put Goodyears on the car."

So we did. We painted the sidewalls white so you couldn't read the Goodyear logo, but everybody knew what we were doing. As I recall, we did that a few times. And I'm sure Marvin cut those tires apart as soon as he got them home, trying to figure out what Goodyear was up to.

That deal with the whitewalls was when we had the Vega, the Lindblad car. We ran that thing for almost four years, and it won all over the place. It was just a great car. Ronnie also won with a couple of my #2X Pintos, first in one of my old cars and later with one that we finished from a Hop Harrington chassis. And then in 1979, once everybody started going to more and more offset cars, Marvin bought a Troyer car that turned out be really fast. That was our black #7 Pinto.

We won our share of races, but, like they say, you can't win 'em all. When Ronnie and I raced together, Geoff Bodine and Dick Armstrong had a great team. It seemed like we butted heads with them constantly, because we usually ran all the same tracks. Bugsy was doing well, too; he won a lot at Stafford in Sonny Koszela's #15, and at Seekonk and Thompson he was fast in Joe Brady's car. And once Richie Evans started spending more time in New England, he and Ronnie had a lot of good races at Stafford and Thompson. Richie and Ronnie were friends, and I had known Richie for a long time myself. There were nights when I'd ask him a question—usually something about handling—and Richie would say, "Well, I'll tell *you*, but keep it just between us."

I miss those days. Ronnie was a top-notch driver, but even more than that, you couldn't ask for a better guy. We just had so much fun.

One year when we raced at Kingsport, we got down there a day early, so we went to the track and practiced. There were only a few cars there, and Ronnie was really fast, way faster than the other guys. I remember Jerry Cook being there, and he was struggling. He must have been having some kind of trouble. We were done for the day, so I was standing there, watching, with Ronnie and Chuck Grime, who helped me for years. Just kidding around, I said, "Geez, I could go as fast as Cookie's going."

Ronnie said, "Well, get out there!"

So I did. And I actually had one or two good laps, but then I almost hit the wall. That was enough for me. It was much better to leave the driving to Ronnie.

Remember what I said about always watching my own car? Well, most of the time I watched *only* my car. When you have a really good driver in your car, and you watch him start in the back and work his way through traffic and get it to the front, you can really appreciate how talented he is, because you watch every move he makes. That's how it was with Ronnie. He was a good outside man; wherever we were, he'd jump to the outside lane and just go. That was the best part of racing, for me. I had done my part, hopefully, by giving him a good car, and now I could watch the driver do his job.

I remember saying something about that to Eddie Flemke when he drove for me, and I also mentioned it to Ronnie later on. I told them both, "I can't see why you guys think driving is so great. There's no way it could more enjoyable than standing here, watching."

Those were good times for me, running with Ronnie. Happy times. I was racing with somebody I liked, and we were winning.

BY GEOFF BODINE

"In a lot of ways, Ronnie and I were kids, racing against all the older guys"

Thoughts on a pivotal time in two great careers

In many ways, the early racing lives of Ron Bouchard and Geoff Bodine were on parallel tracks. Both hit their Modified strides at the dawn of the 1970s, both were young sensations in their respective regions—Bouchard in New England, Bodine in New York— and both proved their mettle in the neutral-turf special events that dotted the division's schedule. Further, both had late-'70s winning spurts that

PAUL BONNEAU

marked them as candidates for the Winston Cup stardom they eventually attained. Yet for all those similarities, these were two very different men. Ronnie, forever the people person, smiled his way through pit conversations and victory ceremonies; Geoff, often doubling as his own crew chief, was usually locked in deep thought, examining the race just run or pondering the next chassis change, and his popularity suffered (unfairly) as a result. Both were key figures in a remarkable Modified decade.

There is no question that racing in New England with Ronnie and the rest of the great drivers out there played a big part in my career. That's where I was taught how to pass, how to maneuver, how to *race*. The fast cars always started toward the back of the field, and both Ronnie and I were usually in that group, so we saw a lot of each other.

I loved the *challenge* of those races, the idea that you had to start in the back and work your way to the front while at the same time racing against so many top drivers. It really gets your heart going to know that you're starting 18th, and you've got 30 laps to try to get past all those other cars. Every night, it was a race just to see which of the fast guys could get to the front first. I can tell you that if Ronnie hadn't been around, all those nights would have been a lot easier, and I'd like to think that he felt the same way about me.

In a lot of ways, Ronnie and I were kids—or at least young guys—racing against all the older guys, the veterans of the Modified division. I'm sure he was learning just like I was learning, even though we were both winning races at the time.

He and I had raced together a number of times before I moved to New England in 1975, mostly at places like Trenton, Pocono, and Martinsville. But, to be honest, I don't have any really strong memories from those days—the early '70s—that involve Ronnie. See, through the early part of my career, it was almost like I had blinders on. I was building my own cars and maintaining them, as well as driving them, so I was pretty wrapped up in what I had going on; I focused on what I was doing and where I was headed, and not much else. But there's no question that I was aware of Ron Bouchard, and that he was one of the up-and-coming guys out in New England. And I remember him in the purple #17, Bob Johnson's Pinto; Ronnie and that car were synonymous in those days, and that was a combination you had to be concerned about when you went to the bigger races.

Back then I had no idea that I'd end up driving for Dick Armstrong, and moving to Massachusetts, and racing against Ronnie every week, in fact multiple times a week. I was still running the #99 car—first a Valiant, then a Vega—all over New York for a fellow named T.K. McLean. Then T.K. wanted to step away from being a car owner, so some friends and I bought his equipment and tried to run the operation on our own. My cars had some pretty trick stuff for those times, and we won some races, but money was tight. Finally, the money just ran out. Then for a while I raced for a guy out of Troy, Pennsylvania, named Al McClure, but that just didn't work out.

Through all of that, I didn't know what the future might hold for me, and of course I was concerned about that. But at the end of 1974, it all started coming together. I went to run a Modified race at Metrolina Speedway in Charlotte, and Ray Hendrick was there driving a car for Dick Armstrong. Ray and I chatted a bit, and I was telling him about my situation, how I didn't have enough money to run my own car and how things with Al McClure weren't working out.

I told Ray, "Man, I would love to find a good, steady ride."

Ray said, "Hey, why don't you talk with Dick? He wants to run more races up North than I can run, living in Virginia."

As I recall, Ray introduced us right then, and Dick and I discussed things a bit, just getting to know each other. In February of '75, I raced the McClure car again on the road course at Daytona, and maybe once more after that, but I knew I had to do something different. So I called Dick, and he said, "Come on out here." That's what started the whole process of me moving to Bellingham, Massachusetts, and working at Dick's race shop in Franklin with Hop Harrington. The idea was that I would drive in as many races as we could run, and Ray would drive a second car for Dick in some of the bigger races.

In 1975 we used a car that the team had been running for a while, along with a Pinto that Hop and I built together, and we had some success. We won races, and we won the track championship at Stafford, which was a major accomplishment for me. And that same year, our team kind of started the switch from the big-block engines to the small-block engines in the NASCAR Modifieds. That basically came about because when I began to drive for the Armstrong team, one of our first races together was a small-block event at Thompson with a Camaro-bodied car that Dick owned. I ended up getting that car on its roof, which is a whole different story. Anyway, the engine in that Camaro felt *so* good, and I told Dick and Hop that we ought to try running that small block at Stafford, instead of the big block. The weight rules back then were determined by how many cubic inches each car had, and my thinking was that with the smaller engine, we'd be able to run a lighter car, so we'd handle better and we wouldn't burn up our tires. Dick and Hop were both old-school guys, so they basically said, "You're crazy. Modifieds run big blocks, and that's what you've got to have to go fast on a half-mile track." But eventually I wore them down, and we not only tried the small-block engine at Stafford, we *won* with it. That was the beginning of the end of the idea that you needed to have a big-block car to run at the NASCAR tracks, and a small-block car to run on Sundays at Thompson, or in any of the small-block shows like the Yankee All-Star League or the Thompson 300.

Those cars we ran in '75 were good, but I was interested in building something different, the same way I'd always done my own thing before. So that winter we built two new cars based on some ideas I had, and those were the Pintos we ran in 1976 and '77. Those two cars were exactly alike, chassis-wise, although one had a longer roll cage to accommodate Ray Hendrick, who was much bigger than me. Anyway, that design worked extremely well, and 1976 was when things really took off. Then we improved things by putting in the three-link rear suspension, which was pretty revolutionary for that period, and we got even faster.

There were a lot of great drivers in New England at that time—Ronnie, Bugsy, Freddy DeSarro, Leo Cleary, Eddie Flemke, George Summers, and several more—but for a couple of years we just out-engineered everybody else. I had learned very early in my career that if my car was better than everybody else's, it was going to be a lot easier to win races, so I worked hard on that. Yeah, I was a good driver, but we had a better car than the rest of those guys did; I'm sure that if those drivers I mentioned had been in cars that were equal to mine, the story probably would have been a lot different. So I had an advantage for a while, and as time went on our success forced some of the other teams to build better cars. Pretty soon, Ronnie and Bugsy and the rest of those guys had great cars, too, which led to some really terrific racing.

You know, I mentioned that small-block scene a moment ago. One of the neat things I remember about those years was going to tracks I'd never been to—Monadnock, Westboro, Waterford, Star Speedway, all kinds of places—and racing against drivers I'd never run against, and in many cases drivers I'd never heard of. That's fun, and when you're winning it's even better.

In those days, there weren't many Modified guys who ran *everywhere*; some guys you saw only at Stafford, or only at Seekonk, or only at Thompson. Ronnie was one of the guys who, no matter where we went, was probably going to be there. In that period, I'd say we had a good relationship, at least from my side. Did we hang out together? No. But it appeared to me that he respected me as a driver, and I certainly had a lot of respect for him. That doesn't mean we gave each other any extra room on the track; the two of us raced *hard*. And, you know, racing hard is its own form of respect.

Naturally, when you race competitively against somebody for any length of time, you're going to have your tough nights. Ronnie and I had some scrapes on the track, just like I had with Bugsy and a few other drivers. It was never anything intentional on my part, and I never felt there was anything intentional on Ronnie's part, either. But every once in a while we'd bump wheels, and someone would get mad. It was never anything where we'd want to get out and fight, just enough to maybe make one of us shake a fist at the other one, and cause a little bit of controversy. And, hey, that's all part of racing. I don't care what sport you're in, sometimes you're going to foul a guy, or you're going to grab a facemask, or you're going to rub wheels. That's just the way it goes.

But Ronnie and I were always cordial. If we saw each other in the pits, we'd say hello, and if we had time we'd chat.

Now, one issue I dealt with when I was in New England was something I created myself, although not by design. I didn't hang out with the other drivers, didn't go to the bars, didn't go to the clubhouse at Thompson, so it got to where I was thought of as being unsociable, or stuck up, or not friendly, or not a nice guy. But racing was how I made my living; I had a young family to feed, and bills to pay, and my racing was the only thing that made all of that possible. So after a race

I'd load up, go home, work on the car a little bit, then get some sleep and work on it again in the morning so I'd be ready to go to the next track that night. My whole thinking was that I wanted both myself and the cars to be at 100 percent, always, so I could do the job that paid my bills. Most of those New England drivers, Ronnie included, had other jobs, other means of income, so even though they were serious about their racing, they could also have fun with it. It wasn't something they *depended* on, the way I did.

So I didn't hang around and party with the other racers, and I didn't spend as much time with the media as I could have, and the result was that I had a bad rap with both those groups while I was there. But I was on a mission. My long-term mission was that I wanted to get to the Winston Cup series, and my short-term goal was to support my family, and the way to accomplish both of those things was to run good, win races, and avoid breaking down. So, yeah, I was serious about what I was doing. When I was at the track, that was a continuation of my work time, so I was constantly checking tires or adjusting the chassis or whatever needed to be done. It was not a time for telling stories and hanging out.

But, again, Ronnie and I would still talk a bit when our paths crossed, or maybe at the drivers' meeting, or in situations like that. We certainly were not *unfriendly*.

Our two car owners, Dick Armstrong in my case and Marvin Rifchin in Ronnie's case, also had an interesting relationship. When I first started driving for Dick we ran Firestone tires, and then we changed to Goodyears, but in either case that automatically would have created a bit of a rivalry because, of course, Marvin owned M&H Racemaster. But it was a friendly rivalry; on almost any night at the track, you'd see Dick and Marvin talking at some point. I think they looked at it as business, as competition, instead of making it into anything personal. And there were even a couple of times when we tried Marvin's M&H tires.

Looking back, I'm not sure how the other drivers felt about me in those days; I suppose you'd have to ask them. But I knew how a lot of their fans felt, because I could *hear* it. They booed me, and in the beginning that was tough to get used to. Then I started saying in my victory lane interviews that all this "boo-power" was helping me, not hurting me. I said, "The more you boo, the faster I'll go." Well, as you would expect, that made them boo louder.

Now, hearing people boo won't actually make your race car faster, or make you a better driver, but it *did* make me work harder. And I think that whole situation also helped people get more involved in what they were watching. Instead of just watching their favorite driver—Ronnie, or whoever—they were watching me, too.

My relationship with the fans in New England was not always smooth, but it was *real*. They were booing because I came in there and beat their heroes, and

I came to realize that this was part of the deal: When you're successful, some people are going to boo you, and that's all right. No, I didn't like having beer cans thrown at me, which happened at Riverside Park, or having beer poured on my family in victory lane, which happened at Seekonk. But in my mind, I had a clear understanding: Those people didn't like Geoff Bodine, the race driver, but they didn't know Geoff Bodine, the *person*. So I honestly didn't take it personally.

That was a great era of Modified racing, and I'm so glad that I can say I was a part of it. I was lucky to drive for Dick and Carol Armstrong, who were willing to spend the money it took to win, and I was also very fortunate to have so many good people on that team: Hop and Randy Hathaway, who was Dick's son-in-law, were right there from the beginning, and in 1978 I brought in Billy Taylor, who was a great worker and motivator. So it wasn't all *me*. I designed the cars, and we built them right there at Dick's, but without good people around me, it wouldn't have been possible. I just had the pleasure of being the guy who sat behind the steering wheel when it was time to go racing.

That 1978 season was when we had 55 victories out of 84 starts—almost all of them with the same car—and I can tell you that the boos that year got really loud. I don't think my success that year won anyone over, put it that way. Once people have an opinion of you, it's hard to change their minds. But as time went by, I think they realized that a lot of hard work went into that season. I know that later, after I'd moved on, I'd run into people from New England who'd say, "Man, I used to watch you every weekend! I remember 1978, when you won all those races!"

I'd kid them and say, "Yeah, I recognize you. You were one of the fans who used to boo me."

They'd say, "No, no, no ..."

I'd smile and say, "Come on, tell the truth!"

They'd say, "Well, okay, maybe I booed a *little*."

Then we'd laugh about it. I enjoyed those conversations, because at least we were getting to know each other a bit.

As it turned out, 1978 ended up being my last season with Dick Armstrong. My plan for '79 was to run for Dick again—I had even flown to Charlotte to pick up a new transporter he'd bought—but I ended up getting together with Jack Beebe to drive his Winston Cup car instead. That all came about because of Satch Worley; Satch had run a few Cup races for Jack in 1978, and Jack wanted to do more, but Satch was involved in his family's construction business and he was too busy for that. Satch and I were good friends, and he suggested that I call Jack, so I did. And that changed everything.

That arrangement ended up not working out, and I only drove Jack Beebe's car in three races. But this story also involves Ronnie Bouchard, and in more ways than one. Harry Gant drove the Race Hill Farm car for the next couple of seasons, and then Ronnie got into it. Everybody knows that.

But when I first got that ride, I said, "If I'm going to run the full Winston Cup schedule, I need to move my family down South." So we found a place near Greensboro; that was step one. Step two was that now we had to actually *move* everything.

I was too busy preparing the cars to keep running back and forth, driving my stuff to North Carolina, and I remembered that the Bouchard family was in the moving business. So, out of the blue, I called Ronnie one day and told him I had a job for him. We talked a little bit about what was involved, and he said, "Heck, yeah," and we started making plans.

When it came time to haul everything down there, Ronnie actually drove the rig himself. The funny thing was, the job ended up being a lot tougher than he expected. The driveway to our new house was pretty steep, and it just so happened that North Carolina had snow and rain that week, so now that steep driveway was muddy, too. Ronnie couldn't get the truck and trailer backed all the way up to the house, and because of the mud he had to lay down all kinds of cardboard and moving blankets so he and his helpers could carry everything the rest of the way.

I was working at Beebe's shop in Connecticut, but at some point I called down there to see how things were progressing. My family said, "You wouldn't *believe* what's going on …"

It sounded like a mess, and I'm sure it was.

They put Ronnie on the phone. I started telling him how sorry I was, but he cut me right off: "You son of a …"

We laughed a bit, and he said, "You're lucky you're not here helping."

But you know something? Looking back on it now, that whole moving episode showed that no matter what might have happened between the two of us on the track, it never transferred *off* the track. Most of the fans at Stafford or Seekonk or Thompson probably wouldn't have believed that. But the fact that I was comfortable calling Ronnie about that moving job and the fact that he agreed right away to take it was proof that we had never let it spill over. Again, whatever happened on the track was nothing personal. It was racing, and we were just two hard competitors.

Each of us respected the other, and from my perspective that never changed. It carried right through the years we both spent racing in Winston Cup cars.

So when I think about Ronnie, there are a lot of fond memories. Gee whiz, I loved racing against him, and against all the New England Modified guys we've been talking about. They were *good* racers, great racers. They were *clean* racers. I enjoyed racing against people like that, and I appreciated what they were teaching me.

Like I said earlier, they were teaching me to race. And I can tell you that without guys like Ronnie Bouchard, my learning curve would have been a lot slower.

BY CLYDE MCLEOD

"We're doing 70, with our bumper right up against Bobby's ramp truck"

Road trips, security slips, and friendships

There was a time in the '70s where if you saw Ron Bouchard, you likely saw Clyde McLeod, too. "It was like I was his damn sidekick for a while there," Clyde chuckles. A product of the same small patch of central Connecticut that produced Steady Eddie Flemke, Bob Judkins, and a handful of other Modified luminaries, McLeod jumped into their chaotic world as soon as he was old enough to get around on his own. He turned wrenches for Flemke, and later helped lead Billy Corazzo's Sherri-Cup team to victories with drivers like Ken Bouchard and Brett Bodine, and a NASCAR Modified Tour championship with Mike McLaughlin. Having relocated to North Carolina some 20 years ago, Clyde served as a Busch Series crew chief for McLaughlin, Todd Bodine and others, and has since held several positions with a number of NASCAR teams, most recently Stewart-Haas Racing.

VAL LESIEUR COLLECTION

It would hard to describe to someone who wasn't there just how much fun Modified racing was in the mid-to-late-'70s. Today I'm around a lot of young guys who work on Sprint Cup teams, and when you mention that you used to go racing three or four nights a week with the same car—and partied your ass off in between—they look at you like they think you're lying. They cannot even picture something like that. But it's all true.

Those were the vintage years, in my mind. The racing was absolutely the best I've ever seen. Stop and think about the drivers you had. You'd go to a regular weekly show at Thompson or Stafford and see Ronnie and Kenny Bouchard, Geoff Bodine, Bugsy Stevens, Eddie Flemke, Fred DeSarro, John Rosati,

Ray Miller, Leo Cleary. If it was a big show—a Spring Sizzler, or the Thompson 300—you'd have all those guys, *plus* Richie Evans, Maynard Troyer, Jerry Cook, George Kent, Charlie Jarzombek, Freddy Harbach. If it was a Yankee All-Star League race on a Wednesday night, you'd throw in the top guys from all the small-block tracks.

In that period, Ronnie was as good as anybody. You hate to say one guy was the best, but there certainly wasn't anybody *better*. I saw him do great things in Bob Johnson's cars, Bobby Judkins's cars, Marvin Rifchin's cars, Lenny Boehler's cars, plus a handful of cars he only drove once or twice. If the car was good enough, he would do the job, no question about it.

He was a great driver, a *hard* driver, but he was clean; I never saw him do anything dirty. He was really good at getting into the other guy's head—I think he learned some of that from Eddie Flemke—and he would use that to his advantage. You could see it when you watched him come from the back of the pack.

Ronnie and I met in the craziest way. I grew up in Southington, Connecticut, and Plainville Stadium was just a few miles away, so that's where I first went to the races. My dad used to take me and Stan Greger, who lived in the same neighborhood, and of course Stanley went on to be one of the top drivers there. Anyway, after a while I started helping Billy Zenobi, who owned a coupe that Ron Wyckoff drove at Plainville, and also a little bit at Riverside Park. At some point in the early '70s, we decided we wanted to go racing at Seekonk. It was two hours from home, but the purses were really good. We tried to buy a car Georgie Summers had been driving, but somehow that deal fell apart, so we bought one from another team and started hauling over there every week. On about our third or fourth week there, Wyckoff was going pretty good in the feature, running in the top five. But Summers and Bouchard, man, they're *coming*, with George just ahead of Ronnie. They had started in the back, but they blasted to the front, and now they're running down the leaders.

So they catch Wyckoff, and George passes him on the high side. Bouchard, trying to be sneaky, goes the other way, and dive-bombs under Wyckoff. I'm still not sure if Bouchard hit Wyckoff—he always swore he didn't—or if Wyckoff didn't see him until the last second, and juked the car right. Either way, Wyckoff lost it, and into the wall he went. Our night is done. Ronnie kept on chasing George, but he never caught him, and George won.

So after the race, back in the pits, I walked over to Ronnie's pit. I said, "Hey, Bouchard, did you win?"

He said, "No, I got second."

I put my finger right in his face and said, "Good! I'm *glad* you didn't win! What'd you wreck us for, you sonofabitch?"

That was all it took. From behind Ronnie, out of nowhere, here came Bob Bouchard, ol' Pepe, with his fist cocked. Well, you know how that goes: Right away there's a pile of people pushing and shoving, but nobody really gets hit because everybody's holding onto somebody else. When they finally got everybody separated, Bob still had his fists clenched, but the Bouchard crew hung onto him by the arms and shoulders until he settled down.

We didn't go to Seekonk for the next couple of weeks, while we fixed the car. But once we did go back there, it was like nothing had ever happened between us and Bouchard. Ronnie and I would kind of nod at each other, and as time went by we'd talk a little bit. As a matter of fact, he even helped us out a few times. He was obviously on top at that place, so we'd say, "Hey, we're not getting around this place. Is there something we should try?" And he always had some little tidbit for us, or for Wyckoff.

I've thought about that a lot over the years. I was the one who had started all that commotion that night. I was the troublemaker. But he never held a grudge over that; he just didn't let it bother him. And when you think about it, that's how he was as a race driver, too. He didn't let anything rattle him, ever.

We only raced Seekonk that one season, so I lost touch with Ronnie for a while, but I knew he was still doing well at Seekonk. By the time he started coming to Stafford with Bob Johnson, I'd already been going there regularly, helping Eddie or helping Billy Corazzo's team, and that's when he and I reconnected. We started talking more and more, and we became friends, and then *good* friends. And our friendship lasted ... well, forever. I think one of the reasons we hit it off so well was that we were pretty close in age. Ronnie was a little older than me, but it seemed like everybody else—all the drivers, all the owners, even the guys on the crews—were a lot older than both of us.

So time went on, and we got into the timeframe where Ronnie met Paula, and they started dating. But no one knew about this yet, especially Eddie, so a few of us were sworn to secrecy. That was a hard thing, because here's Eddie, my hero, and every time I was with him, all I could think about was not slipping up and saying something. Obviously, Eddie found out eventually, and for a while he wanted to *kill* Ronnie. But, you know, Ronnie earned his respect. He had already earned Eddie's respect on the track, but off the track Eddie came to see that Ronnie was a good guy, and that this was a serious relationship, and he accepted it. And, you know, that turned into a really nice story, because even though Eddie and Ronnie were still rivals, they became *friendly* rivals, and when Eddie stopped racing he was as big a fan of Ronnie as anybody was.

When Ronnie started driving for Bobby Judkins, he and I got even closer. See, if you were from that part of Connecticut, Judkins was one of those guys you looked up to; everybody stopped by his garage, and hung around his car at the track. Whenever Ronnie was down this way—whether he was passing through on a trip, or visiting Paula—he'd naturally stop and see Judkins, and he kind of became like an adopted Connecticut guy. He knew all of Bobby's guys, he knew the Corazzo crew, and the Garuti family, which had been involved in racing forever. He probably had as many friends in that area—Southington, Meriden, Berlin—as he had back home.

That reminds me of something. The Corazzo family owned Sherri-Cup, which made paper cups, and I worked there. There was a company in Leominster, Massachusetts, that made lids for our coffee cups. We'd get two or three truckloads a week. Leominster is right next to Fitchburg, so it was a natural thing to ask Ronnie, since his family had a trucking company, if they'd be interested in that business. He talked to Pepe, and they came up with a good price, so we made a deal for them to start delivering those lids. Sometimes Pepe even made the deliveries himself—luckily, he never remembered me from Seekonk—but usually Ronnie did, which got him to Connecticut even more. He'd show up late in the day, then we'd grab dinner and a drink, and he'd stay over at my house and go back to Fitchburg early in the morning.

Well, this one particular week, there was an open-comp 100-lapper at Plainville. Billy Corazzo wanted to know if Ronnie would be interested in driving his car, the Sherri-Cup coupe, which Billy was actually trying to sell. I called Ronnie and said, "Hey, I know you're delivering a load of lids this weekend. If you bring your helmet bag, you can run the coupe at Plainville."

Ronnie didn't even hesitate. He said, "All right, I'll do that."

Today, most drivers would want to bring their own seat, and they'd have you moving the pedals, the steering, you name it. Ronnie rode with us to Plainville, climbed into the car, adjusted the belts, and he was ready to go. Plainville was a flat little bullring, and the regulars there—Reggie Ruggiero, Stan Greger, Ronnie Rocco, Dave Alkas, Jap Membrino—were tough to beat. Bouchard had never even seen the place, and he won the show.

My God, did we have fun back then. Anytime he was in the area, we'd get together—Ronnie and Paula, me and my wife, Ann Marie—and just go out and relax.

For a long time, the four of us were inseparable. We'd drive to Daytona together, and a trip like that can really be fun if you're with good friends. It always seemed like we'd be in a car that had some kind of a problem. Sometimes it was whatever car Ronnie came up with, and one year it was Paula's Chrysler—a Plymouth or a

Dodge, whatever it was—which had a broken heater control. Every time we got too cold or too hot, we had to pull over, open the hood, and turn a valve. We did that all the way to Florida.

That year, Ronnie was driving for Judkins at New Smyrna. One night after the races the girls took off, and Ronnie and I went out with the guys and hit all the usual spots. I don't remember who we were riding with, but we left the Shark Lounge—where all the Modified people hung out—and headed down Route A1A, the main drag along the beach. We're passing a McDonald's, and we see a car backed right up onto a big rock alongside the parking lot. The rear end is off the ground, but the tires are touching just enough that they're smoking, because the driver is trying to power it off the rock. We take a closer look, and it's Paula's car! The girls had gotten that thing stuck, and obviously this was way before cell phones, so they couldn't just call us. We swung in there, got the car off that rock, and we all went on our merry way.

Another year, just when it was time to leave for Daytona, we got *clobbered* by a blizzard. Ronnie had stopped at my house on the way, and now it was looking like we were going to be stuck there. The governor of Connecticut had shut down all the roads. Well, it got to the point where if we didn't get going, we were going to miss the first night or two at New Smyrna, because the snow wasn't letting up. So Ronnie and I just left. We knew there was a good chance we'd get pulled over and arrested, so the girls stayed home, because there wasn't any sense in us all going to jail.

We had this big old Bonneville with a plastic steering wheel, but the plastic was falling apart, so you were pretty much steering with the steel ring inside. Just another clunker Ronnie had found. We made our way out to the highway, through snow so deep we couldn't believe it. The ramps to the Interstates were buried, too, but the highways themselves were decent; the snow was still deep, but the plows had been through earlier, so we could basically see where we were supposed to be going. But there was *nobody* on I-91 or I-95, except us. Finally we reached the New York line, and in New York the roads were open, because the snow had skimmed past and slammed into Connecticut.

So we put the hammer down, and from there it was pretty much the standard drive to Florida. But just as we're coming to Palm Coast, Florida, between Jacksonville and Daytona, we see a vehicle pulled over with the flashers on. It's dark, but as we get closer, we can see that it's a ramp truck. It's Judkins. We pull over to see what's wrong. It was something in the drivetrain, like a clutch or a transmission; the engine still ran, so he had headlights and he had steering, but the damn thing wouldn't move.

Now, Bobby's ramp truck was a big cabover Ford. With the race car and everything on it—all the tools, probably a spare motor—there's no telling how much that thing weighed. But Ronnie says, "Get back into the truck. I'll push you."

And he did. It took a while to get that thing rolling and up to speed, but once we did, Ronnie wasn't about to just push it along at 30 miles per hour. We're doing 70, at least, with the bumper of that Bonneville tucked right up against Bobby's truck. We can't see a thing except the back of the race car. He had told Judkins not to pull off until he saw a place where it looked like he could work on the truck, so down the highway we went, past one exit, two exits, three exits. Finally we saw his blinker come on, and Ronnie eased up and followed Bobby off the exit and into a parking lot. Bobby said he'd be okay, so Ronnie and I kept on going.

That blizzard might have been in 1978, the year Ronnie won the World Series championship at New Smyrna. If I'm right, that was a pretty eventful trip: We start out driving illegally, on closed roads, then we push a ramp truck down I-95 with a passenger car, and nine or ten days later he's the New Smyrna champion.

We always had a riot at Daytona. One year after the Modified race there, a bunch of us are leaving the track in another one of Ronnie's cars, an orange Pontiac Grand Prix. He's driving, and Wally Jackson—a good friend of ours who was a Stafford official—is riding shotgun. There's three of us in the back seat. We're going to leave the infield and go out Gate 7, and to do that you had to drive across the track itself, between turn four and the tri-oval. Well, Ronnie takes a left. He says, "Come on, let's take a lap."

Off we go. Ronnie's giving it the gas, but this damn Pontiac is struggling to go 90 miles per hour, and when we get up on the banking it's bottoming out, throwing sparks. We're laughing our asses off, until we come off turn two, and all we see up ahead are blue lights. Somebody up in the tower spotted this street car out on the track, and called for security. Now every security car in the place has the track blocked, and they're flagging us down.

We stop, and the head honcho says, "Who do you think you are? You can't be on this track! You guys are about to go to jail!"

Ronnie, cool as can be, says, "Gee, I'm sorry. I was in the race today, and my air cleaner fell off. We were hoping we could find it."

The guy says, "You ain't gonna find no damn air cleaner up there on the banking! What's your name?"

Ronnie tells him, and as the guy walks off, we hear him on the radio: "The driver says his name is Ron Bouchard, and that he ran in the Modified race today."

Well, it turns out Big Bill France is in the tower. We hear some mumbling, then the guy comes back and says, "Mr. Bouchard, you can go. But Mr. France said to tell you that this is his track, and he doesn't ever want to see you on it again in a passenger car. Have a nice day."

We managed to keep straight faces until we were well past where all the guards were, and then we all cracked up.

There was always at least one point during Speedweeks when everybody who raced at New Smyrna would end up at JB's Fish Camp, a seafood joint over by the beach. One night we were all there, and Dick Trickle was jumping around in the rafters, with Richie Evans firing beer cans at him.

Speaking of Richie, that reminds me of the time Ronnie drove Richie's backup car at Martinsville. Those two were good friends, and I think there was a mutual respect between them as drivers, because they raced a lot alike. At the end of 1979, Judkins and Marvin Rifchin were ending their partnership. Martinsville was coming up, and Ronnie didn't have a ride. So Richie called and said, "Hey, if you want to, you can run my other car."

Ronnie said, "Let's do it."

I helped Billy Nacewicz, who'd been Richie's crew chief forever, because he and his guys had their hands full running two cars. Richie and Ronnie ended up second and third, behind Jerry Cook. Ronnie was second for a while, and he tried everything in the world to get past Cookie, but Jerry knew how to make his car wide when he had to. At one point, Ronnie's right-front tire even rode up onto Jerry's trunk when things got a little tight. Toward the end, Ronnie's tires were shot, and he knew he wasn't going to get past Jerry. But Richie pitted later than both those guys, so he was on better tires, and he was coming. When he caught Ronnie right at the end, Ronnie just moved up a lane and waved him by. He saw the situation; he appreciated that Richie had given him the opportunity to run that race, and his own chance to win was gone, so he was saying, "Go get him, boss." And Richie couldn't get by Jerry, either, but he had a good day, with his cars second and third.

Ronnie had those kinds of friendships with just about everybody, because he was so good at treating people well. Look at his relationship with Marvin. Those guys were so close; you know, everybody used to joke around and say that Ronnie was Marvin's stepson, but those two really looked after each other. Yes, Marvin really took care of Ronnie, but Ronnie would do anything for Marvin, too.

And how about Ronnie and Lenny Boehler? Lenny, as everybody knows, could be a hard character to figure out, but Ronnie *understood* Lenny. They really clicked as driver and mechanic, and the two of them together were a tremendous force. In a short time, they won a lot of races: Stafford, Seekonk, Westboro, Thompson, Monadnock. They both loved a good party, too. We'd be in the parking lot after the races, and the party would roll until Boehler said, "The sun's coming up, it's time to leave!"

You know, I have so many good memories from those days. Like his kids; until Ronnie went Cup racing, his four oldest kids were almost always at the track. Most of the time we didn't see them until after the feature, because they were in the grandstands with Ronnie's mom and or his sister, JoAnn. But at the end of the night they'd come into the pits to see their dad. I can still picture them running around when they were little, having a good old time. We watched them grow up without even realizing it.

You know, when Ronnie got the call from Jack Beebe, asking him if he wanted to go Winston Cup racing, he asked me what I thought. I remember saying, "Take the shot. Not everybody gets this chance." I was really, really happy for him. *Proud.* I think we all felt that way, because our buddy was going big-time, and we knew he deserved it.

But it was also hard. It was like watching your best friend move away, and realizing that he wasn't going to be around as much anymore. I mean that. He was the best friend I had, for a long, long time.

BY ROB BOUCHARD

"I didn't know how lucky I was to be in that era, around all that great racing"

A well-traveled son looks back on some memorable nights

BOUCHARD FAMILY COLLECTION

Rob Bouchard is the second oldest of the Bouchard kids, and among longtime race-goers he was probably also the most visible. If he wasn't at the track cheering on his dad, he was there cheering on Uncle Kenny, or, as he came of age, driving himself in various divisions at New England speedways. Away from the track, Rob passed a portion of his teenaged years working in the machine shop his dad operated in partnership with Dave Rossbach. "When Dale Earnhardt stayed at my father's house," Rob says with a chuckle, "he came to the shop and couldn't believe I was grinding cylinder heads at that age. He wanted to take me home." Having held a variety of positions with his father's businesses, Rob today serves as operations manager for Ron Bouchard's Auto Stores, and has a hand in everything from overseeing outside purchasing to communicating with manufacturers.

When I was a kid, my father was just my father. Even though you look up to your father, you don't see him the same way other people do. The older I got, the more I began to realize that a lot of people followed his racing, and that he always made an effort to accommodate those people. He'd talk with them, sign autographs, or whatever it took. And it wasn't just when the night was over; he'd sign autographs between the heats and the feature if there were kids at the pit fence. That was just his personality, and I'm sure that's why he became so popular.

What really put that into perspective for me was meeting some of the drivers *I* looked up to. For a long time, I was a huge fan of Maynard Troyer. Maynard had beautiful cars, but I think I liked him mostly because he was an invader, a guy I didn't see every week. I didn't take him for granted, the way I took for granted my father and Bugsy and the drivers I saw every week. I remember Maynard winning three Spring Sizzlers in a row, and just being in awe of him. Well, my uncle Kenny introduced me to Maynard, and it turned out he was a down-to-earth guy, a regular Joe. Then Kenny introduced me to Charlie Jarzombek, another outsider I'd been in awe of, and he was a regular guy, too.

Talking with Maynard and Charlie was no different from talking with Kenny or my father. That helped me understand how some people looked at my father the same way I looked at those guys. To me, he was Dad, someone I was around every day, but to those people he was a hero.

By the time I was old enough to really know what was going on in racing, he was already winning on a regular basis. I remember him driving Bob Johnson's car at Westboro when it was a Friday track—Stafford still ran Saturdays—and winning so many races that they put a bounty on him.

My father was already running a pretty busy schedule, and I loved it. You know, back then there wasn't as much to do for entertainment, especially for a kid—no Facebook, no Internet, just a few channels on television—so going to the races was such an exciting thing. It was everything to me.

After my parents split up, I spent most of the time at my grandmother's house, because that's where my dad stayed until he bought a home and moved. Half of the time us kids rode to the races with my dad, and the other half with Nana and JoAnn, my aunt. I didn't care *how* we got there, as long as we got there.

For a long time, I couldn't wait for Friday to come. But there was one season, 1980, when Monadnock went to Thursdays, and that year things *really* got good, because my father would pick me up early from school on Thursday afternoon. And the best part of that year was that he and Kenny won a lot of the Monadnock features. Kenny had his own car, a red #35 Pinto, and that thing was a rocket. I just couldn't believe we got to go to the races four nights a week: Monadnock, Stafford, Westboro, and Thompson.

I had a group of friends I knew just from the races. My brother Gene and I hung around with Brian Brady, Joe Brady's son, and with Brian Ross's son Chris, and several other kids whose parents were involved. If one of their parents won, whether as a car owner or a driver or whatever, we were all happy. Of course, my father won as much as anybody, and that was fine with me.

At Stafford we got friendly with a group of eight or ten kids who lived close by. They were mostly Gene's age, just a bit older than me, and they were big fans of my father. Richie Schlaefer's dad ran the beer garden at Stafford, so naturally he was there every week, and Richie was part of that group. We're friends to this day.

What's funny is that I also had a crew of old-timers who were my pals. As soon as I got to the track and saw them, they'd quiz me on everything I knew about what all the teams were doing. I found out later that those guys would bet on all the races—heats, features, everything—but they never went into the pits, so they were using me for inside information! One guy in particular used to show up at all the tracks, and he always had a crowd of people around him because he was running a betting pool for his friends. He would seek out us kids to find out stuff not just about my father, but about Geoff Bodine, Bugsy, Richie Evans, everybody. They figured we had the scoop, although I'm not sure if anything we told them ever worked in their favor.

My sisters liked going to the track as much as Gene and I did, but probably more for the social part of it. They hung around with Anne Brady, Dick Armstrong's daughter Kim, Bugsy's daughter Debbie, and Jean Michaud's girls, Kathie and Julie, and a few others. By then my dad was driving for Bobby Judkins, who had a lot of daughters, and later, when he drove for Lenny Boehler, it seemed like the guys who hung around that car had a hundred kids. So there were always plenty of friends around, which was fun, but I was the real "racing guy" in the family. I always paid attention to what was on the track; I didn't want to wander off and miss the consi, or something like that.

I liked going to the races no matter where they were, but Stafford was the best time just because of all those friends we had there. Stafford had switched to Friday nights, and even for the weekly shows the crowds were really good, which made everything more intense. We always sat down low, just behind the flagstand, and you could hear the crowd behind you getting into it. I would get the same feeling at those races that I'd get today going to see the Boston Bruins in an NHL playoff game: that uneasiness, that feeling that you don't know what's going to happen.

I enjoyed Seekonk, too. You had guys like George Summers, Leo Cleary, Eddie St. Angelo, and Johnny Tripp, plus my father, Bugsy, Fred DeSarro, sometimes Bodine, sometimes Kenny. The atmosphere was fantastic; you could smell the hamburgers and onions cooking, and Seekonk had those cement grandstands just about all the way around the place. The fans there really liked my father, and the Venditti family, from Anthony down, were the nicest people in the world. If we got there early, my dad would stop at their house and we'd visit with Irene, Anthony's wife.

It seemed like Seekonk was a party place. In the grandstands, everybody was having a great time, and after the races a lot of the teams hung out for hours. Then again, maybe that was just a Saturday-night thing, because Westboro was the same way. Westboro was the closest track to Fitchburg, but that didn't mean we ever got home early, especially when my father drove for Lenny. That Boehler crew would hang around all night long.

Thompson was also a place I liked, because it was so fast. My father won a lot of races there, especially when he ran the #7 Vega for Judkins and Marvin Rifchin. The only thing bad about Thompson, as a kid, was that it was the last race of the weekend.

But I'd have to say that my favorite track, just for racing, was Monadnock. It's a tight bullring with very different turns and banking on each end, and that layout just seemed to promote good competition. Both my father and Kenny won a lot of races there, so that probably made me like it more. But I also paid attention to the guys who came from up that way, like Dunk Rudolph and Jack Bateman. And I liked watching Marty Radewick when he drove Freddy Felton's Modified, because that car was so different.

I wish I had been a little bit older through those years, because I didn't know how lucky I was to be living in that era, and to be around all of that great racing. You can't really appreciate that when you're seven or eight old. But by 1978 and '79, I was beginning to understand the sport more, and on the ride home I would ask my father all kinds of questions. I had started to realize that race cars handled differently on different nights, so I would ask about that, and sometimes he would explain that he ran certain lines so he could get through the corner better. That was really interesting to me, and I learned a lot by listening to him.

Plus, as I got older I started to feel more like one of the gang when we hung around after the races. Bobby Judkins was the nicest guy when it came to making you feel welcome, and Chuck Grime and Steve Kalkowski, who were always with him, were the same way. I even rode in their ramp truck sometimes if we were traveling someplace far off. I remember riding to Oswego with Bobby and Steve, and that was really cool.

My father won a lot of features driving for Judkins and Marvin, but two of the races I remember best were times they ended up finishing second. One was the Spring Sizzler in 1979, when Troyer won that race for the third year in a row. My father was driving the black #7 Pinto, which the year before had been the red #2X, but they repainted it. It was getting toward the end of the race and Maynard was leading, but my father had come from a long way back and was all over him. Maynard had a big block, and the #7 had a small block, so my father would lose all kinds of ground on the straightaways and than catch Maynard again in the turns. It was a great battle. I was pulling for my father, but, I will admit, it did kill me to have to root against Maynard.

Later that year, Marvin bought a Troyer car for Judkins and my father to run, and of course I loved that thing. The first race for that car was the Ferrara 100 at Stafford, and my father was having a great battle with Geoff Bodine—who was driving for Lee Allard—until the #7 lost the brakes and ended up second. But I remember it being a fantastic race up until then.

After Marvin and Judkins split up, my father started driving for Boehler and also running the bigger races for Dick Armstrong. He won the Thompson 300 in 1980 with Armstrong's car, and to me that was his biggest Modified victory. I know he won a lot of big races when he was with Bob Johnson—Martinsville, Pocono, Oswego—but I was too young to remember those. So to me, that 300 was his signature Modified victory, because it was just the next spring that he left to go Cup racing.

Paul Bonneau, a photographer who was good friends with our family, took a great picture of the victory lane ceremony after that Thompson 300. He shot it from the flagstand, and even though my father is surrounded by people, he's looking right up at Paul. It seems like everybody in the world is in that shot, except *me*. You can see Paula, my sisters, Dick and Carol Armstrong and their family, Hop Harrington, and this giant crowd, but not me. That photo pops up on Facebook sometimes, and people always ask me how come I'm not in it. I'm not sure, really, but I always say that I knew everybody would be going to the clubhouse to celebrate, so I was getting a head start.

There's another race that stands out from 1980, and it was at Westboro. That season everybody ran there on Saturday nights because Seekonk wasn't running Modifieds. My father was leading the feature in the Boehler #3, and Greg Sacks was running second in Lee Allard's car. It was one of those situations where the second-place car was quicker, but Westboro was such a tough place to pass, so Sacks was all over my father. Finally, coming out of turn four, Greg ran into his back bumper, and my father spun. The caution came out, and when my father got back on the track he ran half a lap in the opposite direction. You knew he was mad, and the fans were going crazy, wondering what was going to happen.

You know how sometimes the officials would give a guy his spot back if they thought he'd blatantly been spun out? Well, my father kind of forced them into it. He pulled into line in front of Sacks, and stayed there. They ran a few caution laps like that, and finally whoever was in charge must have decided to leave him there. They restarted the race with my father leading and Greg second, and that's how they finished. The funny part was that Sacks was still faster, but he never really tried another move. I don't know if he felt bad, or if he just thought it was smart to give my father a little bit of breathing room.

Even though my father and Lenny were only together a short time, they did a *lot* of racing. One Sunday there was an afternoon show at Thompson and a night race at Monadnock. They won at Thompson, and then we all took off for Monadnock. Kenny was there with his own car, but he also practiced the other Boehler car for my father. In the feature, my father was leading until Kenny passed him. Then Kenny got a flat tire, pitted on a caution, restarted at the rear, then got *another* flat tire. Kenny's crew didn't have any tires left, so Boehler gave them one. Kenny drove back to the front, and passed my father for the win. It was a great race.

I honestly thought my father would end up driving Modifieds forever. He'd had a chance to go Winston Cup racing earlier and turned it down, and I figured that was the end of that. When he took that Cup ride with Jack Beebe in 1981, it definitely changed things. I was so used to watching him run three or four nights a week, and it was different not having him around.

But I never stopped going to the local tracks. Not all of the Cup races were on live TV yet, and even when there was one I'd usually skip it and go watch the Modifieds instead, at Thompson or Monadnock. Fortunately for me, Kenny was going really good in that period, so I just started pulling for him more. Obviously, I had always cheered for Kenny, anyway, although in the past I'd kept an eye on both him *and* my father.

So the feeling was still the same, really. I was just pulling for one Bouchard instead of two!

BY RICH BONNEAU

"I'm 16, announcing at one of my favorite tracks, interviewing my hero"

Pit areas, parking lots, and picnics, with eyes wide open

PAUL BONNEAU

Rich Bonneau is best known to New England fans as an announcer at Thompson Speedway, where for years his warm voice welcomed them to another Sunday. But long before he took to a microphone, he was attending races as the son of noted photographer Paul Bonneau, whose stealthy approach —linger, linger, linger, shoot!—produced terrific candid images. If you ever wanted proof that Ron Bouchard's people skills cut across all personality types, you needed just one visit to the postrace gatherings that were a hallmark of his Modified years. Look one way, and you'd see the Judkins or Boehler crews and their friends engaged in rowdy shenanigans; look the other way, and you'd see Paul Bonneau and his smiling wife, Alice, quietly taking it all in. Close by, always, was their observant son Rich, who through the years knew Bouchard as a hero, interview subject, and friend.

My parents' relationship with Ronnie goes back longer than I can remember. My father had always been a race fan—he'd gone to Seekonk Speedway in the '50s—and after I was born in 1964, he started going again. I even have vague memories of the Bouchard crew wearing those red and white polka-dotted hats.

I have to say, though, that the first driver I rooted for was George Summers; I even had a Bulldog Stables #31 shirt, the first piece of racing apparel I ever owned. And my favorite *car* was Eddie Hoyle's, because instead of a number it had "FORD!" written on the door, with the "O" a little bit bigger so it was a zero. When you're a kid, that kind of thing grabs your attention.

But my father instantly liked Ronnie. I think part of it was that Ronnie was so young—that whole Kid from Fitchburg thing—and part of it was that, like everyone else, he recognized that Ronnie had a special talent. So anywhere Ronnie went, we went, and that meant going to Stafford when he started racing there on Saturday nights. We lived in New Bedford, Massachusetts, so Seekonk was close by, but if Ronnie was going to Stafford, we were, too. Through all of that, Ronnie kind of took over as the guy I rooted for, because George Summers was still at Seekonk.

My father installed television antennas for a living, but what he really loved was photography. He had taken correspondence courses when he was younger, and had some kind of a degree in it. He enjoyed taking photos at the track, but for a long time it was just a hobby; he'd shoot from the grandstands, and never bothered asking for press credentials. But after we started going to Stafford and then Thompson, he got more involved; he started sending his photos to a magazine called *ProSpeed Revue*, run by Phil Harris, and then Val LeSieur's paper, which was *New England Speedway Scene* and later just *Speedway Scene*. I'm sure that's how he got to be friendly with Ronnie, just by being around and shooting photos.

When Stafford switched to Friday nights in 1977, that was perfect for us, because all of a sudden we could see Ronnie, Bugsy Stevens, and all those guys three nights a week. We'd start there, then on Saturdays we'd go to Seekonk or Westboro, and of course Thompson on Sundays. It made for a long weekend, starting at 3:00 p.m. on Friday, when we'd leave for Stafford, and not ending until my father got his photos mailed to the papers on Monday morning.

Photography was a lot different then. Digital cameras didn't exist; it was all film, and film was expensive. On Friday my dad would load one roll of black-and-white Kodak film, 36 exposures, and try to conserve that roll through the entire weekend. He'd have a spare roll with him, just in case, but he usually didn't need it. He must have been really good at what he did, because you always hear photographers talk about taking dozens of shots to end up with a few great ones, but my dad's stuff was really good. He'd just wait until something caught his eye. He generally didn't shoot action photos; before the races he'd walk through the pits, and later he'd shoot victory lane. That was it.

When we got home from Thompson on Sunday nights, he'd drop my mom and me at home and then drive to his business, where he kept his darkroom. That's when the real work started. Back then you'd put the film in a canister with some kind of chemical, then look at each negative in an enlarger, expose an image on a sheet of photo paper, and bathe the photo itself in three different trays of chemicals. Then you'd hang the prints on a line to dry. Finally, you had to mail the prints; no one had ever heard of e-mail.

Then the next week, we'd do it all again.

All those speedways had a different feel to them. In the '70s, Stafford was *the* professional track in this area, in terms of the caliber of cars and drivers and the way things were presented. I mean, Jackie Arute and Mike Joy were in the announcer's booth, together, and you had the drama of seeing Ronnie, Kenny, Geoff, Bugsy, Freddy, Flemke—go right down the list—start toward the back and come to the front. Incredible. I'd usually sit with the Bouchards at Stafford, and I can remember Lorraine, Ronnie and Kenny's mom, being *very* nervous. That's something I understood better as I got older and became a parent myself.

Seekonk, especially from 1977 through '79, was also a special place. Robbie Bouchard had a set of flags, and he and I would sit in the front row, close to the track, waving those flags: green, yellow, white, checkered, even the passing flag. Seekonk always had lots of side-by-side action, and you had guys like Summers, Leo Cleary, and George Murray mixing it up with Ronnie, Bugsy, and Freddy. And Ronnie and the Judkins team won the championship in '78, which made that a good year for me!

Even though Seekonk was close to home, I enjoyed going to Westboro in 1980, when a lot of the Seekonk guys went there. That was such a fast track, considering that it was a bullring, and I loved it. By then Ronnie was in the Boehler #3, Kenny was strong in his own car, Bugsy was in Joe Brady's car, and Greg Sacks was in Lee Allard's #66. Then you had guys like Joe Howard and Gomer Taylor, who were very competitive at Westboro.

With Thompson, the first things you think of are the speeds and the high-banked turns. The neat thing about their Sunday-night program was that because they only ran small-block Modifieds, you saw guys from several different Saturday tracks. Thompson has a special place in my heart anyway, because I later worked there for so long, but even before that, I absolutely loved the Thompson 300. For me, that was *the* race. There were guaranteed starters from just about every track in the Northeast, and giant fields. It was such a special event.

Once my dad started spending more time in the pits and getting to know more people, that's when we began hanging around after the races, and joining in some of the parties in the parking lots. My mom always had a cooler full of sandwiches, and other people had coolers full of beer, and everybody would shoot the breeze, and laugh, and joke around. To me, it was an amazing thing; in 1977, I'd have been 13, and at that age guys like Ron Bouchard seemed like big-league sports stars. Yet here I was, watching the races with his family and then hanging out with him and his crew—Bob Judkins, Chuck Grime, Steve Kalkowski, and whoever else was with them—and also with other drivers and teams. It was like a Red Sox fan hanging around in the players' parking lot after a game. I really felt like I was plugged into something, getting behind the scenes.

We were friendly with a couple named Bruce and Kathy Sturdevant, who lived in Fair Haven, just east of New Bedford. Bruce and Kathy would go to Seekonk every Saturday, and they were part of that group that hung out after the races. One weekend they invited Ronnie, Paula, and the whole Judkins crew to a Sunday-afternoon picnic at their house. They backed the hauler into the driveway, and that Sunday afternoon felt just like being in the Seekonk parking lot, except, obviously, there was a lot less beer drinking. Lenny Ellis and his brother, Bobby, who both raced at Seekonk, showed up and had a beer, but for Ronnie and the team it was a workday. I've got a bunch of photos from that picnic, and in the background you can see Bobby, Chuck and Steve working on the car.

It was so relaxed, and so laid back, and it was amazing to me—again, at that young age—to think you could have a picnic during the day and then go racing at night. But at some point my parents and I jumped into our Plymouth Fury, Ronnie and Paula jumped into what I think was a big Mercury, Judkins and the guys jumped into the hauler, and we all took off for Thompson.

When Ronnie started driving for Boehler in 1980, that social feeling was still there. Lenny was pretty reserved and kept to himself a lot, but because he lived not too far from us, my father would visit his garage once in a while. So they were friendly, and because of that, I always felt comfortable with Lenny. So we still hung around with Ronnie; only the car and the team had changed.

I can't say exactly what got me interested in announcing, but fairly early on, at Thompson, I'd sit in the grandstands with a tape recorder and describe what I was watching, then listen to those tapes during the week. There were some great announcers in this area—Mike and Jackie at Stafford, as I mentioned, and John Janisaitis at Thompson—and I'm sure that had some influence on me, but it's hard to say for sure.

There was a fellow named Chuck Jeffries, a radio host from out near Springfield, and in the late '70s he would occasionally sub for John Janisaitis if John had some other commitment. Chuck knew my parents just from being around the tracks, and I guess he saw that I had an interest in announcing, so he'd ask me to help him. I wasn't on the microphone, but I'd hand him lineups, rosters, and things like that. Then at the start of 1980, when Ben Dodge took over, he allowed

Cheese! Gene, Robbie, Michelle, and Tracey Bouchard join their dad in victory lane after a 1976 Monadnock 100, Ron's first win for car owner Bob Judkins. (Bouchard Family Collection)

(Top) Few racing relationships had greater impact on Ron's career than the one he shared with M&H Tire boss Marvin Rifchin. (Paul Bonneau)

(Right) Back on familiar turf, Ronnie parks the M&H Vega in victory lane at Seekonk in 1977. (Dave Dykes Collection)

Small-block heaven: Ron Bouchard and Geoff Bodine on a Sunday evening at Thompson. (Paul Bonneau)

It's 1977, and a high-speed battle on the Thompson Speedway banking. That's Ed Flemke down low, and Bouchard in his customary groove upstairs. (Mike Adaskaveg)

Killing time before a Thompson 300, Ron Bouchard and the future Mrs. Bouchard, Paula Flemke, lounge in the infield grass. (Mike Adaskaveg)

(Top) Taking a break from a backyard picnic, Bob Judkins, Steve Kalkowski (kneeling) and Chuck Grime prep for Thompson. (Paul Bonneau)

(Left) Tight quarters: Bouchard takes the long way around Bodine in the 1978 Seekonk closer. (Paul Bonneau)

Wheeling this Judkins Pinto in 1978, Bouchard won from New England to Florida. (Dave Dykes Collection)

(Above) Father and son: Long after Ronnie left the family racing stable, Bob Bouchard was still there to back his elder son. (Paul Bonneau)

(Above) Ron and his mom, Lorraine Bouchard. (Paul Bonneau)

(Right) In 1979, Ron accepted the Spring Sizzler's Fred DeSarro Award from Fred's sons, Gary and Bryan. (Val LeSieur Collection)

(Above) Always a fan favorite, Bouchard indulges a group of kids on the prowl for autographs. (Paul Bonneau)

(Left) Stafford promoter Ed Yerrington congratulates his track's 1979 Modified champion. (Paul Bonneau)

(Below) Talented team: Bouchard (outside) wheeled a Richie Evans backup car at Martinsville in October of '79. Their one-off pairing yielded two podium finishes. (Coastal 181 Collection)

Nine years after he'd first driven for Dick Armstrong, Bouchard climbed into the gleaming red #1 and captured the 1980 Thompson 300. (Howie Hodge)

Photographer and friend Paul Bonneau climbed the Thompson Speedway flagstand to snap this shot of the Bouchard/Armstrong gang's 300 celebration.

(Above) Bouchard in the Boehler #3, which in 1980–81 took him to multiple wins at Stafford, Westboro, Thompson, Monadnock, Waterford, and New Smyrna. (North East Motor Sports Museum)

(Right) Though their partnership was relatively short, Bouchard and Len Boehler were a dynamic Modified combo. (Paul Bonneau)

(Left) Ron and Ken Bouchard will go into the record books as two of New England racing's most successful and most popular siblings. (Paul Bonneau)

me to do some announcing during the warm-ups; in the past, they had usually just played music until it was time for the heat races. That was a good way to get used to being on the microphone without the pressure of actually calling the race. By summer, I started co-announcing with Ben, and I announced for several years at Thompson with him and with Russ Dowd.

Of course, 1980 was Ronnie's last full season in Modifieds. Not long after I started announcing, he won a feature in Boehler's car. Ben usually handled the victory lane interviews, but as the race was ending I asked Ben if I could do it this time. Ben knew why that meant so much to me, and he said, "Sure, go ahead." For me, it was the greatest thing: I'm 16 years old, I'm announcing at one of my favorite tracks, and I'm interviewing my hero.

That September, Ronnie won the Thompson 300. Because that race was such a big deal, Ben did the winner's interview. But I had a great day anyway, because when Ben headed toward victory lane with a few laps to go, that left me alone in the booth, so I called the finish of one of Ronnie's biggest Modified wins.

I was always careful to be impartial on the microphone, but I do think that getting to know Ronnie and his teams, and becoming good friends with guys like Lenny Ellis, helped my announcing. It gave me an insight on how hard people like Judkins and Boehler worked to get those cars ready each weekend, and I tried to pass that along to the fans, because they don't see that. The average fan doesn't realize that most weekly racers are regular people who have jobs; Ronnie worked for his dad, Summers ran a trucking company, Bugsy owned a junkyard, Freddy had an office job, Judkins had a gas station. If you give that information to the fan, I think it helps him relate better to the people he's seeing.

And getting to know those guys when I was so young, particularly Ronnie, made it easier later on, when I was doing both announcing and some PR work at Thompson. I'd go through the pits and visit with the drivers, and I wasn't at all intimidated to talk with a Richie Evans or a Reggie Ruggiero because by then I understood that even the top drivers were just *people*.

That period had a huge influence on my life. Obviously, hanging around race tracks led to the announcing and the PR stuff, and I feel lucky that I got to do all of that. But it taught me things beyond that; as a young person I was always hanging around with adults and meeting new people, and that helped me in school and later helped me as I became an adult myself. And Ronnie was a big part of that. I watched the way he treated people, and I'm sure that, without even knowing it, I learned something from it. In the beginning I was just this kid, this starstruck kid, and he always found time to talk with me, always put me on his level. He made a big, big impression on me.

At the time, though, I mostly just loved watching him race. Everybody talks about him running the outside, but what I remember is that he always seemed to know where to go, no matter what lane that might have been. He just had that knack, especially at Seekonk, where everything depended on being in the right lane at the right time, because it was a multi-groove track. One great example was the last race of the 1978 season, when Ronnie pinned Geoff Bodine behind a lapped car and won with the Judkins #2X. That was Geoff's big year, when he won 55 races with the Armstrong car, and you almost figured that once he got the lead, no one could possibly beat him. So that was a big day, especially at Seekonk, where Ronnie was so popular. When he got by Geoff, the place went crazy.

There's another Seekonk story that always make me laugh. Ronnie's team always had to turn their #7 into a #7X or a #71, because Frank Federici already had that number. With the Vega, they'd use a couple strips of duct tape. But in 1979 they had that beautiful new Troyer Pinto, and I just couldn't imagine them slapping duct tape on the sides of that thing. Well, one of my suppressed desires was to be a sign painter, because I loved the way Brian Frederick, better known as Brian Signs, used to letter some of the Modifieds. So I went down to the local sign shop. They had this magnetic material that was almost like a thick decal; you could stick it on, and peel it right off. I didn't have any money, but they were nice enough to give me some scraps. I took that stuff home, and I made these really nice "1" magnets, two of them, in the same style as the #7 on that Troyer car. I painted them silver, and I even painted the trim to match. I brought my numbers to Seekonk, and Judkins and his guys let me put them on the door.

I was 15 years old, and there were my numbers, riding on Bouchard's car. Coolest thing ever, right? But there was one problem: The Modifieds back then had real doors, so there was an indentation where the Pinto's door handle would have been. The magnet didn't stick very well in that spot, and in warm-ups the number started blowing off. It wrapped itself around the nerf bar, and then started flapping against the tire. When Ronnie got back to the pits, it was beat to crap, ruined. All my hard work, down the drain.

That might have been the only bad night I ever had watching Ronnie Bouchard.

BY DICK WILLIAMS

"If you were a promoter, Ronnie was at the top of the list of drivers you wanted"

Thoughtful words on friendship, business, and racing

In the late 1970s and early '80s, Dick Williams was among New England's most popular promoters. He was also one of its busiest, commuting from his home in Westerly, Rhode Island, while operating as many as four speedways. Williams promoted the Waterford Speedbowl on and off from 1978–85; Westboro Speedway from 1979–83; Monadnock Speedway from 1980–83; and Thompson Speedway in 1981.

STEVE KENNEDY

His generous, good-guy nature occasionally bit him; more than once, he boosted payoffs when the grandstands were full—"At Thompson we had a great crowd for the Icebreaker, and I added $10,000 to the purse," he recalled—only to discover that loyalty was not always a two-way street with some racers. But it's hard to get promotion out of the blood; after nearly 30 years away from the sport, Dick has recently been a key player in New England's Tri-Track Modified series.

Ronnie was just the greatest guy. His parents both had a hand in that, I'm sure. His father was a hardworking man, and he obviously taught Ronnie all about hard work and dedication. But I know his mother must have influenced him, too, because Ronnie was so good with people, so hospitable.

When we first met in the early '70s, I was working as the handicapper at Stafford, and he had just started driving for Bob Johnson. He was a young guy—the Kid from Fitchburg—and people were talking like he was going to come in and beat all the big Modified heroes. I said to myself, "Well, *that* ain't going to happen." But he showed up there, and, boy, did he run. And before you knew it, he *was* beating those guys.

I can't say I knew him too well in those days, but we were definitely friendly; he was the easiest guy in the world to get along with. Then I left Stafford, but for years I was the handicapper at Thompson, so we still saw each other all the time. I think we sort of became friends without realizing that it was happening.

In the winter of 1977–78, there was talk going around that the Waterford Speedbowl wasn't going to open. I had gone to Waterford since I was young, and a fellow I worked for, Sam Cherenzia, said, "I'll bet you'd really like to run that track."

I said, "Boy, would I ever."

That was because, having been around the sport and having seen some good ideas, I was sure Waterford could be successful with the right effort behind it. So we met with Harvey Tattersall, who owned the track, and we made a deal to lease it. It was a gamble; you never really know everything that's involved until you make that leap. You can have rainouts, you can have all sorts of problems. We certainly didn't have a great season, but we didn't *lose* money. If I remember correctly, Sam and I ended up with $600 apiece at the end of the year.

Ronnie won the first race I ever promoted, the 1978 Blast-Off 100, driving for Bob Judkins. That was no big surprise, because a lot of outsiders came in every year for the Blast-Off. But then Bob and Ronnie came back for the first two weeks of our regular season, and that was unusual. They were never Waterford guys, and it's not like we paid a big purse. But they came to support what I was doing there, because they were friends of mine.

Ronnie won both of those regular shows, and then he said, "You know, Dick, we're going to be running Seekonk on Saturday nights, starting next week." I told him that I *expected* him to leave, because the money was better at Seekonk. But I'll tell you how smart Ronnie was: He said it wasn't going to help me if he stayed at Waterford, anyway, and he was right. Waterford had a lot of good racers, but they were mostly low-dollar teams that were not of the same caliber as Ronnie and Judkins. It was a great place for the little guys, but it wasn't going to be too good if Ronnie Bouchard showed up and beat them every week.

I said, "Look, I know why you've been coming here. You did it to help me, and I appreciate that."

I had a similar conversation with Fred DeSarro. I had helped him build his first race car, and we lived two or three miles apart. We were *good* friends. After I got Waterford, we were having coffee, and Freddy said, "You know, I'm not going to be able to run for you on Saturdays." I told him I understood that completely.

The only thing I added was that if he and Lenny Boehler were free when I had a special event, I'd love to have them. And all those guys—Ronnie, Freddy, Cleary, Bugsy—supported my big shows.

In 1979, I took over Westboro, which was another good track for low-buck guys. But then Anthony Venditti decided he wasn't going to run Modifieds at Seekonk in 1980, so all the top Seekonk guys came to Westboro. We opened with a big show, the Busch 100, which was a story in itself. I had spent a lot of money there; I replaced the old wooden fence with new guardrail, and I had arranged to have the track paved in certain spots, because it was really rough. Then I got a call from a banker, asking if I'd like to lease Westboro Speedway again. That was a surprise, because the owner had told me he was having some tough times, so I'd already paid him half of my lease money for the year. Then the bank foreclosed on him, so technically *they* now owned the track, and I had to pay a second time to lease the track.

Lee Allard, who was one of the top Modified owners at that time, was going to do the paving. I called Lee and told him I'd have to cancel the job. He said, "Dick, I don't want to race there if you don't pave the place. You've got to do this." Well, one day I was up there, and here came a whole fleet of paving trucks. Lee paved that place without getting paid up front, because he said I had a good enough name that he trusted me. So we opened with that big 100-lapper, and Greg Sacks won it ... in Allard's car!

By then, Fred DeSarro had died, and Ronnie was driving for Boehler, and they ran for me every Saturday night. I got along great with Lenny, probably because I had been so friendly with Freddy all those years. Lenny was a little bit different, but, let me tell you, he was a square shooter.

It was great to have Ronnie at Westboro, because Fitchburg wasn't far away, and he was very popular with the local people. Of course, he was popular everywhere, because he was great with the fans and great with the press. If you were a promoter, Ronnie was right at the top of the list of drivers you wanted to have, along with a small handful of guys; Bugsy was another, and so was Richie Evans, although I usually couldn't get Richie at Westboro because it wasn't a NASCAR track and he was busy chasing points.

I used to love to go into the pits and talk with everybody after the races, and that included Ronnie. I was always so glad he and Paula got together, because they were such a good pair. I'd known her father, Eddie Flemke, since I was 20 years old. For some reason, Eddie took a liking to me, and he would talk to me, and I never forgot that. So to see her and Ronnie become a couple, that was awesome. I just enjoyed being around them.

That same year, 1980, I took over promoting Monadnock for Bill Davis, who owned the track. Monadnock had always been a Friday-night operation, but Stafford was so successful that Bill didn't want to go against them. So we settled on Thursdays, because that was the best open night. Monadnock was another track that could draw from that Fitchburg area, and, luckily for me, Ronnie and Boehler came there, too. We had some great racing that year—a lot of it was between Ronnie and his brother, Kenny, who had his own car—but it ended up being too hard to get cars and fans on Thursdays. The season wasn't a total loss, but it wasn't good.

I have good memories from my time at Monadnock, and a lot of them are directly connected with Ronnie. Anytime I had to go to Monadnock during the week, my route from Rhode Island would take me right through Fitchburg. I'd always stop at Red & White to see Ronnie and Kenny and their father, Bob. A few times, Ronnie called his mother and said, "Ma, I've got this pain-in-the-ass friend who's passing through town, and I know he's hungry," and Mrs. Bouchard would set an extra place for dinner. What a nice thing to do, and what a great family that is.

In 1981, I added Thompson to my plate. That was another track where Ronnie was really popular, and I obviously would have loved to have him there every week, but before the season even started he made his deal to go Winston Cup racing with Jack Beebe. My only reaction was that I was happy for him. A lot of promoters might have worried about losing one of their top guys, but I looked at it a different way. I knew that as long as things were going well for him, he'd be back to help when he could. And that's just the way it worked out. He ran a few races for me that year—not just at Thompson, but at Westboro and Monadnock—and whenever he was coming, there was really a buzz to it. It was a big deal to a lot of New England people that they had a chance to see him again, or maybe even see him for the first time.

But the biggest thing for me was that I knew getting that ride was a great break for Ronnie, and I wanted the best for him. We were friends, and that was the most important thing.

It just so happened that Seekonk brought the Modifieds back that same year, so a lot of the big names left Westboro. But there were several times when Ronnie had a weekend off from the Cup stuff, and he would drive Lenny's car at Westboro. That meant the world to me. I mean, here I had one of the hottest drivers in the country running at my track on a Saturday night. But, just to show you again the way he was, after he'd won a few times he said, "I'm not sure I'm doing you any favors." He meant because he was beating the little guys, just like in '78 at Waterford.

He really did see the big picture. I used to tell everybody—and I still tell them today—that there are three parts to short-track racing: the fans, the track, and the racers. If one of them is getting a far better deal or a far worse deal than the other two, it won't work. We all have a stake in this; we have to take care of one another. When it comes right down to it, we all want the same thing: the drivers and owners want to be treated fairly, and so does the promoter. With Ronnie and I, it was never about *money*. He saw what I was trying to do, and whenever he could, he would be there to help, even after he was running in the Cup series.

He understood racing, and he understood the *business* of racing. He knew that you couldn't just *take*. You also had to *give*.

And I'm going to tell you something: Ronnie never asked for a nickel. All those times he came and helped me, he would not take a penny.

There was one exception, and that's another good story.

Ronnie would always try to help if he knew you *were* struggling, and there was a period when we were struggling at Waterford. So not long after he won at Talladega, he said that he'd come down one Saturday night, and he would arrange for the guys from Race Hill Farm to bring that winning car to the Speedbowl. So we advertised this Ron Bouchard Night, with an autograph session, and a special match at intermission: Ronnie against me, in Late Models, which he thought was great.

He said he didn't want any money, but I told him. "Look, this time it's going to be *your* night. If you don't take something, you and I are never going to do anything else together."

He said, "Okay, you're the boss."

Now, I had raced a little bit, way back when, but I wasn't too good at it. In the early '60s I had a Modified coupe, and I think I qualified for two features at Waterford. You've got to remember, they had over 35 cars a night back then, so a lot of guys missed the show every week. Those two times I qualified, they felt like victories to me. I was probably the most underfunded, least talented guy there, but I loved to race.

Anyway, the night came around, and as Ronnie and I were making our way to the pits for the match race, we walked past the security guys at the pit gate. A couple of them, just kidding around, said, "Hey, Dick, are you really going to put it to him? You're going to beat him, right?"

Ronnie grinned at me and said, "Hey, bossman, have you been shooting your mouth off to these guys?"

I said, "Well, maybe a little bit. I can't let you come to my track and think you're just going to walk all over me!"

He said, "Oh, so this is for *real*, huh?"

I said, "You bet it is."

We were both having a lot of fun. We had two Late Models ready for us, so we climbed in and rolled out for our pace laps. Dick Brooks was the starter, and when Brooksie waved the green flag, we took off. I was on the outside, which turned out to be a good thing, because when we got to the first turn, my right-front suspension broke and I went straight into the wall. It was really a hard crash; it folded the right-front corner back to the firewall. It also jammed my leg, so I was in a lot of pain. And I was thinking, "Okay, now what?"

Ronnie came back around and stopped by my car. He asked the track-crew guys if I was okay. I didn't want to complain that I'd hurt my leg, so I said, "Yeah, I'm all right."

And Ronnie said, "Good. Get him another car, so we can finish this!"

So we did. We got somebody else to lend us a car, and we ran our match race. He made it look good—played with me until the last lap—and then dusted me coming down for the checkers.

At the end of the night we were off by ourselves, and I handed him a big paper bag that I had stuffed with money. He said again that he didn't want anything, but I insisted, so he took it. Well, I had put a handful of big bills at the top of the bag, but everything else was singles. Naturally, he didn't go through it while we were standing there. But I guess on the way home he opened it up and saw all those big bills, then dug down a bit and saw that it was all singles, and he laughed like hell. For weeks I had people telling me, "Ronnie said that was one of the best tricks anybody ever played on him. You really got him."

I still smile when I think about that.

You always remember the good people in this sport, the ones who are there to do something for you, and who appreciate it when you do something for them. Ronnie Bouchard was one of those guys.

PART FOUR

Big League, Big Times

BRYANT MCMURRAY

Ron Bouchard's most transformative decade began, ironically, with business as usual. And why not? Life was good. In ten seasons, 1971–80, he had driven for Dick Armstrong, Bob Johnson, Bob Judkins, and Len Boehler, four owners who'd make anyone's Modified hall of fame. In that span he'd won something north of 150 races; if those numbers fell short of those racked up in the '70s by full-timers like Bodine and Evans, they didn't miss by much, and they dwarfed those of just about any part-time racer, which is exactly what Bouchard was. He was still hauling furniture and freight when he wasn't hauling a race car deep into the corners.

Often he'd enlist out-of-work racing pals to help him on those moving jobs; he enjoyed their company, and this way they might make a buck, too. Chuck Grime and Ed Flemke Jr. tell a hilarious story about the three of them, using a combination of muscle and moving straps, shouldering a piano up a steaming-hot stairwell "somewhere in New York City," as Flemke recalls.

"It was upstairs from a funeral parlor," says Grime. "As we got to the top of the landing, Eddie and I were pulling from above while Ronnie was lifting and pushing from below, hollering, 'Don't you two let go! Don't you *dare* let go!'"

Flemke adds, "It wouldn't have mattered if we had let go. The straps had already lifted both me and Chuck off the ground."

You get the sense that if things went like that forever, 40-hour weeks and 30-lap features, that would have been fine with Bouchard. And as the calendar flipped to 1981, that's how things were looking. In February he went to New Smyrna with Boehler, grabbing a World Series win, and come March, as usual, Ronnie went to Martinsville, where he would drive Armstrong's car.

He and Paula stayed at the Dutch Inn. One night, the phone rang. It was Bob Johnson. The call changed both their lives.

After their parting in 1976, Johnson had raced infrequently, mostly contesting the bigger Modified races with Satch Worley. He passed his time in a shop beside his home, welding up woodstoves for a friend's business and daydreaming about doing once again something he and Bouchard had done: tackling some of the richer events in NASCAR's Late Model Sportsman division, in the days before it morphed into the Busch Series. Through a friend, Johnson casually knew Jack Beebe, who lived not far away and operated Beebe School Transportation, the biggest school-bus company in Connecticut. Jack's son Mike raced at Waterford, so he was no stranger to the sport. One day the friend shared Johnson's idea with Beebe, who wanted to know more.

"So I went to see Jack," Johnson says. "And as we got talking, he said, 'Listen, if we're going to do that, why don't we just get a Winston Cup car?' I said, 'Well, okay, that works for me!' I was never afraid to try something."

So Johnson and Beebe, suddenly much better friends, flew to Charlotte and bought an ex-Harry Ranier Chevy.

"We got the car, an engine, and 20 wheels," Johnson chuckles. "Now we were ready to go Cup racing!"

They set up a shop at one end of the bus-company building. Beebe named the team after his estate in Madison: Race Hill Farm. With Worley at the wheel, Beebe's #47 made its debut in May of 1978 at Dover; though 19 laps down at the checkers, they finished 14th, leaving all involved "pretty satisfied," says Johnson. In three more starts that season, they placed 18th at Daytona, a better-than-respectable ninth at Pocono, and 14th again at Martinsville.

Beebe and Johnson wanted to run more in '79, but Worley declined, citing obligations to his family's construction firm. At some point Bouchard was asked if he wanted the ride, no surprise given his ties to Johnson. As far back as 1974, national magazine stories identified Ron as a future Cup star, and he'd always called it a goal. But, like Worley, he put family first, and said no.

"He had children at home," says George Summers, "and he was still involved with his father's moving business."

Son Gene Bouchard says, "That was a huge sacrifice on his part, to give up something he really wanted. As a kid that's not something you understand, but it couldn't have been easy to do."

In 1978, the hottest man in asphalt short-track racing had been Geoff Bodine, and Johnson was familiar with his work. Bodine had not put down roots as deep as Worley's or Bouchard's; he'd relocated to Massachusetts just four years earlier to drive for Armstrong, and racing was the only business Geoff was interested in. Offered the Race Hill Farm ride, he parked his motorhome outside Beebe's shop and went to work.

Even in the winter of 1978–79, this seemed a combustible combination. When it came to racing and setups, neither Johnson nor Bodine was used to consultation; each had succeeded on his own will and guile. The old "too many chiefs, not enough Indians" cliché was applied, and some predicted the pairing would not last beyond the season-opening Daytona 500. Those forecasts were wrong … by a whopping two races. After leading six laps at Daytona, breaking a rear end at Rockingham, and having a feisty radio debate about the car's handling at Atlanta—"Jack looked at me," Johnson recalls, "and said, 'Tell him to pull that sonofabitch in and *park* it!'"—driver and team went their separate ways.

Neither man sounds bitter about it today.

"There were several people who told me I'd never get along with Bob Johnson," Geoff laughs. "Those people were right."

Johnson says, "Geoff thought that right away, we'd be a front-running car. Well, that ain't going to happen."

So Beebe and Johnson looked at the other end of the intensity scale and hired Harry Gant, who had won Late Model Sportsman and Modified races all over the South and whose agreeable nature made Andy Griffith look positively crabby. Across the next two years with Race Hill Farm—54 races in all—Gant scored 18 top-ten finishes, ten of them in the top five. Harry's steady hand gave Johnson room to grow the team.

Each Thursday, the Race Hill Farm transporter—a Kenworth with a double sleeper that "would take four or five people," says Johnson, who often drove it—left Connecticut with all vital personnel. On Friday night or Saturday morning, a van would take the same route, shuttling in the weekend crew, along with Gussie Johnson. ("Everything they say about how there's a strong woman behind every successful man, that's Gussie," says Ed Flemke Jr.)

But 1981 brought great disruption to the Beebe team. First, new NASCAR rules downsized the Winston Cup cars, heaping a load of work on Johnson and company. Next, the deep-pockets Skoal Bandit team owned by actor Burt Reynolds and Hollywood stuntman Hal Needham, having gotten off to a shaky start with driver Stan Barrett, lured away Gant in March. Harry's last start in the #47 came at Atlanta, where he finished second.

Needing another steady hand, Johnson turned again to Bouchard. Though he'd never started a Cup race, he was a driver in whom Johnson had enormous faith. When you win together as much as they had, you don't forget how it felt.

Today, there isn't a short-track driver alive who wouldn't crawl over broken glass for a shot at a full-time Cup ride. But in 1981, salaries and race purses weren't what they are today; a sixth-place run at Richmond, two races before Gant's departure, had netted Beebe's team just $4,770, almost a grand less than Bob Polverari earned in winning the 1981 Spring Sizzler. On top of that, Bouchard had steady employment at Red & White Movers. So, as hard as it might be for Gen-X and Millennial racers to comprehend, this was not a slam-dunk decision.

"I don't think he doubted himself," says Clyde McLeod. "He was just concerned about whether it was the right situation."

Ultimately, Bouchard took the gig. In the two-week gap before the next race, he visited the shop and got to know the team. He made his debut on the daunting Tennessee hills of Bristol Motor Speedway, shocking everyone by qualifying third behind Darrell Waltrip and defending series champ Dale Earnhardt, each of whom had already won there twice. Come Sunday he led laps 145-150. A hundred laps later, worn out, he radioed his pit to ask how much of the race remained. About half, Johnson replied. Bouchard toughed it out until the engine blew after 349 laps.

His problem wasn't conditioning, but an ill-fitting seat. McLeod recalls Bouchard stopping to visit as he passed through Connecticut on his way home. "He pulled off his shirt," says Clyde, "and his back was raw from top to bottom."

So in his first race, he'd learned the value of personalizing his cockpit. Oh, and there was another lesson: Preparing to leave the track, he spied a crowd in the pit area. At its center was Richard Petty, signing autographs. Richard's race, too, had ended with a dead engine, but there were still fans to please. This, Ronnie saw immediately, was how this new game was played, or at least how it ought to be played. He returned to his team's transporter, grabbed a marker, and sat down. The line that formed for his signature was shorter than Petty's, but no less appreciative.

Four months later—a stretch that included five top-ten finishes in ten Cup races and, back home, four Modified wins—Bouchard went to Alabama for the Talladega 500. It was August 2, 1981. You know how the afternoon ended: with Ronnie, pushed into contention by drafting help from his friend Ricky Rudd, diving low through the tri-oval of NASCAR's fastest track and surprising Darrell Waltrip and Terry Labonte, who'd thought they had things to themselves. Bouchard said he'd learned that move from another new chum, Buddy Baker, in a garage-area tutorial.

"When you think about it," says his old Brookline mentor, Pete Salvatore, "third place would have been a great finish for him. But he had the nerve to go for the win. That took some balls."

Sure it did. In those pre-restrictor plate days, the cars had huge horsepower, and their new downsized bodies were no sleeker than bread trucks. They slipped and danced as they negotiated that final bend at 200 miles per hour, and headed for the checkers.

It looked more like the finish of a horse race than a stock car marathon, their three Buicks crossing the line three abreast, with Bouchard's in front by about the length of Secretariat's neck.

On pit road, Steve Kalkowski, who'd worked with Bouchard in his Judkins/Rifchin years, could scarcely believe his luck. He had joined the Race Hill Farm team that very week. He says, "One day I'm thinking, 'Holy cow, I made it to the big show.' The next day, Ronnie pulls off one of the biggest upsets in history."

The Beebe/Johnson camp erupted with joy. So did the pits at Thompson Speedway, where Bouchard had so often won. During a break in the action, folks had gathered around ramp-truck radios to catch the finish; Bugs Stevens, suited up for the night's Modified action, exclaimed, "That little shit! He *won* it." The Modifieds were also running at New York's Oswego Speedway, where Ronnie had once shown up as an outsider and whipped all comers in a 100-lapper. *Speedway Scene* columnist Bob Echo was at Oswego, 12-year-old son Jared in tow. Jared, now 46, older than his dad was that day, was checking out the Richie Evans pit when news of Bouchard's win crackled over the loudspeaker. He recalls seeing crewman Kenny Hartung, who was unloading tires, "toss a Goodyear up in the air" in celebration.

If you happened to be watching the race on television, things were a bit different. There was disappointment when the live CBS feed famously lost its video in the closing laps, turning lots of Sylvania and RCA sets into big, clunky radios.

In Connecticut, lots of old friends were watching. Make that *listening*. Ed Flemke Jr. says, "I was in my apartment, by myself, jumping up and down." Clyde McLeod remembers, "Ann Marie and I had tears pouring out, saying, 'Can you *believe* this?'"

And in Fitchburg, where a big chunk of the clan was gathered in Lorraine Bouchard's living room, "The house just *exploded*," remembers son Rob. "Everybody went crazy."

Louie Roy, who in years gone by had loved driving Ron's hauler to Seekonk, appeared in the driveway, whooping to the heavens. "It was mayhem," says sister JoAnn.

Ah, but in the office at Red & White Movers, where Bob Bouchard had seen his elder son creep into the lead battle, there was no joy. Accounts vary, but when the TV picture went black, Bob either put his foot through the screen or hurled the set into a wall. Ken Bouchard says, "I got to work Monday, and that TV was busted into a million pieces. Pepe really took care of that thing."

There were a half-dozen more top tens, and a Michigan pole, between Talladega and the end of the Cup season, and at year's end Ronnie was voted Champion Spark Plug Rookie of the Year. At the NASCAR awards banquet, held at the Waldorf Astoria in glittering Manhattan, he and Paula were joined by George and Maggie Summers, Clyde and Ann Marie McLeod, and Don and Terry Smart. Don Smart, nicknamed "Maxwell" after the bumbling secret-agent from the '60s TV sitcom "Get Smart," had done a bit of racing and was Stafford's track welder, but it was his close association with Boehler that bonded Max and Ronnie; his wife, Terry, drew equally close to Paula.

"I'll never forget that night," says Clyde McLeod. "It was a big, big, big moment. I'll never forget it. We were all so happy."

History compresses time, so there is a tendency to recall 1981 being as good as it ever got in the big leagues for Bouchard, as if nothing later came close to that Alabama day and that New York night when he was the toast of two very different towns. But that's not quite true. Across the next four seasons—1982–85, the rest of his tenure with Race Hill Farm—there were 45 more top-ten finishes, 14 of which were top fives. A break here and there, and a top-five run turns into a victory, as at Martinsville in '84, when Geoff Bodine's first Cup win came at Bouchard's expense.

"That was cool, a couple of Modified guys running one-two," says Geoff. "We both beat Allison, we both beat Earnhardt, we both beat Waltrip, and all the rest of those names."

There was also Rockingham in the fall of 1985, when Ron finished just a second behind winner Waltrip, that year's Cup champion. And there were third-place runs in the 1982 Firecracker 400 and the '85 Talladega 500, either of which, but for the whims of the drafting breezes, might have produced a second Cup victory for Bouchard, Beebe, and Fitchburg.

So things weren't all bad. Every so often his kids were able to come, and JoAnn might turn up with future husband Bob Bergeron, who always found a way to lend a hand. And Barbara Savitsky, still running the Ron Bouchard Fan Club, organized bus trips to Cup events at Dover, Pocono, and Martinsville. Familiar faces turned decent days into good ones.

And there were friendships made and deepened along the way, with drivers like Baker, Rudd, and Dale Earnhardt finding Bouchard as easy to hang with as Summers, Bugs Stevens, and Richie Evans had in the Modified days.

But, yes, there were some bumps in the road. Crew chiefs came and went: Johnson left in mid-1982, then David Ifft was on board from late '82 through July of '84. Wayne Baumgardner filled the role for the first five months of 1985, before Beebe replaced him with Jake Elder. Any gaps were filled by committee; Vic Kangas, who knew Bouchard as well as any chassis man could, often pitched in. But by 1985, Kangas, too, had cleared out, gone to massage IMSA road-racing cars for Florida owner Billy Dingman. It had to take a toll on Bouchard, whose racing career had been marked by productive long-term relationships.

On the bright side, the longest-term relationship in his private life, aside from those with his kids, was further solidified on June 14, 1983, when he married Paula Flemke. Two years later, in July of '85, she gave birth to a son, Chad, and when they took the baby—Paula's first, Ron's first since 1970—to a handful of Cup events that summer, he beamed like every day was the '81 Talladega 500.

Every so often, as if reminding all that he could still make magic with a steering wheel, he'd jump into something other than a Winston Cup car. Bouchard grabbed a pair of 1984 Busch Series wins at Darlington in a Pontiac fielded by DuBee Racing, a partnership between Beebe and friend John Dufour. And there were Modified wins with Boehler at Westboro and Thompson.

"Whenever my father came back to run Boehler's car," son Rob recalls, "it was a huge deal around here."

Not quite as huge, though, as some other Bouchard escapades. In 1982 and '83 he took part in Thompson Speedway match races with Bobby Allison and Geoff Bodine, respectively, all of them steering full-blown Winston Cup cars. Then Ronnie got really adventurous, partnering with Russ Conway and Ken Smith to promote the Budweiser Showdown of Champions, which over four summers found Cup drivers taking on New England's top Pro Stock racers. Bouchard turned on the charm and convinced seven-time champion Richard Petty, future seven-time champ Dale Earnhardt, three-time champs Cale Yarborough and Darrell Waltrip, and 1984 champ Terry Labonte, plus Buddy Baker, Tim Richmond, Kyle Petty, and assorted regional heroes to jump into unfamiliar cars at tracks in New Hampshire and Connecticut.

As often as not, those Winston Cup visitors bunked at the Bouchard home in Fitchburg. Says Paula, "I remember asking Lynda Petty what Richard liked for breakfast. She said, 'Oh, just get him some Ring-Dings and Coke.' He wasn't hard to shop for!"

That situation prompted the question: What on earth were Mr. and Mrs. Ron Bouchard still doing in Fitchburg, anyway?

"He and Paula were constantly traveling," says sister JoAnn. "I remember saying, 'Ronnie, why don't you move to Charlotte, or at least get an apartment there to use during the season?' He said, 'Nope. Fitchburg is my home.'"

You could take the Kid out of Fitchburg, but you couldn't take Fitchburg out of the Kid.

But if changing his address was out of the question, changing teams no longer was. From 1982–84, Bouchard's name came up in Silly Season whispers; he was linked with a couple of established teams, and even with a one supposedly being formed by actor/racer Paul Newman. Paula says, "There were offers, including a couple of really good ones. In hindsight, maybe he should have taken them. But he was very loyal to Jack."

Come the end of '85, however, he moved on. A 1986 deal with Mike Curb, the former lieutenant governor of California who'd fielded cars for Richard Petty, looked stable enough. But rising-star crew chief Mike Beam quit after just three races, and from there the team had neither speed nor reliability.

"To be honest," Bouchard told beat writer Ben White, "1986 was my worst year in racing."

He should have added the words "so far," because '87 was worse. Offered a limited schedule with Hoss Ellington—whose cars had won five times between 1976 and '80 with Donnie Allison and David Pearson—Bouchard told White, "Hopefully we can win some races [and] maybe a few poles."

He signed for 18 races. He only stayed for five. Progress had overtaken Hoss, a good-time guy whose best days had come when life, and the sport, moved at a slower pace. Aerodynamics was the new NASCAR obsession, but Ellington had booked no pre-season wind-tunnel time. And Bouchard complained to friends about showing up on race weekends ready to go, only to find that his cars were not. Though their results were not bad—12th at Atlanta, eighth at Darlington—morale in the driver's seat was down.

On May 3, 1987, at Talladega, of all places, everything ground to a halt. Early in the Winston 500, Bobby Allison cut a rear tire; his car spun exiting the tri-oval, got airborne, and ripped out 100 yards of catch-fencing. A dozen cars, their drivers scrambling to miss Bobby's mauled Buick, spun and crashed. Among those wrecked too badly to continue was Hoss Ellington's Bull's Eye Barbecue Sauce Chevrolet.

Its driver, Ron Bouchard, climbed out unhurt.

Unhurt and, at last, unmotivated.

He was 38 years old, and a retired race driver.

BY BOB JOHNSON

"I'm not sure if people realized what an underdog situation we were in"

Wrenching, coaching, winning, and battling the Establishment

VAL LESIEUR COLLECTION

When Bob Johnson moved to NASCAR Winston Cup racing as a crew chief for Jack Beebe's Race Hill Farm team, he brought with him every bit of the fire that had made him a winning Modified owner. Paired once again with Ron Bouchard, they scaled heights neither had ever dreamed of when Ronnie was flinging Bob's purple #17 around tracks all over the Northeast. After leaving Beebe's team in 1982, Johnson eased back to the short-track life, guiding young Randy LaJoie to a 1985 championship on the rugged NASCAR North Tour circuit. Later, Johnson returned to the Cup garage and helped shape the early careers of drivers like Ken Schrader and Ernie Irvan. These days, Bob leads a quiet life—no, seriously—in North Carolina, with wife Gussie by his side, as always. It was at their Lincolnton home that Bob was interviewed for this book.

When it came to Winston Cup racing, the hardest thing for me to get used to was that you didn't win every week. If you've ever gone through a period in short-track racing where it felt like you *had* won just about every week—like Ronnie and I had—it's hard to suddenly realize that now you're going to be lucky to run in the *top five*. That was the biggest transition I had, getting into the frame of mind.

Harry Gant had driven for us at Race Hill Farm for basically two years: most of 1979, all of 1980, and the spring of '81. Things had been going pretty well. We had a lot of top-fives, and a bunch of top-ten finishes, and by 1981 we were pretty competitive. We ran good at Daytona, but had a distributor go bad. After we fixed the distributor, he got back in the race and checked out on the field, which showed that we had the speed. At Richmond we sat on the outside pole and finished sixth. We ran good at Rockingham. Then we finished second at Atlanta, which was Harry's last race for us, because Hal Needham and the Skoal Bandit team had come along and hijacked him.

I got wind of that about a week before Atlanta. It was a much better deal for Harry, financially, and I understood that to some degree. But I wasn't happy; I was madder than hell, to be honest. I mean, at Atlanta we started on the front row, led the race, got a lap down, got the lap *back*, led again until we had a flat tire, and still finished second. We were fast. We were ready to win races, and now Harry was leaving. Yeah, I was mad.

So we needed a driver. I called Ronnie from Atlanta and said, "Hey, would you be interested in driving for us?" He came down to Jack Beebe's shop the next week, and we made a deal.

Our first race together was at Bristol, and we qualified third. Man, I was happy. But, to tell you the truth, I wasn't surprised. When you have as much confidence in somebody as I always had in Ronnie, you just figure he can do it. Sure, you understand that it might take a little bit of time to get adjusted, but I never had any doubt that he could drive those things.

Bristol is a tough place. It's tough on the car, tough on the driver. He said later that he was surprised how long the race felt, but I don't remembering him complaining. We eventually had an engine problem and fell out, but until then Ronnie did a great job.

From there, everywhere we went, we ran good, especially when you consider what we had and what we were running against. And you know something? The older I got and the longer I was around, the more I learned about what we were running against, and it wasn't always legal stuff. If I had known then what I know now—what you could get away with and what you couldn't—it would have been a whole different story.

Communication-wise, Ronnie and I got along great. That was the nice thing about us having been together, and having had success: It made it easy for me to understand what he was telling me, and for him to understand me. We knew each other so well.

When we went to Talladega in August, I didn't know what to expect; we'd been okay there in the first race, but not great. But as the weekend went along, I knew we were in pretty good shape. We practiced good, we qualified good—tenth—and Ronnie was happy.

In the race itself, we were fast all day. In fact, we were even better than it looked. Ronnie poked his nose out front a few times during the day, and I remember telling him on the radio, "Don't worry about leading. Just cool your jets. I know that's probably hard to do, but a lot of things are going to happen between now and the end of the race."

The other thing you've got to remember is that the sport was different back then. This was before drivers and teams started coming into NASCAR from all over the country; it was more of a *closed* thing, a clique, and as an outsider you could feel that. This was our third full year of Cup racing, but we were still outsiders, especially now that we had Ronnie driving. We were a New England team with a mostly New England crew and a rookie driver from Massachusetts. So that was on my mind; I worried that if we charged to the front and looked really dominant, we'd get a strange pit-road penalty or something like that. I'd seen that kind of thing happen to people, and I wasn't sure "the Establishment" wanted this little team of outsiders leading a bunch of laps.

At one point late in the race Ronnie lost the lead draft and we fell back a bit, but he came on strong toward the end. And once he got back to third, I felt like we had as good a shot as anybody.

I know Ronnie always talked about how he'd picked Buddy Baker's brain about drafting, and that was true; I saw it myself. He talked with Buddy that weekend, and I'm sure he talked with other guys at the first Talladega race and the July race at Daytona. Ronnie was smart that way. And it definitely helped him, because at least on that last lap he knew exactly what he wanted to do.

When they came by for the white flag, he was right with Darrell Waltrip and Terry Labonte. They were single file, with Darrell leading. But when they came back around the last time, Labonte made a move to the outside, and Darrell moved up with him. That's where Ronnie went to the bottom, in the tri-oval, right in front of us. But at Talladega the start/finish line is between the tri-oval and the first turn, past the end of pit road, so we had no idea whether we finished first, second, or third. It looked like he made the right move, but then he was gone, out of sight.

I distinctly remember turning around, looking up at the scoreboard, and seeing our number flash to the top. It didn't happen right away, because I'm sure the officials were looking at replays. But when I saw that #47 flash up there, it was pretty awesome. It was a major deal. I said, "I'll be a sonofabitch!"

Even today, I can't really explain how that felt. I had won lots of Modified races, and with the Cup car we'd run in the top five, and even finished second several times with Gant. But to win at that level—especially the way we won that day, on the last lap—was just so fulfilling.

Most of the guys, and Paula, too, jumped onto the car and rode there along with Ronnie. I walked alongside, and maybe ran a little bit. Every so often I'll see photos of that, and I'll think, "*That* was real racing." By that, I mean just a genuine racing moment. I know people say this all the time, but when the really big money came into the sport, it took away a lot of the fun. Don't get me wrong, it's cool that the guys who work on those cars make good money today, because back then almost nobody did. But today a guy wins a race, and the whole celebration seems scripted, or done just for television. That day at Talladega, we reacted with genuine emotion. It was such an amazing moment for all of us. It was *real*.

Most people don't know this, but we had an issue with the engine after the race, during tech inspection. I'd gone upstairs with Ronnie for the press box interview—something I'd never do, but somebody in victory lane persuaded me to go—and by the time I got back to the garage my guys had pulled the cylinder heads. That's standard procedure; no big deal. But the inspectors, Art Krebs and Joe Gazaway, said, "Bob, this motor is big."

I said, "Bullshit, it's big."

They said, "It's on the large side."

This gets back to what I was saying about us being outsiders. I was thinking, "Here we go."

The maximum engine size was 358 cubic inches. Ours was 357.5, and I knew that, because I had *built* it. When I was with Jack, I built every engine except two; when J.D. Stacy sponsored us in 1982, I was sick with the flu, so we got a couple of engines from one of Stacy's other teams. My point is, I *knew* this motor.

Gazaway said, "You've got a 3.5-inch stroke."

I said, "Don't tell *me* what it is. It's a 3.490. You'd better check it again."

So they did. They went through the whole process of rechecking that engine, and when everything was done they said, "Okay, it's 357.5 cubic inches."

That was that. We were legal. We had won the race.

A little later, Bill France Jr. wandered by. He said, "Bob, you were a little close on that motor."

I said, "Bill, the rule says 358 cubic inches, and I'm 357.5."

He said, "Yeah, but what if you made a small mistake?"

I said, "You can't make any mistakes if you're going to run with these guys." I think he liked that.

The funny thing was, the race after Talladega was Michigan, and, don't you know, Ronnie wins the pole. After qualifying we were pushing the car through the garage, and there was Bill Jr., standing at the back of the NASCAR trailer. He said, "I hope you're not as close on that motor as you were last week!"

I laughed and said, "We're plenty safe."

We yanked the motor out for them to inspect it, and here came Krebs and Gazaway. To check the stroke on an engine you use a dial indicator, but first you have to put one of the pistons at bottom dead center by turning the crank with a breaker bar. Art set the piston at bottom dead center, and after he set the dial indicator both him and Joe turned their heads to look at me. When they did that, one of my guys—George Colwell, who had worked for a lot of Modified guys, and worked with the Pettys for years—bumped that breaker bar, just messing with them. I saw him do it, but they didn't. He didn't bump it much; maybe enough to move the piston 15 or 20 thousandths. Anyway, Art went back to his dial indicator, and ran the piston up. Then he got this strange look on his face.

He looked at Joe Gazaway, and then he looked at me, and said, "How big is this motor?"

I said, "Art, you just checked it. You tell me."

He looked at Joe and said, "This thing checks out at 331 cubic inches!"

Joe Gazaway turned and said, "Bob, how big is this motor?"

I said, "Joe, Art just *told* you!"

Gazaway said, "Check it again."

Well, until then it was funny, because George was just playing around. I knew that motor was legal, but now I was thinking, "Wow, if this thing comes up a different size, they're going to tear it apart trying to figure out what's going on."

So Art gets the piston back to bottom dead center, and sets the dial indicator. He's being real careful. But just as he's about to check it, he and Joe turn toward me, and, sure enough, George nudges that bar again. Now, the odds of him bumping that breaker bar the exact same way twice were about a million to one. But Art runs the piston up, takes his measurement, and I'll be damned if it's not 331 cubic inches *again*.

They said, "Bob, are you really running a 331-inch motor?"

I said, "Yeah, but please, guys, don't tell anybody else!"

They turned and walked right out of that truck. The motor really was a 357.5, but those two guys never knew that.

I'm not sure if people back then realized what an underdog situation we were in with that team. Very few people really understood what we accomplished, and how hard that was. We were racing with so little, against so much. And that's not an excuse for the times we didn't run good. It's just a pure fact.

Just about every race we went to, I rode in the transporter, all the way from Madison. Once in a great while I'd fly, if I had to catch up on work at the shop. But most weeks, when the truck pulled out of the driveway, I was in it. If I had to do all that traveling now, I couldn't. But when you're caught up in it, when you're trying to win, you'll do whatever it takes.

I ended up leaving Race Hill Farm during the '82 season, because I had some personal differences with people behind the scenes. When you're working seven days and 70 hours a week, you get fed up over things that might not have bothered you in ordinary circumstances. So the easiest thing was to just go. I know that caught Ronnie off guard, but I don't think it ever caused any kind of a problem between us, because it had nothing to do with the two of us. I went off and did some NASCAR North racing with Randy LaJoie for a few years, and by the time I went back to Winston Cup racing, Ronnie was just about to get out.

It's nice that people remember me and Ronnie for the big moments we had, like Talladega and all the Modified wins. They stand out in my mind, too. But just being involved with him—*both* times—was pretty big for me. We had so many great days.

BY PAULA BOUCHARD

"*I embraced it all with open arms; I looked at it as a new chapter in our lives*"

A girlfriend, wife, and expectant mother reflects on a time of change

Paula Bouchard is the daughter of the late Modified driver Steady Eddie Flemke, a legend in his own time, and the big sister to Ed Jr., himself a winning driver and noted fabricator. Had she come along a few years later, when female drivers became commonplace, she might have been a racer herself; Daytona 500 winner Pete Hamilton, one of Steady Eddie's protégés, still marvels at the "natural timing" she dis-

BOUCHARD FAMILY COLLECTION

played as a girl when the Flemke gang rode go-karts. Later, Paula raised eyebrows by hot-lapping her dad's and her brother's Modifieds in a period when some old-timers were still getting used to seeing women in the pits. So, like her future husband—Paula and Ron wed in 1983—she'd led a long and much-traveled short-track life before the two of them dove headlong into the very different world of NASCAR Winston Cup racing.

On the morning of that Talladega race, Ronnie found a praying mantis in the hotel room. Well, technically, it really wasn't *our* room. When we got down there for the weekend, it turned out that there weren't enough rooms reserved for the whole team, so Ronnie and I gave up our room, climbed into the hauler, and stayed in the sleeper. In the mornings, when the crew left for the track, we would use one of their rooms to shower and get dressed.

Well, when we walked into the room on Sunday morning, Ronnie saw a praying mantis on the floor. He was going to step on it, but I said, "Don't you kill that praying mantis! Those things are supposed to bring good luck."

So he picked it up gently, brought it outside, and let it go.

And, of course, he won the race.

We knew Ronnie had won even before *he* knew it. We saw the numbers change on the scoreboard, and Ronnie didn't see it until he got around to the backstretch.

The joy was just beyond words. It was euphoria. I remember him coming down pit road with a big smile and reaching out to me. I looked into his eyes, and I just felt so proud, so happy for him. Then I hopped up and sat on the window ledge, and all the guys climbed onto the car, and we rode to victory lane. I still remember everybody pounding, pounding, pounding on the car, and people from other teams stepping out to wave or give a thumbs-up. It was just a happy moment. I had never felt anything like that in my life.

I remember every second of that ride, but I don't remember anything about the actual victory lane ceremonies. You're shoved and you're pushed—stand next to Ronnie for this photo, get out of the next photo—and it's more like a process that you're going through. That was all new to me; Ronnie was used to posing for photos, because he'd been doing it for years, but only once or twice was I ever in any victory lane photos with either Ronnie or my father. But at Talladega, I *wanted* to be in that picture. It was such a big moment.

By the end of the day, when it was just the two of us alone, I think we were both speechless.

It took us almost a week to get home. We stopped at Clyde and Ann Marie McLeod's house in Connecticut, and they had a big party. Then we stopped to see my father, who was as proud as a peacock. My father had basically stopped racing by then, but he got so much happiness out of keeping track of how Ronnie was doing. Anytime I called just to say hello, after a few minutes he'd want to talk with Ronnie to find out the details of the last race.

When we finally got back to Fitchburg, there was a bridge decorated with signs congratulating Ronnie, our house was decorated, and Red & White was decorated.

A couple of nights later there was a big party at what used to be the Thunderbird Motel, right across the street from Red & White. That was a great night, because most people who followed Ronnie's career—not just people from Fitchburg, but from all over New England—weren't able to go to the Winston Cup races. So this was their chance to be part of the celebration.

We did a lot of celebrating that season, because Ronnie also won the Rookie of the Year award. That was something that was decided by a NASCAR committee, and not just by points, so we didn't find out about it right away. The last race on the schedule was at Riverside, California, then Ronnie and I went to Las Vegas to meet up with Clyde and Ann Marie, plus our good friends Max and Terry Smart. That's where we were when we heard that Ronnie had won the rookie award, so we partied a little bit extra.

Then came the banquet in New York City, at the Waldorf Astoria, and there's a good story that goes with that. Because of Ronnie being Rookie of the Year, we'd been given a free room at the Waldorf. We invited Max, Terry, Clyde, and Ann Marie to stay with us, because the rooms there were quite expensive. We took the mattress off the bed and put it on the floor, and then Max grabbed some cushions off the couches in the hallway and put those on the floor, too. It was no different than the way everybody did things when we traveled to the Modified races, because you had to watch what you were spending. But they were not used to that at the Waldorf; we heard one of the housekeepers in the hallway say to her co-worker, "They're all piled up in there!"

Ronnie had to give an acceptance speech, which we had worked on together before we left for New York. We wrote everything on index cards, and he practiced it over and over. The most nervous I ever saw him was just before he had to get up and make that speech, but he did a great job.

In that year, so much had changed for us. We were at Martinsville when Bob Johnson and Jack Beebe called Ronnie about driving their car. They were racing that weekend, too, at Atlanta, and Ronnie said he would talk with them when we all got back to New England.

I know it had to be a huge decision for him. When he was younger he'd really wanted to go Winston Cup racing, but then several years later, when he actually had a chance to do it, he turned it down. He did that for his kids. Ronnie's thinking was that between working for his dad and being very successful with the Modifieds, he was able to take care of his children, but there was always the chance that if he took that offer and things didn't work out, his family would have suffered.

Once that happened, he never talked anymore about Cup racing. I'm sure he realized that those chances usually don't come more than once, but he was okay with that. Ronnie was very strong-willed that way; once he made a decision, he lived with it.

But when the opportunity came around again, he obviously did think about it. A few more years had passed, and the kids were older, and he felt like it was something he had to consider. He went to Connecticut and met with Jack and Bob, and then he came home and talked with his dad. His dad said, "Go ahead, take it. Don't worry about the kids. We're here, and we'll take care of things."

Then he spoke to *my* father, and asked him what he thought. My father said, "Ronnie, you got asked once, you got asked twice. You may not get asked again."

So that was it. Off he went, and off *we* went.

In the beginning, it wasn't any big, wonderful adventure. We rode back and forth to the races with Bob Johnson and Steve Bird and maybe another person or two, all of us in the big truck. They all took turns driving, including Ronnie.

I couldn't always get away in time to go with him. Robbie was living with us, and sometimes I'd take Michelle and Tracey to gymnastics; you know, life doesn't stop just because Dad has a Cup ride. On those weeks I'd get everything figured out at home, then I'd drive to our friend Wally Jackson's house in Connecticut, and he'd bring me to the race shop so I could ride down in the van with Gussie Johnson and the crew.

During the races, I'd stay in the pits and time the car. In those days there were no computers, so I had my stopwatch and my lap chart, and I kept track of exactly when they pitted for gas. At the end of the day, we'd pile back into the truck or the van and head home. And on Monday morning, Ronnie and I would both go to work. Ronnie was still helping his dad at Red & White, and I was doing secretarial work for our friend Jean Michaud's body shop.

So a lot of what I remember about those days is just being worn out. But it was also an exciting time, because things went pretty well right from the start. Qualifying up front at Bristol, in his first race, had to be a nice jolt for Ronnie, a confidence-booster. But, honestly, I don't think he ever doubted that he could do it. He was a very confident person.

For me, going Cup racing was like a lifestyle change. You're very aware that you have to keep up appearances, because there are always sponsors and VIPs there. So you find yourself dressing differently, instead of just wearing whatever you had on, like we did in our Modified days. I remember going to dinner with some sponsors, and they took us to a restaurant where the menu was printed in French. Ronnie was kicking me under the table, as if to say, "How do we order?" Finally we decided that if we just said "steak," the waiter would know what we meant.

But I embraced it all with open arms. I looked at it as a new chapter in our lives. In a lot of ways it made us more rounded, and prepared us for life after racing, because in business you're always meeting new people. In that way, it was a wonderful experience. And we developed some nice relationships, too. We socialized with Ricky and Linda Rudd, and Dale and Teresa Earnhardt, and early on I made friends with Kim Labonte, Marcia Parsons, and a few of the other wives and girlfriends. I also remember Lynda Petty being very, very nice to me.

We had a lot of good days after 1981, and some that weren't so good. I think some of those periods were difficult for Ronnie, because for years he'd been used to winning races. But he never let on publicly that he was disappointed. He would climb out of the car, smile for any reporters or photographers who might be there, and always have a word of encouragement for the guys on the team. That was his way. He always had a positive attitude; Ronnie's cup was half full, not half empty.

But he was a very competitive person, and when he was focused on racing, he was *really* focused. I remember being at a track when I was pregnant with our son, Chad, and on Sunday morning I was crying; during a pregnancy your hormones take over sometimes, and you get very emotional, and you don't even know why. It just happens. Well, Ronnie didn't even ask what was wrong. He just said, "Can you find me something to eat?"

So I did. Our truck didn't always have food on it, so I used to go to Harry Gant's team and ask if I could raid their refrigerator. On this particular day I stopped crying, dried my tears, and went and got him a sandwich. And I never cried again on a race day, because I knew I wasn't going to get any sympathy!

Chad was not even two months old when I took him to his first race, at Dover, with little earplugs and cotton to protect his hearing. Dover wasn't too far, so we might have driven to that race, but sometimes we'd fly because by then NASCAR and Eastern Airlines had an arrangement that let drivers and their families fly at a discount. Ronnie would go early, and I'd fly a day or two later with Chad. That was always interesting, because I'd be walking through Logan Airport in Boston with a baby in one arm and a diaper bag in the other, dragging a suitcase. If the race happened to be at a track where it wasn't practical to bring a baby, I'd drop Chad off with Maggie and George Summers, and go to the airport myself. It's hard to leave your baby, but I knew Chad was in good hands with George and Maggie.

Like I said, a lot changed for us in a very short period of time.

Here's something to think about: In February of 1981, Ronnie and I were going to drive to Florida with Clyde and Ann Marie, like we always did. We were taking our Ford Country Squire wagon, but Ronnie discovered that the frame was cracked. So on our way to Clyde's, we stopped at Max and Terry's house in Monson, Massachusetts, to have Max weld the frame.

Ronnie was driving Lenny Boehler's Modified at New Smyrna every night, but one day we decided we'd go to Daytona to watch Winston Cup practice. Money was tight, like always, so we didn't want to buy four infield tickets. Ronnie and Clyde had two of those old-style pit passes that were used at all the NASCAR tracks, and Ann Marie and I hid in the back of the station wagon with blankets over us. It worked *almost* perfectly. The guys waved their passes at the ticket-takers and drove through the tunnel, but when we got to the other side

Ann Marie and I popped our heads up too soon, and one of the guards saw us. He started yelling for us to stop, but Ronnie pretended he didn't hear him until we got out of sight. Then he stopped the car said, "Hurry up, you two, jump out and run!"

Ann Marie ran one way and I ran the other, and that guard never did find us. So we got away without paying to watch practice for the Daytona 500.

And the next year when we went back there, Ronnie was *in* the Daytona 500!

BY STEVE BIRD

"I can still picture that view, rolling down pit road on the hood of that Buick"

A decorated mechanic recalls some wonderful racing days

STEVE BIRD COLLECTION

With the exception of some Bouchard family members and Pete Salvatore, it's likely that Steve Bird knew Ron Bouchard longer than just about anyone in racing. Both were teenagers when Ron was a rising star in the cutdown division and young Stevie manned the pit gate at the Pines and Hudson tracks, not far from his home in Salem, New Hampshire. Later, Bird spent almost enough time in Fitchburg to qualify as a resident; he was by then turning wrenches for Modified driver Pete Fiandaca, who earned his "Travelin' Man" nickname by hauling everywhere from Maine to Florida. Bird spent more than five years as part of Jack Beebe's Winston Cup team, including Bouchard's tour of duty as driver. Later, as a crew chief in what was then called the NASCAR Busch Series, Steve was a four-time championship crew chief with drivers Rob Moroso, Johnny Benson, and Randy LaJoie.

Here's the thing about Ronnie Bouchard: No matter how things were going on your race team, even if people were arguing and hollering, whenever Ronnie came around he just had a knack for getting everybody in a better mood. That guy, he had a way of putting a smile on your face. I'm proud to have known him as long as I did and as well as I did, and super proud to have won Talladega with him.

I'd seen him a lot when he raced at Pines and Hudson in the '60s, because my father was the pit steward. I was just a kid, but Ronnie wasn't much older. Then he moved on to Seekonk and started winning races and championships, and you knew he was going to be a big star. By then I was helping Pete Fiandaca, and

Peter's house was just a mile or two from Red & White, so we were there quite a bit, borrowing stuff or just seeing what was going on. Then Ronnie started running Bob Johnson's Modified, and he became one of the top drivers in the whole Northeast. Peter and I didn't always race at the same tracks where Bob and Ronnie ran, but I always paid attention to how they were doing. Obviously, I had no idea that we'd all wind up working together on Jack Beebe's team. It's kind of unreal, when you think about it.

I ended up at Race Hill Farm through Johnson. Bob used to build some of Peter's engines, so I'd known him a while, and one day in 1978 I was at his shop. In that period, he wasn't racing his Modified very much; the day I was there, he was building wood stoves. He happened to mention that he'd gotten tied up with Jack, and that they were in the early stages of putting together a Winston Cup team. We talked about that, and Bob told me to let him know if I ever wanted to go to work for him. I said I'd think it over, and then I thanked him and went on my way.

I got down the road a little bit, and I said to myself, "Man, I think I'm going to go Winston Cup racing."

That was an incredible thought to me. From the time I was a kid, all I'd really wanted to do was work on race cars, and with Peter I'd gone just about anywhere you could go with a Modified. But the idea of doing it full-time, for a living, was something I'd only dreamed about.

I called Bob a few days later, and not long after that I started working for him and Jack. I only went to one race when Satch Worley drove the car in '78. Then Jack decided he was going to run the full season in '79, and to me that was another dream come true. Especially pulling into the Cup garage in Daytona for the first time; I'd been to Daytona before, sitting in the grandstands, but now I saw Richard Petty and his team parked over here, and over there was David Pearson and the Wood Brothers, and Junior Johnson's team with Cale Yarborough. Unbelievable. It was unbelievable.

Those first couple of years were tough. First we had Geoff Bodine driving, but he and Bob were like oil and water. They just didn't see eye-to-eye, which was too bad, because they were obviously both very smart. Then we had Harry Gant for a long time, and on top of being a great driver, Harry was a great guy; when he came up to visit the shop, he'd sleep on my couch.

With Harry, we just kept getting better and better. At the same time, I think we were realistic about things. We were still way behind the big teams, and not just in terms of resources. We also had a lot less experience when it came to working with those cars. All the people in the garage, from the Pettys down to J.D.

McDuffie, were nice to us and always gave us straight answers—or at least what sounded like straight answers—but we had a lot of catching up to do. And being based so far away from the Charlotte area made it just about impossible to hire experienced people.

In fact, out of our six or seven full-time workers at the shop, there were only three or four, including Bob and me, who had any real racing experience. The others were local people who thought it might be fun to work on a race team. Fortunately, on the weekend crew we had a handful of guys who'd worked on short-track cars. But it wasn't like it is today, where teams have one set of guys who work on the car, and another set just for pit stops. I changed rear tires, and Johnson himself changed the front tires.

Plus, all the traveling we did really worked against us. If you look at the NASCAR schedule back then, just about every Winston Cup race was in the Southeast, so we were putting in a *lot* of miles, and also a lot of time. Let's say the race was at Atlanta; we'd pull out of Madison at 5:00 p.m.—with five or six people in the hauler—and drive all night, straight through, to get there at 8:00 a.m. for tech inspection. Then, naturally, after we worked all weekend at the track, we had to make that same trip in reverse.

A team based in Charlotte could leave Atlanta after the race and be home in four hours. At that point, we weren't even a third of the way back to Connecticut. Everybody took turns driving, usually in three-hour shifts, and when you weren't driving you'd try to sleep. Just about every Monday morning, we saw the sun come up before we got back to the shop. That takes a toll.

With Gant we finished second or third half a dozen times, and I think we proved to everybody, including ourselves, that we could run with those Southern boys. It's funny, but the first couple of times we finished second, it felt really gratifying, because we knew how far we had come. But then that competitive nature that's in all of us takes over; pretty soon you finish second and you're not satisfied, because you want to win.

Then Harry left just a few races into the 1981 season, which was really disappointing. I remember a bunch of us on the team sitting around, saying, "Geez, who can we get to drive this thing?" And somebody—I don't know if it was me, but it very well could have been—said, "Hey, what about Ron Bouchard?" I didn't know what kind of relationship Bob and Ronnie had, because you're never sure with guys who have worked together in the past. But Bob ended up calling him, and Ronnie came down to the shop a few days later. Jack and Bob and Ronnie took off for a while, and when Bob came back he told us we had a new driver.

When Ronnie qualified third at Bristol, first time out, I'm sure that for the whole team there was a sigh of relief. Changing drivers is always a big deal, especially when you're going with a rookie in the middle of the season, but after that qualifying session it felt like we hadn't skipped a beat. Then he did a really good job in the race until we broke, so again we had that feeling that everything was going to be okay. Ronnie and Bob meshed together like they had never been apart, and Ronnie was such an easygoing guy anyway that he meshed well with the other guys on the team, too.

The next week at North Wilkesboro, we qualified in the top ten again and finished eighth, and that just built everybody's confidence even more. That's important, because it makes the hours in the shop a lot easier. It even makes the traveling easier, because you're just in a better mood. And, you know, in those days Ronnie and Paula rode to the races with us, in that Kenworth hauler, back and forth from Connecticut. There definitely weren't many other Winston Cup drivers traveling to the races that way.

We were qualifying good and racing good, and I felt like every week, the top guys knew we were there. But we were still underdogs. The way I look at it, no matter how good you run, you're an underdog until you win.

So I guess maybe we stopped being underdogs at the Talladega 500.

We were in the mix that whole weekend. We qualified tenth, and all through practice Ronnie ran with the best cars. We knew we were competitive, and in the race he showed that. He kept himself out of trouble, but he was around the leaders all day long.

Still, we wouldn't have had a chance to win that race if it wasn't for Ricky Rudd. The two leaders, Darrell Waltrip and Terry Labonte, had gotten away from everybody with eight or ten laps to go. But Ricky, who'd had some mechanical trouble and was many laps down, drafted with Ronnie and pushed him right up to Darrell and Terry.

We saw Ronnie make his move on the last lap, because it was right in front of the pits. Watching him turn down to the bottom, I thought, "Hey, maybe we've got a shot at this." But the last I saw of him before the three of them drove out of sight, I figured we'd come up maybe a car-length short. And, listen, even if he'd ended up second or third, that still would have been a great day. We'd have been happy.

I thought I heard the announcer say something about Bouchard winning, but I couldn't tell for sure because it's noisy in the pits. I was thinking, "Did I hear that right?" Then I looked at the scoring tower, and there it was. That was a big, big moment for me. Here I am, a kid from New Hampshire who never had any idea that he'd get to go racing at that level, and now I'm working on a team that just won a Winston Cup race.

I remember riding into victory lane on the hood of the car, happy beyond belief. You always hear people talk about "the thrill of victory," and that's exactly what I was feeling. It's indescribable. I can still picture that view, rolling down pit road on the hood of that Buick. We were a small team with a rookie driver, and we had just won Talladega.

After that we went to Michigan and won the pole position, and to me that was another great moment. It was a way of saying to everybody in the garage area, "We're here. We're for real."

We had some really good races in the rest of 1981, and we had some good ones in '82, also. But it was probably hard to see that just by looking at the results, because the competition had gotten tougher. In 1979, when Jack Beebe started Race Hill Farm, there were five or six big teams: the Pettys, Junior Johnson, the Wood Brothers, Bud Moore, DiGard Racing, Harry Ranier's team, and that was about it. But by 1982, J.D. Stacy had cars, Richard Childress was building up his team, Bill Elliott was there with Harry Melling, and let's not forget Harry Gant in the Skoal car. Before, if you did everything right you could possibly run in the top five, and maybe even win, like we did at Talladega. Now it was getting harder just to run in the top ten.

Plus, that was a complicated year. It's hard now for me to remember the exact order things happened in, but at some point Jack decided that it might be a good idea to move the team to Charlotte, so there was some planning going on for that. Jack also hired David Ifft, who had worked with some of those big teams, and I think that made our team better. But it looked like maybe there was some friction between David and Bob, which happens sometimes when you've got two people with their own ideas.

It's okay to have a little bit of friction, because even the best teams have that sometimes. But when you add in all the traveling we were still doing, all those hours on the road, it just makes those situations worse. You're tired, you're in a bad mood, and anytime there's a small problem it becomes a big problem. I look at that situation today, the way we were always worn out, and I wonder how there wasn't *more* friction.

Bob left Jack's team in 1982, and I only stayed until '84, when I left to go to work with David Pearson. But, honestly, almost all of my memories from working on that Race Hill Farm team are good ones. How we did the things we did, I can't really explain, except to say that the adrenaline and the excitement must have kept us going.

I still feel lucky that I was able to do it at all. Like I said earlier, it was a dream come true. I was lucky enough to know Bob Johnson right at a point when he and Jack Beebe were getting that thing going. If it hadn't been for that, I probably would have kept racing for several more years with Pete Fiandaca, and I'm sure we'd have had fun doing it. But I'm glad it happened, glad that I took a shot at it, and glad Ronnie came along. Because I can tell you this: There aren't many race teams that did what we did.

BY RICKY RUDD

"Ron was always the kind of guy you wanted to see in the garage area"

They were fast friends, in every sense of the term

TOM CARR/NE MOTOR SPORTS MUSEUM

Ricky Rudd's extraordinary career began ominously, at a high-banked Virginia kart oval nicknamed the "Blood Bowl." With no kiddie class, the 7-year-old took on tough-guy steelworkers from the Norfolk shipyards. "Good training," he says, for what followed: a national karting title at 14, motocross at 15, stock cars at 18. His first auto race, in March of 1975 at Rockingham, North Carolina, was a NASCAR Cup event, but this was no rich brat. His salvage-yard owner dad had shelved his own racing adventures because, with five kids, groceries took priority over tires. When things improved and Ricky came of age, buying a used Cup car from journeyman Bill Champion, a family friend, seemed a better bargain than campaigning a Late Model Sportsman. Says Ricky, "We just blindly stumbled into the Cup stuff because it was cheaper." Some stumble: It covered 32 years, 906 starts, and 23 wins.

Back in 1981, the Internet didn't exist, so you got all your racing news from reading *National Speed Sport News* and some of the other weekly papers. But unless you ran a lot with a particular series, you probably didn't know too much about it. My career path never took me toward Modifieds, so I didn't know much about Ron Bouchard when he first showed up in the Cup series. I had seen and heard his name, but I knew of him only vaguely.

I was driving for DiGard Racing that season, and it was kind of interesting how that all came together. I had raced with my family's team for several years. In 1980 we built a Monte Carlo, but for some reason we hadn't run it very much.

My wife, Linda, and I had made a temporary move to Kannapolis, North Carolina—about 300 miles south of Chesapeake, Virginia, where we come from—and I took that car with me, because nobody at home wanted anything to do with it. I was determined to run the Monte Carlo in the October race at Charlotte Motor Speedway, almost as a Hail Mary, last-chance attempt to make something good happen for my career. We rented an apartment in Kannapolis for two months, and I started getting that car ready.

There was an open test at Charlotte a week or two before the race, and I turned what I thought were some really decent laps. Harry Hyde was there, watching, and he stopped to talk to me. Whatever situation he'd been in had just fallen apart, so he said, "Hey, I've been looking at your car. It looks pretty good, but I think I can help you with some things. My shop is across the street, and you can bring it over there if you want to."

Harry was a legendary crew chief, and anybody would have wanted that kind of help from a guy like him. But I barely had enough money to go racing with. In fact, Linda had taken a job in the ticket office at the race track.

I told Harry, "I'd really like that, but I just don't have the money to pay anybody."

He said, "Don't worry about that. I've got some guys who aren't working right now, and I need to keep them sharp."

Harry's shop was where the Hendrick Motorsports complex is today. A day or so later, I brought the car there and unloaded it. My brother, A.J., had built the engine, and Harry took it out and ran it on his dyno. He and Randy Dorton, who was relatively unknown at the time but went on to run Rick Hendrick's engine program, made some improvements by changing the carburetor and intake manifold. Meanwhile, I worked on the car with Tommy Johnson and Jimmy Makar. Just like Randy, Jimmy was still very new to racing, but he later became a great crew chief.

Well, we ended up with an amazing car. At that Charlotte race I qualified on the outside pole, stayed on the lead lap all day, and finished fourth. Early on, I had gotten together with somebody and almost knocked a fender off; if not for that, I think we probably had a car capable of winning.

In a perfect world, I would have loved to keep that deal going with Harry Hyde, but I knew I couldn't afford that. I was thinking about all that, and then the very next morning Bill Gardner, who owned DiGard Racing, called to see if I was interested in driving his #88 car in 1981. I said yes, of course.

Our first race together was at Riverside, on the road course. I had never driven on a road course in anything bigger than a go-kart. But we qualified third, led a bunch of laps, and I was going to win that race until the motor blew with just a handful of laps to go. The funny thing was, later on Robert Yates—who was building the engines for DiGard—told me, "I knew it was your first road-course race, and I didn't think we'd be in contention, so I didn't put in a real fresh motor."

It was definitely a big honor to be hired for that DiGard ride, but I got there at the wrong time. If you really look at the history of most race teams, you'll see that as they build, they get good, then they get better, and then they peak. As a driver, you want to catch them on the upside, right before they peak. Well, I caught DiGard Racing *after* the peak. Darrell Waltrip had left to drive for Junior Johnson, and I think that caught the team unexpectedly. The other thing was, with NASCAR downsizing the Winston Cup cars like they did that year, we couldn't use the setups the team had run in previous years, when that #88 car had been so good. We still had Jake Elder as a crew chief, and I was excited about working with him, but after two or three races Jake and Bill Gardner had a big blow-up, so he left.

Ronnie came to the Cup series that spring with Jack Beebe's team, and right from the beginning he was just a real pleasant guy. He always had a smile on his face, and, no matter what kind of day you'd been having, you'd talk to him a while and find yourself laughing about it.

And Paula was such a down-to-earth, grounded girl, a really neat person. I didn't find out until later who her father was; Eddie Flemke was a short-track legend even back then. Anyway, Paula and Linda just hit it off real well. They were both on the quiet side, and they got to be good friends. So they hung around, and they had a little group they would socialize with. Linda and Paula and some of the other wives would get together and shop, and that naturally brought the guys into the picture, and we'd all end up having dinner and things like that.

You know, racing was different back then. There was no such thing as a VIP motor coach lot for drivers at the track; everybody stayed at the nearby hotels and motels. Some of the areas we raced then, there were only two or three hotels in town, so you'd all find yourselves in the same places. And, again, when that happened it just made sense that you'd go to dinner together. It made for good company; Linda and Paula got along good, and so did Ron and I.

On the day he won at Talladega, I had a car that could run up front, but we had some kind of a mechanical issue and lost a lot of laps getting it fixed. But we got it back out there, and I was riding along with the fast cars. There was a little bit of a breakaway group, maybe five cars, and I could run right with them, tagging along at the back of that pack. It made no sense to get up there and race with them, because I was so many laps down; I didn't want to be a factor in anybody else's day, so I just sat back and watched them run. Ron was in that group, along with Darrell Waltrip, Terry Labonte, and a few other guys. In fact, Ron led some laps during the day. Most people today only remember the finish, but he was really having a great run.

Then, late in the race, a couple of the guys in that lead pack fell behind, and eventually Ron did, too. I'm not sure if his car slipped, or whatever, but he lost the draft. The final pit stops had already been made, so this wasn't the time for something to go wrong. But he was falling back; he'd been right there in the thick of things all day, and now Darrell and Terry were alone up front. I could see that without anybody to draft with, Ron was going to end up third, fourth, fifth, or wherever. That still would have been a great result, but not the finish he probably deserved.

He had fallen back about half a straightaway, and that's basically where my car was, too. So I tacked right onto Ron's bumper and just worked the draft, pushing him back toward those guys up front. I'm not sure why I did it, except that the race win was out of the question for me, and I had seen him up there, having the run of his life—at least up to that point—only to fall back. And, you know, I'm sure I had been in that position before myself, hoping somebody might come along to help *me*.

So it all worked out. I got him up to those two guys right at the end, but then I hung back and let the three of them go. Ron was on his own then, and he ended up winning the darn thing. Yes, I pushed him up there and gave him the opportunity, but *he* won the race. I think Darrell and Terry forgot about him; they weren't paying any attention to him because they'd seen him fall back, and all of a sudden he was right back in it.

You know, it was a neat feeling to see Ron win that thing. I never had an opportunity to race against my brother, but I would imagine that it would have been a similar feeling. To be able to see someone who's such a good guy win a race, especially when he's in an underdog situation, was really special. Let's face it, he wasn't somebody most people would have chosen to win that day. But Ronnie, Jack Beebe, and all those guys, they were great people.

I hadn't even won a race myself at that point, and I'd been trying for several years. But there was never that kind of feeling toward Ron where I said, "Hey, what about me?" I'm sure I dealt with a feeling like that earlier in the day, when I had that mechanical problem, because I really think my car was good enough to win, too. So I was frustrated at that moment, yes, but I was over it by the end of the day. I was just happy for Ronnie; I'd have much rather seen a guy like him win than, say, someone like Darrell, who had already won a few dozen races by then.

Ron won the Rookie of the Year award that season, and as I recall we went out on the town after the banquet ended. It seems to me that we visited some Irish pub, maybe me and Linda, Ron and Paula and some of their friends, and Mike Joy. And we might have hit a few clubs that night, too, but we've made a few trips to New York over the years and it's difficult to remember exactly when all that stuff happened.

It's hard for me to say exactly what happened with Ronnie and Jack Beebe's team after that season. I moved over to drive for Richard Childress in 1982 and '83, and then I went with Bud Moore for four years. You get so caught up in your own world, and I'm not sure I realized at the time that Ron's team had sort of faded a bit. You're so busy trying to be sure that you're making the right choices for yourself that it's hard to know what's happening elsewhere.

But it's like I said earlier: All these teams are going to have their good years and their bad years. And, you know, it's usually all about people. So much depends on who's working on the cars, and who's going in and out the door. It seemed like at that time, people didn't sit real still at one race team as long as they do today. So maybe that was part of what went on with his team, but I don't know. Ron never asked any advice from me; he was smart enough that he didn't need *my* advice.

The sad thing about racing is that you get so caught up in the week-to-week stuff that you don't always notice people coming and going. I raced Cup cars for 32 seasons, and when I look back sometimes it's like, "Man, where did all those years go?" You end up with tunnel vision, looking only at your own program, and one day you look around and some of your buddies are gone.

The sport can be cruel that way. That's why I was always careful not to get too close to too many people. Because if you let yourself do that, eventually you look up and say. "Wow, when did *he* leave?" That's kind of how it was when Ronnie quit.

I still saw him when he did come to races, especially at New Hampshire and Daytona. Anytime he came through the garage, he'd stop and talk. Of course, he had a lot of other friends there, too, but we'd always spend at least some time together. We'd always talk about getting together—about Linda and me going up to visit them, or him and Paula coming down to see us—but we never quite got that put together. You know how it is: People get busy with everyday things. Ronnie got busy with one car dealership and then another, and I'm sure Paula got busy with their son, Chad, and watching him grow up. But we would always exchange Christmas cards, family photos, and things like that.

What I remember most about Ron is that he was always the kind of guy you wanted to see in the garage area. If you got there in the morning, and on the way to your car or your hauler you only had time to talk to two or three people, you'd put Ron in that category.

It's like Linda says: You always picture him smiling. That's just the way he was.

BY DAVID IFFT

"I'd be mad enough to throw things, but Ronnie would always calm me down"

A winning NASCAR crew chief recalls a driver and a friend

David Ifft was one of the top NASCAR Winston Cup crew chiefs of the 1970s and '80s. Born in Youngstown, Ohio, to a family of 12 kids, David inherited his mechanical ability from his father, who kept food on the table by working in a local steel mill and moonlighting as a welder for legendary open-wheel car builder Floyd Trevis. David eventually built race cars himself and even briefly tried driving, "but I knew how much work went into building those things, and I just couldn't tear 'em up." Having read magazine stories about "all the big-time NASCAR shops in the South," he gunned his 1965 Buick down the West Virginia Turnpike and went job-hunting, ultimately hiring on with Bud Moore. Later, as a crew chief, Ifft won with Darrell Waltrip, Benny Parsons, and Cale Yarborough before pairing with Ron Bouchard on Jack Beebe's Race Hill Farm team.

BRYANT MCMURRAY

Ronnie was the kind of driver who, as long as you got him close, he'd make up the difference. He reminded me of Cale Yarborough; Cale couldn't tell you if a car was pushing or loose, but if that thing was in the ballpark, he'd take it from there. Ronnie was a lot better about describing what the car was doing, but he'd be the first to tell you he wasn't a chassis man. But get him in something that was halfway decent, and he'd get you the rest of the way.

The first time I really learned anything about him was at Bristol, when he got into Jack Beebe's car. I'd seen the Modifieds at Martinsville, so I was familiar with the top names—Bugsy, Evans, Bodine, Ronnie—but I was always too wrapped up in my own deal to pay close attention. At Bristol I was looking at the time sheet after qualifying, and in third place I saw his name.

I knew Jack had good cars and that Bob Johnson must have known his stuff, because I'd seen Harry Gant run well with that #47. Harry was there driving another car, so I said, "Harry, how about this rookie starting third? Is he going to do anything crazy?"

And Harry, who had run with Ronnie in Modifieds, said, "No, you don't have to worry about him. He's a good racer."

Harry was right.

The weekend Ronnie won at Talladega, I was working with Cale Yarborough, who was driving for M.C. Anderson. There was another practice left to run, but we'd already parked our car. If the car was right, Cale would say, "Cover it up. I'm going to the motel." I was leaning against the car, and along came Ronnie. I don't think we'd ever even said hello before. He told me his car was wandering in the turns, so I asked about his front-end settings. He said I should come over and talk with Bob. Well, there's a thing about crew chiefs: You don't ever want to step on somebody else's toes, because you don't want them stepping on yours. But Ronnie said, "No, no, come on over. It'll be okay."

I talked with Bob, and he was very friendly. They were fast, but the car wasn't just right. So I had Pete Peterson, who worked with me, bring over our toe plates, and we helped Bob make some adjustments. Ronnie ran the last practice, and he liked the car better now, so he walked over and thanked us. We said it was no big deal, and it wasn't.

On Sunday Cale fell out early, so me and Pete jumped in our car and started home. We were listening to the race on the radio, and, of course, Ronnie passed Waltrip and Labonte right at the end. I remember Pete saying, "That sonofabitch *won*."

Later, after we got to be good friends, I asked Ronnie, "What made you come talk to me that weekend?"

He said, "I saw Cale Yarborough's crew chief standing there, and I said, 'He's got to know *something*.'"

That was Ronnie. He always knew who to talk to, just like he talked with Buddy Baker that same weekend about how to work the draft. After that we would talk, and I really liked the guy. We had an instant connection.

The next year M.C. Anderson was getting out of racing, so I took a break for a while. I played golf every day, had a drink any time I wanted to, and lived like a normal person. In that time, Jack Beebe called me several times, and Ronnie called me, and finally my wife said, "Either tell those people to stop calling you, or go to work for them."

I said, "You know they race out of *Connecticut*, don't you?"

I ended up going there for a week and helping them, and then I went back a couple more times, but my wife was not big on all that back-and-forth stuff. Jack said he'd move me up there, so my wife and I talked it over, and that's what we did. In fact, Ronnie came down with one of his dad's moving trucks and hauled our stuff to Connecticut, to an old farmhouse I believe Jack owned.

We stayed there just a few months. Bob Johnson had left, and I was getting ready to leave, too. My wife was not happy living so far away, and I wasn't, either. I liked working with Ronnie, and I told Jack, "If you guys ever move the team down South, I'd love to work for you, but I can't do this anymore."

Jack said, "Let's find a building."

And he did. He had a realtor who found an old carpet warehouse near the Charlotte airport. Jack flew down, we looked at it, and he bought it. And in that winter of 1982–83, we moved the team down there.

We had a good group of guys at that point. Steve Bird was there, and so was Vic Kangas, and Cheech Garde had come down from Connecticut, and I had Jim Murray—who everybody knew as "Two-Can"—and some other guys from this area. But early in '83, we had a lot going on. The move had put us behind, and I was still getting used to Ronnie. When you work with a new driver, it takes time to figure out what he's telling you. I'd had a lot of success with Benny Parsons, but only after I learned to listen to the way he said things. We got to where all Benny had to tell me was that the car was loose, and I knew just *how* loose by the sound of his voice.

I started learning Ronnie that way, too. First I had to get used to his accent. If he said we had "the wrong *bah* in the *cah*," I knew I needed to change the sway bar. But we figured each other out.

What also complicated things for us was that the technology was changing on those Cup cars. NASCAR had downsized the cars in 1981, and things were still evolving. I was always the type of guy who wasn't afraid to build a new car, or to saw off a snout and build a new one. But it was difficult to talk Jack into that mindset, simply because he wasn't a race car guy. Engines were something he could understand, but it was hard to convince him that you sometimes needed new cars.

We skipped the June race at Riverside, California, just to play catch up. Sometimes, a team needs a break. And I think it helped us, because right away we finished fourth in the Firecracker 400 at Daytona and sat on the pole at Nashville.

Racing is all about people anyway, and as the people at that team got smarter, the cars got faster. Don't forget, some of those guys were only in their second or third year of racing these big, 3,400-pound stock cars. A lot of them had grown up around Modifieds, so with these Cup cars they were learning something new. By 1983 and '84, they were at the point where all of them—Birdie, Cheech, Vic, the whole gang—had really gotten used to the bigger cars.

In a way, it was the same with Ronnie. I didn't always like it when, on a weekend off, he'd run two or three Modified races. I'm sure that as a driver that was fun, because he was winning with Lenny Boehler. But whenever he came back, he'd jump in that heavy Cup car and say, "David, this thing won't turn," or, "This car feels lazy coming off the corner."

I'd tell him, "Ronnie, you've got a thousand pounds more weight and a lot less tire than you had last week with that Modified!"

Both Jack and I urged him to get away from doing that, and eventually he did. I really think that helped him get even better in the Cup car, because now it was his only reference.

Although, now that I think of it, along the way Ronnie decided he wanted to run some of the bigger Busch Series races, and he convinced John Dufour, a good friend of Jack Beebe, that owning one of those cars would be really fun. They had Mike Laughlin build them one, and Vic Kangas finished it up, with some last-minute help from Boehler.

That thing was faster than hell. Ronnie sat on a few poles and ended up winning twice at Darlington, and he led just about every race he ran in that car. We had 'em all at Charlotte until the engine broke; he led 102 laps, and he was out front when it blew up. That was when the Busch Series ran V-6 engines, and we were doing a lot of development work for Buick. Naturally, when you're developing a new engine, all kinds of things can happen. At Dover that thing blew up so bad that we couldn't even find the starter!

I remember John Dufour saying, "They told me this was going to be *fun*. I've never worked this hard in my life."

But we did have fun. Ronnie and I were getting closer as friends, and also as driver and crew chief. His feedback just got better and better. In 1983 and the first part of '84, we had good speed in that Cup car; aside from that pole at Nashville, we had a bunch of other top-ten qualifying runs.

I'm probably too hard on myself sometimes, but I believe I cost us a couple of possible wins. At Bristol, Bobby Allison was leading, and Ronnie was running second. Bobby was flying; we were the only car on the same lap. I convinced myself that the only shot we had was to get fresh tires whenever Bobby did. I saw him come down pit road, and I hollered to Ronnie, "Pit now." Well, it turned out something was wrong with Bobby's car, and he pulled behind the pit wall. By that time Ronnie was already on pit road, so we went ahead and changed tires.

That would have been fine, except as soon as we were done pitting, the caution came out. Now instead of being on a lap of our own, we were back in the same lap with a bunch of other guys. We ended up third, as I recall.

The other thing that hurt us was that I about killed myself in a car crash coming back from Dover in September of '83. I woke up in a hospital in Emporia, Virginia, then got moved to Richmond, but I had terrible neck pain. I ended up signing myself out of there and having my wife drive me to Charlotte, where they discovered that I had a broken neck. They wanted to put me in one of those halo deals, with the screws going into my skull, but I said, "Not me." Instead they put me in a device with straps that went under my arm and a big collar that held my chin absolutely still.

As soon as I was up and around, I went to the shop every day, even with that brace on. I couldn't do any physical work, but I could make sure we were on schedule with things. I was always a good organizer, and I was still able to do that.

Plus, I felt like the team needed me. We were shorthanded, because, let's face it, Jack wasn't operating with the budget the bigger teams had. And some of the guys still had homes and families back in New England, so every so often they'd have to go back there for a day or two. A guy would tell you on Sunday night, "Hey, I'll be back Wednesday." Well, we'd have to leave for the next race on *Thursday*. It was just a struggle.

In 1984, we started off strong. In the first dozen races we had four top-five finishes, and we were in the top ten in the points. I felt like we were finally on top of things. Ronnie was doing a great job, the team was getting better, and we had a good engine program. We were knocking on the door.

Then we had four straight races where we had trouble—Riverside, Pocono, Michigan, Daytona—and it was like everything had gone the other way again. We were back to struggling.

You think you're ready to hit a home run, but every time you hit a long drive it goes foul. It was the same here: problems on pit stops, or silly things going wrong with the cars. And I just didn't see it turning around.

I was burned out, and worn down. I hadn't given myself enough time to heal up from being hurt, so I wasn't feeling good, and when you're frustrated on top of not feeling good, it's miserable. I told Jack and Ronnie that I was leaving. I promised Jack I'd get the car ready for the next race, which was at Nashville, and I did. And then I left.

But Ronnie and I stayed friends. Long after he retired, we'd still call each other once a month. When I was his crew chief, he had a way of keeping me cool.

There were times when I'd be mad enough to throw things, but he'd always calm me down. I knew he had my back, and I had his, and you don't forget that.

As a driver, he was right there with the best of 'em. Think about those Busch races: Whether he was at Darlington, Charlotte, or Daytona, Ronnie showed he could run with Darrell, Bobby, Earnhardt, all the guys who were winning Cup races.

And as a person, he was as nice a guy as anyone I ever worked with. He *cared* about you. He was like Benny Parsons that way; you wanted to do more for them just because of the way they were.

You don't get close with every driver. With Ronnie I did.

BY TRACEY BOUCHARD DiNARDO

"It was much harder to watch on television than to be there in person"

A lifestyle change: From speedway grandstands to sofa cushions

BOUCHARD FAMILY COLLECTION

Born in 1970, Tracey Bouchard DiNardo is the youngest of Ron's children from his first marriage, but she was old enough to appreciate the dynamic changes to his career in the '80s. The decade began with his kids cheering him on at tracks like Westboro Speedway—"There's a shopping mall there now," she says, "and whenever I go by, I look over and think of all the fun we used to have"—but within just a few years, watching Dad race meant gathering around the television. Long after his retirement, she'd still catch the NASCAR Cup events on Sunday-afternoon visits with her father. Today, between husband Al, son Anthony, and her physical-therapy job, Tracey has less time for racing. "But when I had Dad or my uncle Kenny to watch, or Dale [Earnhardt], because he was a friend of my father's, I wouldn't miss a lap."

When my dad left to go Winston Cup racing, I was 10 years old, almost 11. I was happy, and proud, and also relieved. Even at that age, I knew he'd had the chance to do that previously but chose not to take it, because he had a lot going on here in Fitchburg. I was excited for him to be able to realize a dream he had probably given up on.

Let's face it, that was the pinnacle of racing, and we were all so excited for him to get there.

We got to go to some of the Cup races, but not many, because you had to be gone so long and we were still in school. I do remember going to the closer tracks like Pocono and Dover, and we went to Daytona in February and also in July, when we were out of school for the summer. I remember Paula keeping after Michelle and me to put on the sunscreen, but, being kids, we knew better. We slathered on the oil instead. Big mistake. We got sunburned.

When we couldn't go with him on the weekends, we still made our way to the Modified tracks, because Kenny was doing very well. But as we grew up, I played basketball and other sports, and it just seemed like different things started filling up my time.

In a way, though, my father's racing was still the biggest part of our weekends. There was no Internet back then, and no cell phones for texting, so we had to wait for the telephone call to find out how he qualified. If he was starting on the front row, or even in the top ten, that got us all pumped up. Then on Sundays we'd sit and wait for the race to come on television, just like we sat and waited for the feature in the old days at Seekonk or Stafford. The only difference was that instead of being at the track, we were at Nana's house, with our snacks and our drinks.

The highs and lows were the same: If he was running good, we'd sit there cheering him on; if a motor blew or somebody put him in the wall, we were all dejected.

I have to say, it was much harder to watch on television than to be there in person. When you're at the track you can follow *your* driver through the whole race. On TV they focus on the leader or any interesting battle, and anytime my father wasn't on the screen I felt lost. I wanted to know more about how he was doing.

I probably didn't realize at the time how big a difference it was in our weekly routine, not going to the races all the time. But when I look back on it now, it was a major change. It's almost like it was a loss; something fun and exciting had gone out of our lives. We didn't see a lot of our friends nearly as much as we had, and there was no longer that excitement every Friday about starting another weekend of watching my father race.

It never felt like any kind of earth-shattering difference, but it was, because that had been our whole lives until then. Honestly, as young as it's possible to have memories, that's how far back I can remember him being a race car driver. I remember seeing his helmet bag on the floor at home, and things like that. And all of us kids started going to the tracks when we were very young, which I'm thankful for now, because we had that time with him.

I guess I just figured that racing was what people did on the weekends, because that's all we ever knew. We were either riding to the track with him, or riding with

(Right) In his Winston Cup tenure, Bouchard fit right in with the hot dogs, in this case Cale Yarborough. (Howie Hodge)

(Below) The biggest day in the racing lives of three men: From left to right, crew chief Bob Johnson, 1981 Talladega 500 winner Ron Bouchard, and team owner Jack Beebe. (Bryant McMurray)

(Above) Good friends, all dressed up at the 1981 NASCAR banquet. Standing, left to right: Max and Terry Smart, George Summers, Ron Bouchard, Clyde McLeod; seated, left to right: Maggie Summers, Paula Flemke, Ann Marie McLeod. (McLeod Collection)

(Above) Back in New England for a 1983 Modified race, Ron joins "Nana," sister JoAnn, and brother Ken. (Paul Bonneau)

(Right) Crew chief David Ifft, at left, confers with Beebe and Bouchard in 1983. (Val LeSieur Collection)

(Left) Bouchard and Geoff Bodine thrilled a 1983 Thompson crowd with a match-race demonstration aboard Winston Cup cars. (Paul Bonneau/Val LeSieur Collection)

(Right and below) It's hard to believe today, but a mid-'80s New England Pro Stock series co-promoted by Bouchard lured several Winston Cup legends, among them Buddy Baker and Richard Petty, shown with Ronnie at Hudson Speedway in 1984. (Russ Conway Collection; Val LeSieur Collection)

(Right) This Busch Series machine led often, won twice (both times at Darlington) and indirectly got Bouchard into the new-car business. (Val LeSieur Collection)

(Below) A 1986 Winston Cup gig with Curb Racing offered much promise, but within a handful of races the team was in disarray. (Rick Nelson/Val LeSieur Collection)

Last ride: Although he finished a fighting eighth at Darlington, a frustrated Bouchard left Hoss Ellington's team after just five races in 1987. His driving career was over. (J&H/Val LeSieur Collection)

(Left) Wheeling and dealing, Bouchard founded a solid used-car business while still very active as a Winston Cup racer. (Bouchard Family Collection)

(Middle) The Honda Store, Ron's introduction to the new-car game, opened in Fitchburg in 1986. (Bouchard Family Collection)

(Bottom) Today, this sparkling Nissan dealership is just a piece of the multi-brand Ron Bouchard's Auto Stores universe. (Bouchard Family Collection)

(Right) 1998: The inaugural class of the NEAR Hall of Fame. Top row: Bill Slater, Tara Evans (for father Richie Evans), Ed Flemke Jr. and Paula Bouchard (for father Ed Flemke), Gene Bergin, Ron Bouchard, Harvey Tattersall III. Bottom row: Bugs Stevens, Ernie Gahan, Rene Charland, Florence Tattersall (for father Harvey Tattersall Jr.), Pete Hamilton. (North East Motor Sports Museum)

(Middle) Full circle: Ron and Ken Bouchard flank father Bob, as Pete Salvatore tries on a modern Modified painted in his honor. (Bouchard Family Collection)

(Bottom) Who kept score? This golfing foursome included ex-Fitchburg police chief Charlie Tasca, obvious ringer Chad Bouchard, George Summers, and Ron Bouchard (Summers Family Collection).

September 24, 2015: Bob and Gussie Johnson were among those joining Ron and Paula Bouchard at the opening of the RB Racing Museum. Built on the Fitchburg site where the Bouchard family's racing history began, the museum showcases significant cars, trophies, and memorabilia from Ronnie's career, as well as celebrating other area drivers. (Dick Berggren)

A life well lived. Ron Bouchard strolls the links, that winning smile undimmed. (Summers Family Collection)

other people to get to whatever track he was at. Little by little, I started to realize that my friends had other activities, but I'm not sure if most of them had any idea what we were doing, because racing just wasn't as big as it became later on.

I did have a few close friends who wanted to come and see what it was all about, and then—just like you'd expect—once they came, they wanted to come again. They'd say, "Are you bringing us? Can we come this weekend?"

But it was hard to really plan things with people, because racing was mostly something we did as a family. Plus, you always had to be ready for a last-minute change, like a rainout or even a rain delay. A lot of my friends had church on Sunday morning, so if the races ran very late on Saturday night and you didn't get home until some crazy hour, that was no good. And, of course, Sundays for us meant Thompson Speedway or sometimes Monadnock. For us, that *was* church, meaning something you did with your family, something you just couldn't miss.

I think people who aren't into racing can't understand that everything else in life tends to get scheduled around whatever's happening at the track. They say, "Wow, racing, that's a dysfunctional way of growing up."

I tell them, "No, it was the best way to grow up."

I loved going to the races. *Loved* it. The worst thing in the world was to not be able to go, for whatever reason. In fact, that happened to me once, and I still haven't gotten over it.

My father only had a couple of rules for how we were supposed to behave at the track, but they were very strict rules. First, Paula, Nana, or JoAnn needed to know where we were at all times, and who we were with. Second, he told us, "Don't ever, ever, go outside the fence," out into the parking lot. Well, one night at Stafford I really wanted to see Kenny. My father's teams were always parked on the side of the pit area that was closest to the grandstands, so I could see him anytime I wanted to, and even talk with him. But on this night the team Kenny was driving for was parked on the opposite side, and the only way to get close to his car was to go out in the parking lot and walk *around* the entire pit area. I figured I wasn't doing anything wrong, because I was only going to see my uncle. Well, somebody saw me out there, and word got back to my father. I realize now that whoever told him wasn't trying to cause trouble; they just understood that he wouldn't have wanted me out in the parking lot.

My punishment was that the very next week, I was not allowed to go to any races. I can remember standing in the window as they drove away, screaming, "No! Don't leave me behind!" That's the truth; I was crying and screaming. I could not wait for that weekend to be over. But I can promise you this: I never went outside that fence again!

I liked the Saturday and Sunday races, because then we could ride with my father. On Fridays we were still in school when he left for Stafford, so we rode with Nana and JoAnn. Going with my grandmother and my aunt was nice, and God knows they took us everywhere. But, naturally, we loved riding with our dad. That also meant we spent a lot of time with Paula, because when we got to the track and he went into the pits, she was the one responsible for dragging all these kids around. I used to tell her and my father that they should have written a book on how to raise children, because we were always taken care of, no matter what.

Those were the best of times, they really were. I loved everything about those days.

Obviously, I was proud of the fact that my father was a great driver. It was easy being proud when we'd watch him win a race. But as I got older, I started to see the sides of him that I'm even more proud of. Then there came a time when he showed that he was a great brother, too, because I watched him stick up for Kenny whenever something happened. I could also see that he was a great partner to Paula. And he was a great dad, even at the track, and today I'm so proud of the fact that he always made sure we were *involved*. His family was part of his racing, because that was the way he wanted it. Even back then I could see that, and I knew how lucky we were.

You know what I remember? After the races, there was always a crowd of people around him, and as a child in that situation you could almost feel left out. But my father had a way of reaching out and putting a hand on your shoulder, even as he was talking with those other people, almost as a way of reassuring us kids that he was right there for us. And he did that for the rest of his life, that *touch*.

You hear sometimes about athletes—not just in racing, but in all sports—treating people badly. That wasn't my dad. He always believed that the people, the fans, made everything possible. I can't ever remember a night when he said, "Sorry, I don't have time," and left somebody standing there. I think he understood that if some little kid came up looking for an autograph, that kid had no way of knowing whether my father was having a good weekend or a bad weekend. And that little kid wouldn't have known it when he walked away with that autograph, either, because even if my father *was* having a bad weekend, he would have kept it to himself.

Even years after he retired, anytime somebody recognized him somewhere, he would oblige them with that big smile and chat with them for a minute. He was just that type of guy. He knew it was important to those people, so it was important to him.

When I think today about some of his biggest moments—not just Talladega, but also the pole positions and the Busch Series wins—I just remember being so full of pride. It's funny now, but when it comes to Talladega that pride was mixed with anger, because the television picture went out, so we didn't get to *see* him win. I remember everything about that day; I can still see the color of Nana's living-room carpet and where each of us was sitting. My father was getting closer and closer to the leaders, so we were on the edges of our seats. And then, all of a sudden, the picture was just ... *gone*.

We could still hear the sound, so I remember the announcers talking about this three-wide finish, and how it looked like my father might have won it. Then they talked about looking at the replay, and Ken Squier said, "Yes indeed, give it to Ron Bouchard of Fitchburg, Massachusetts."

I remember the screaming, and stuff being thrown around, and everybody hugging and crying and jumping around the room. Then, within seconds, the phone started ringing. It seemed like everybody in the whole world was calling Nana's house. And when my father and Paula finally called, everybody there was like, "Let me talk," and "Okay, my turn."

Some of my friends who never understood racing before started to understand it after that, because his Talladega win was in all the newspapers, and there was a big celebration in Fitchburg. Later he had all kinds of requests to come and talk to school groups, and he did a lot of that stuff. As a matter of fact, a new school year started just a couple of weeks after he won that race, and I can remember seeing his #47 car get rolled into the auditorium at St. Bernard's school for an assembly. I was in seventh or eighth grade, sitting there listening to my dad talk to all the kids. I'm sure I was absolutely beaming. I was so, so proud of him in that moment.

You know, when you're that age you always hear kids say, "Well, my dad owns *this*," or, "My dad is the president of *that*." I'd always say, "Well, my dad drives race cars, and he wins a lot." I don't think any of them really got it until that day, when the whole school was in that auditorium, listening to him speak.

I know it was hard for him sometimes, racing in the Cup series and struggling. I think anyone who watched my father's whole career knows he was a lot better than his Winston Cup results say he was. It's just that there were only a handful of teams that won most of the races in that period. In my mind he deserved to be in one of those cars, but there were other great drivers who had been there a long time and were locked in with those teams, and that's just the way it was.

Still, it was really something to see how big he had become in the racing world, especially around here. I don't mean that to sound boastful, because my dad was never boastful at all. But when he passed, some acquaintances of mine who saw all the newspaper stories and news reports said, "Gee, we never knew all this about your father, and how accomplished he was in racing. You never told us any of that."

Well, I just never really felt a need to talk about him that way. To me, he was more than Ron Bouchard, race driver. He was Daddy.

BY RUSS CONWAY

"Earnhardt didn't jump into that Pro Stock just to race in New England"

Spectacular promotions, with some help from a friend

HARTFORD/NE MOTOR SPORTS MUSEUM

In the Northeast, Russ Conway is regarded as one of the most creative promotional minds ever to walk through the gates of a short track. For years, he and Ken Smith ran the rollicking New England Super Modified Racing Association (NESMRA), which blew past the confines of its own name to stage races from Florida to Nova Scotia. They also launched the annual autumn event that morphed into Thompson Speedway's popular World Series, had a long tenure steering the weekly program at New Hampshire's Star Speedway, helped Charlie Elliott give new life to what is now Lee USA Speedway, and operated homey Hudson Speedway, scene of some of Ron Bouchard's earliest victories. But Conway's most audacious idea was the mid-'80s Budweiser Showdown of Champions, which, with a little help from Bouchard, brought several of NASCAR's brightest Winston Cup stars to tracks in New Hampshire and Connecticut..

R onnie knew his place in racing, his role, and he had a personality perfect for that role. He felt as though it was the fans who ultimately paid the bills, and he always made time for them. He was what I would call a perfect "fan's driver," because he gave them what they wanted, on the track and off it.

The Showdown of Champions thing started because Ronnie had shown that he was willing to compete in short-track events when he wasn't busy with his Cup schedule. He had run a bunch of races with Lenny Boehler's Modified, and won several of them. He had run a match race at Thompson with Bobby Allison, both of them in their Winston Cup cars, and that went pretty well.

Big League, Big Times   177

My outlook as a promoter was always: How can we top the other guy? Ken Smith, Charlie Elliott, and I were operating Hudson Speedway, and we were open to trying things. Ronnie and I got talking at Daytona in February of 1983. He had run at Hudson when he was 16 years old, so he had some history there, and I'd known him since the '60s. I said, "Why don't you come up this summer? Pick a date that works, and we'll make it worth your while."

Ronnie said, "Yeah, I can do that."

Almost as an afterthought, I added, "And maybe, if we can afford it, we'll bring in another Cup driver, and have the two of you run with our Pro Stocks."

We talked several times after that. Ronnie mentioned that he and Buddy Baker had become good friends, and that he thought he could get him. Buddy was running a limited schedule for the Wood Brothers, which was helpful, because that opened up more possibilities. So Ronnie started putting things together with Baker, who liked the idea. We got a date sorted out, I recruited sponsorship from Anheuser-Busch, and we organized what was called the Budweiser Showdown of Champions. We did a lot old-fashioned promoting: I hung posters anywhere I could, handed out flyers at every track I could get to, and things like that.

We lined up Fran Colson's Pro Stock for Ronnie, which was perfect because Fran was winning races and they knew each other. The Colson crew repainted their car yellow and white and put a blue #47 on it, so it matched the color scheme of Ronnie's Race Hill Farm car. But we had a major problem with Baker; he was six and a half feet tall, so we had to find a car he could fit in. When I talked to Buddy on the phone, he said, "It's simple. Just find me the best car driven by the biggest guy."

It was Ronnie who suggested Mike Murphy. Mike wasn't as tall as Baker, but he was a big, strong guy. Murphy's crew made some changes inside the car—shortened the steering post, moved a few things around—and we hoped for the best.

Baker did us a big favor by winning the Firecracker 400 at Daytona a week or two before our race. Buddy was a popular guy, but prior to the Firecracker he hadn't won in three years, so suddenly he was hotter than he'd been in quite a while.

Race night comes around, and we get a great crowd. Baker climbs into the car, and he basically fits, but it's tight. He goes out for warm-ups, and right away he's turning some pretty good laps. He pulls into the pits, and I notice that his head is cocked a little bit sideways. Ronnie and I lean into the car to talk to him.

Bouchard says, "What do you think, Buddy?"

Baker says, "The car feels good, but my eyes hurt."

Right then, I realize that the reason his head is tilted is that his helmet is right against the roof. He'd been out there hot-lapping like that! Between the vibrations of the car and the fact that he was looking at the track sideways, no wonder his eyes bothered him. So the Murphy clan goes to work with a rubber hammer, banging the roof from the inside, and they get Baker a little more headroom.

We had twin 25-lap features for the Pro Stocks. As I recall, Paul Richardson and Pete Fiandaca were the winners. Bouchard and Baker both put on a good show, and, all in all, it was a very successful night.

Afterwards, we all ended up at a Pizza Hut. Everyone was in a good mood, and we started talking about how we could top this the next year. Somebody said, "We'll get Richard Petty!" That was a joke, because rarely had Petty ever run anything but a Cup car. He just didn't do any extra races. But Bouchard said, "Maybe Buddy and I can talk to him." Buddy had driven for the Pettys, so he and Richard were friendly. We went home thinking that Petty was very unlikely, but he was certainly on our minds. I started thinking that if we *could* get Petty, maybe we'd have two dates. Right away I thought of Don Hoenig at Thompson, because Ken Smith and I had a great relationship with Donald. But all of this, of course, would depend on getting Petty.

Well, in November of '83, I went to the Cup race at Atlanta. It never hurts to be optimistic, so I had contracts in hand, hoping to somehow get Richard on board. Ronnie had mentioned this thing to Richard, but only briefly. On Friday, Bouchard, Baker, and I had breakfast. I asked Baker if he'd had a chance to feel out Richard, and he said, "Not much. I've been busy, and he's been busy ..."

Saturday we had breakfast again, and Buddy says, "Well, I really haven't had time to get together with Richard."

Sunday rolls around, and Baker still hasn't talked with him. I go to Petty's hauler, with my contract in a big manila envelope. George Colwell, who was working for Petty Enterprises by then, says, "You just missed him. He's over at the chapel service."

I'm not going to leave Atlanta without some idea where we stand with Petty. So I walk over to where they're holding the chapel service, wiggle my way through the crowd, and stand *right next* to Richard. He sees me, and he sees this envelope under my arm. When the service ends, he says, "This must be awful important for you to come see me at church."

I start telling him about our races, and he says, "Oh, I'm coming. Ronnie talked to me, and Buddy said he had a good time last year, and I'm sure my wife would like to visit that area."

I tell him, "Well, I've got this contract …"

He says, "I'll give you *my* contract." He sticks out his right paw, and we shake hands.

I say, "Richard, wait. What do we pay you?"

He says, "If we do good, we'll *all* do good. If we don't do good, *none* of us will do any good. But we've got a deal."

I was as happy as I could be. Think about it: Richard Petty doesn't do these things, but he's coming to Hudson Speedway. We made a deal with Don Hoenig, so now the second annual Budweiser Showdown of Champions would be Sunday evening at Hudson, followed by Tuesday night at Thompson.

We also did something else: Ken and I made Bouchard a partner in the Showdown of Champions. That was a great move, because Ronnie was instrumental in everything that followed. For example, in February of 1984 he lined up Steve Byrnes—who was still fairly new to TV—to tape some interviews we could use in the days leading up to the Showdown. Steve did separate interviews with Bouchard, Baker, and Petty, with all of them talking as if the event was happening that very week. Then all three teams lined up their Cup cars so we could take a publicity photo with the word "Daytona" on the wall behind them.

Ronnie made that all happen. He was a people person, and that was just what we needed. He said to me in the beginning, "Look, I don't know about advertising, ticket prices, or anything like that. You guys handle that, and I'll make sure Richard and Buddy are happy, and we'll work together just fine, win, lose, or draw."

Just like Baker the previous year, Petty goes to Daytona just before our Showdown and wins the Firecracker 400. Better yet, it's the 200th victory of his career. If you can't promote *that*, you're in the wrong business. We had Bouchard and Baker do a press conference for the Boston media, where we announced that Petty would be at both Hudson and Thompson. We held that press conference at the Boston Garden after a Bruins hockey practice, and some of the players stuck around to meet Ronnie and Buddy. The Commonwealth of Massachusetts even declared a Richard Petty Day.

We did our Sunday race, and drew what is still the biggest crowd in the history of Hudson Speedway. Richard's only stipulation was that he had to drive a Pontiac, so a friend of mine named Lucky Young built him a car from scratch. That was quite a night. In addition to Petty, Baker, and Bouchard, we had Gordon Humphrey, the U.S. Senator from New Hampshire, driving a Pro Stock owned and normally driven by Lew Boyd. Instead of a number on the door, Lew's car had the word "No" follow by the "cents" sign. If you read it out loud, of course, it was "no sense," perfect for a rookie driver straight from Congress. Humphrey got almost as much media attention as Petty, which was great.

In one of the features, Petty knocked Baker right over the sandbank and into the woods off the back straightaway. Well, video from that incident made every TV sportscast in Manchester, New Hampshire, as well as in Boston, which is the biggest media market in New England and one of the biggest in the country. It was terrific advertising for our Tuesday-night show at Thompson, and it was free!

In the meantime, Ronnie and Paula held a lobster feed on Monday at their house in Fitchburg. So Petty's in the pool, and Bouchard says, "Watch this." He grabs a live lobster, sneaks around the pool, and puts it in the water behind Richard.

Somebody says, "Hey, Richard, turn around."

Petty lets out a yelp, takes off swimming, and climbs up that ladder faster than you could have believed. He says, "Man, I didn't know those things could swim in *pools*, too!"

Now we go to Thompson, and, boy, did we put a crowd in there. The racing was terrific—Dave Lind swept both features—and the autograph line for the Cup guys snaked farther than we ever could have imagined. Petty signed until almost two o'clock in the morning, and never complained. Later, when we were all sitting in the track office, I said, "Richard, I've got a poster here that Ronnie and Buddy have already signed. Would you mind?"

Petty gave me that famous toothpaste-ad smile, and said, "You know, when my day finally comes and the undertaker has me in the box, just before he closes the lid he's going to lean in and say, 'Richard, do you think you could do just *one* more autograph?'" Bouchard laughed so hard that he started crying.

Anyway, Petty had a ball, and Baker enjoyed himself again, and we knew we were going to do it all again in 1985.

Now, that year we had some complications. Jim Libbey, another top Pro Stock racer, built a beautiful Firebird for Petty, but Richard suffered a concussion in the Firecracker 400. I knew he'd crashed, but, strangely enough, it was Richie Evans who tipped me off how bad it was. I'd lined up Richie to run a Pro Stock at Thompson, so on Monday, the day before, I called to confirm everything. Richie said, "Yeah, I'll be there, but are you sure about Petty? He's got two black eyes. He looks like Rocky Raccoon."

See, Daytona was on Thursday. On Saturday, Petty had an appearance at Shangri-La Speedway in New York; Richie won the Modified feature, and Petty presented the trophy, so they had talked. I knew Richie well enough to tell when he was being serious, and he said, "Honestly, I don't think he should be racing."

Wow. I called the doctor from the Boston Bruins, who I knew quite well. I said, "Doc, let's say a guy suffered a concussion on Thursday. Could he drive on Tuesday?"

He said, "A *race* car? I'd say definitely not, Russ. Are we talking about one of your regular guys?"

I said, "No, Richard Petty."

The doctor said, "I hope you've got a lot of insurance, in case he gets hurt again!"

I thanked the doctor, and I called Ronnie, who agreed that we needed to line up a replacement. We already had most of the top regional names—Evans, Bugsy, Bentley Warren, Reggie Ruggiero, just a hell of a supporting cast—so it had to be a Cup driver. Bentley suggested Tim Richmond, who'd won a few NASCAR races by then and was starting to become a star. Tim had run for Ken and me in Florida, when we'd promoted our NESMRA winter series for Supermodifieds in the '70s, so I already knew him. I mentioned him to Ronnie, who said, "Yeah, Tim might want to do this."

Ronnie and I had different phone numbers for Richmond. He tried the one he had, and got no answer. I called the other number, and Tim picked up. He was on his boat in Fort Lauderdale.

I laid it right out there: "Listen, Tim, I'm in a tough spot. We're promoting a race with Ronnie Bouchard, and Richard Petty was supposed to run it, but he's banged up. Do you think you can come?"

He said, "What kind of car?"

I said, "A Late Model, at a track in Thompson, Connecticut."

He said, "When is the race?"

"Tomorrow night."

Richmond laughed and said, "Geez, why didn't you just wait until tomorrow morning to call me?"

Then he said, "Where's the nearest airport?"

I told him, "Hartford or Boston."

"Give me ten minutes," he said, "and call me back."

So I did, and he said, "Have somebody at Logan Airport at 4:30 tomorrow afternoon. I'm coming."

I said, "How much is this going to cost?"

"We'll figure that out later," he said. He gave me his flight number and what airline he'd be on, and he hung up.

I remember Bouchard saying, "Tim's got a big personality. He'll be fun."

Well, I guess he was. He was almost the whole show. He started in the last row of both features at Thompson, and finished second twice. Bouchard won one of them, I remember that.

By the way, Petty came, and he still managed to pull off something special. He and I were standing in the little office right at Thompson's front gate, the one that doubles as a ticket booth. We took a peek around the corner, and there were five long lines. Richard said to me, "You know, I've done everything there is to do around race tracks except sell tickets." He sat right down on one of the stools, and said, "Next!"

Before long, people caught on. You could hear them saying, "Richard Petty is selling tickets in that window!" And just like that, you saw all five lines trying to merge into one, so they could buy their tickets from Richard.

During intermission, we had Mike Joy interview our special guest drivers from atop the flagstand. He gets to Richmond, and Tim says something like, "The promoter called and told me Ronnie Bouchard and these guys were having a big race tonight, and they needed me to replace Richard Petty. I told him, '*Nobody* can replace Richard Petty.' But I'm here, and I'm single, and, ladies, I'd be more than glad to meet you after the races!"

A month later we had three of our Showdown dates close together: Lee Speedway on Friday night and Hudson on Sunday—between those two, Dale Earnhardt won three of the four features—and then Stafford on Tuesday night. Ronnie was a phenomenal help with that Stafford race. We had Earnhardt, Richmond, and Baker again, and Cale Yarborough was there. Plus, I had a brainstorm: a Grand National Demolition Derby, featuring all these NASCAR drivers. Ronnie said, "Bill France Jr. is going to love us." We could just picture the president of NASCAR hearing that his biggest names were in a Tuesday-night demo derby.

Ronnie got together with the Fullers—Jeff, Bobby, Rick, that whole racing family—and had those guys haul eight junk cars to Stafford. We had great racing that night, but that damn demo derby had everybody going wild. Baker won it, but along the way he'd gone flying down the front straightaway in reverse and pulverized Richmond's car. In fact, Tim ended up going to the hospital with a broken nose. What a crazy night.

We ran the Showdown one last time in 1986, and then we pulled the plug. We had done pretty well promoting this thing, and I think we all knew—because the big money was starting to roll into Cup racing—that we weren't going to be able to keep drawing those guys as cheaply as we were, even with Ronnie's influence. You could see that a series like this was going to become too big a financial risk. We were in Fitchburg, having a couple of beers, and we agreed that enough was enough.

But that whole thing was *so* much fun. I remember Earnhardt and Richmond banging wheels at Hudson in a 25-lap Pro Stock race, and laughing about it later. Bouchard said, "See? We didn't know if this would work, but they're enjoying the hell out of it!"

Most of those guys over the years stayed at Ronnie's house, and he and Paula were such great hosts. Baker kept saying, "She's so nice, I can't believe it. Anything I want for breakfast, that girl will make it." Dale and Teresa Earnhardt obviously felt very comfortable there; they were great friends with Ronnie and Paula. I remember Dale talking about his 10-year-old son, Dale Jr., who was in military school.

So you can see how much all of this happened because of Ronnie. Yeah, I had the original idea, but he had the connections. Let's face it, Earnhardt didn't jump into that Pro Stock just because he wanted to race in New England. Same with Baker, same with Petty, same with Cale, same with everybody else who ran for us. Again, Ronnie made that happen. Those guys just liked him.

BY MIKE JOY

"Ronnie had an easygoing nature, but, let's face it, everybody wants to win"

A broadcaster and friend traces the deceptive arc of a Cup career

THIBODEAU BROS

Just as New England's short tracks prepared Ron Bouchard for Winston Cup racing, they honed Connecticut native Mike Joy for his current role as play-by-play man for the Fox Sports TV coverage of NASCAR's top series. Joy got his announcing start calling football and basketball games while at the University of Hartford, then broke into stock car racing by chance: Riverside Park Speedway owner Ed Carroll overheard his call of an amateur autocross meet and hired Mike to announce his track's Saturday-night Modified action. In the coming years, Joy moved to Thompson (where he first encountered Ron Bouchard), Stafford (sharing the booth with Jack Arute Jr.), and several other Northeast tracks before a radio stint with NASCAR's Motor Racing Network and TV gigs with ESPN, CBS, TNN, and ultimately Fox. In 1981, Bouchard's rookie Cup season, Mike was MRN's executive producer and co-anchor.

One of Ronnie's greatest gifts to New England was getting all his rowdy friends together—some of the top stars in the sport—and bringing them home to Stafford, Thompson, and those other tracks, whether it was for match races or the Showdown of Champions races that Russ Conway and Ken Smith promoted. Let's face it, Dale Earnhardt didn't do that stuff, Cale Yarborough didn't do that stuff, Tim Richmond didn't do that stuff, and Richard Petty *definitely* didn't do that stuff. But those guys and several others did those races for Ronnie. That, more than anything, tells you how well respected he was among his peers down South. And I honestly think those events helped pave the way for what Bob Bahre did when he built New Hampshire International Speedway, because it showed everybody how crazy New England was for racing, and how there was room there for Cup racing.

That's a great legacy. Ronnie helped advance the sport in the region where he grew up, and also helped advance the reputation of the Modified division. Think about this: If Ron Bouchard had not been fast in the Cup series, would Rick Hendrick have hired Geoff Bodine? Would Jimmy Spencer or Brett Bodine have gotten close attention? Without Ronnie, I'm not sure the opportunities would have opened up for those guys.

I was happy to see Ronnie get that ride with Jack Beebe, and happy with the idea that we'd be seeing each other on a regular basis again. We knew each other well from Stafford, Thompson, and the Modified tracks. When Jackie Arute and I came into Cup racing as broadcasters, we were the two leading proponents of the Modifieds; I'm sure both of us pointed people in that direction, and said, "This is where the next generation of talent is coming from."

You know, in 1981 there were not very many people from the Northeast in Cup racing. Pete Hamilton had come and gone years earlier; Geoff Bodine had run a few races, but he was not yet in a full-time situation. Ronnie, Jackie, and I were all pretty close in age, and the neat thing was that we'd all had the same dreams, and we were very fortunate that we had the talent, the drive, and the good people around us who helped make those dreams come true. And when Ronnie got to the Cup series, I think he was as happy for me and what I'd been able to do as I was for him. We did kind of have a kinship, and a friendship that lasted for decades.

So on the personal side, my thinking was: Ronnie's a friend, and I know he's a very talented driver. But as a broadcaster, I wanted to get his story out there, because he was an outsider. There were not many drivers from outside the South, so getting his story out would make him more familiar, both to people in the garage area and to the fans. It was not unlike when he'd arrived at Stafford as this young kid, this exciting new driver. People like to see that young star coming along.

Race Hill Farm was an interesting team. Jack Beebe was a great guy with a terrific passion for racing, and he built himself a solid organization. Harry Gant had done a nice job in that car, but when he left to drive for Burt Reynolds and Hal Needham—which was not an opportunity Harry could walk away from—my guess is that everybody on that team, from Jack to Bob Johnson to Steve Bird, just said, "Hey, Ronnie Bouchard is ready."

He was an easy choice. Ronnie was very adaptable. No matter the track, no matter the speed, he got the job done, and that was true whether we're talking about Modifieds or Cup cars.

When he qualified top-five at Bristol, that pretty much stood everybody on their ear. Then he went to North Wilkesboro the very next week, qualified in the top ten again, and *finished* in the top ten. Next he goes to Martinsville and gets another top-ten finish. After that, I think everybody's eyes were on him.

The Southern teams really didn't take Beebe's operation all that seriously, because he still had the team based in Connecticut. But Ronnie seemed to fit in very quickly. When people started making jokes about his accent—"*pahk* the *cah* in *Hahvahd Yahd*"—that's when I knew he'd been accepted.

Ronnie was a charmer, in the best sense of the word. I don't think he ever met a stranger, and he projected a great deal of likeability, a sense of humor, and talent. There was little question in my mind—actually, there was *no* question in my mind—that he would make it in Cup racing.

People forget this, but in the three races prior to his victory at Talladega, he'd finished in the top ten. At Michigan, he started fifth, finished tenth; Daytona, he started seventh, finished ninth; Pocono, started 14th, finished tenth. So they were competitive.

At Talladega, I was in the radio booth with Barney Hall. As a broadcaster, you really have to work to be objective. When you spend as much time within the sport as we do, that's often difficult—you naturally make friends, and you spend more time with some drivers than others—but you have to be objective, and call the race that's right there in front of you. But how could you have been any happier at that moment, if you knew Ronnie Bouchard?

I'll be honest, when they came into the tri-oval on that last lap, I would not have given you a nickel for Ronnie's chances to win. In fact, when Terry Labonte made his move on Darrell Waltrip and it looked like Ronnie might go with Terry, I wasn't sure there was enough distance between the tri-oval and the start/finish line for Ronnie even to get to second. But when he double-drafted those guys and made that elevator move, top to bottom, it was hard for me, at that moment, not to be a fan.

We called it at the line, Barney and I: "It's Bouchard, by about a foot!"

Then he got to victory lane and, so typical of Ronnie, he didn't even want to take credit for that move. He made sure he told everybody the story of how he'd been garaged near Buddy Baker, and basically asked him, "Buddy, how do you run Talladega? How do you pass here? What do you do?" Baker took Ronnie under his wing, and, boy, did that pay off.

But that's where Ronnie's likeability added to his talent, and made him a winner. If he hadn't been the kind of guy a fellow like Baker wanted to help, I don't know if he could have won that race.

Then Ronnie went to the next event, at Michigan, and won the pole, so that had been an awesome stretch.

One thing that worked in his favor was that there weren't many multi-car teams. A small team like Jack Beebe's could do really well if they did their homework. Race Hill Farm was not a championship-caliber team, but they were a real threat to be a top-ten team every week. They even had a stretch in the fall when, in four races, Ronnie had three top-five finishes and a sixth. They even went out to Riverside, California, which had to be the first time Ronnie ever raced on a road course, and finished tenth.

So, clearly, that team had its act together in 1981. But every year the top teams are developing, and while Race Hill Farm was a very good team operationally, maybe they just didn't develop fast enough to keep pace. They started out the next season with three top-ten finishes, but then the good results got harder and harder to come by. It seemed to me that they were fine on the short tracks and the big superspeedways, and even on the road course; it was at the intermediate tracks that the other teams got better. Ronnie did win another pole at Michigan in '82, but on Sundays they struggled. The same was true in 1983: They qualified in the top ten in about a third of the races, and even sat on the pole at Nashville, but the good finishes just were not there. In that entire '83 season, they only had one top five.

Now, 1984 was certainly better. Ronnie finished second at Martinsville, third at Bristol and Charlotte, and fourth and fifth at Nashville. But he also had a bunch of mechanical issues toward the end of the season: three engine failures and a transmission problem in the last nine races. If you look at all those things and read between the lines a little bit, it's easy to think that the team was starting to get behind.

Ronnie had an easygoing nature, but, let's face it, everybody wants to win. In 1984 he had those two Busch Series victories at Darlington, and that had to boost his spirits. If nothing else, when you win a race you prove to yourself that you've still got it.

He ran another year for Jack Beebe, and then in '86 he left to drive for Mike Curb. I know Ronnie had some other opportunities, but, as I recall, he took that deal for two reasons: There was a solid national sponsor in Valvoline, and the financial package was very attractive, with a guarantee and signing money. I remember him telling me, "I don't know if I can win here, but I've got to look beyond racing. I've got some things I want to do."

Like, say, open up some car dealerships.

That was another case where Ronnie's personality led him to greater opportunity. He'd met Jack Billmyer, who was Honda's head of dealer development as well as a race fan. Jack got to know a number of drivers; some of them had an interest in the car business that they wanted to pursue, and Jack got them Honda franchises. But to be a Honda dealer, you needed to have a certain amount of liquid assets, and I know the money he made by signing with Curb helped Ronnie in that regard.

Now, in the beginning that Curb operation was not a limited-schedule team. In the first half of the season, they did skip Martinsville and the June race at Riverside, but they ran 13 of the first 15 races. However, the results just were not there, and I think that by then the team was on life support. After the Fourth of July, they ran only four races: Talladega, Darlington, Charlotte, and Atlanta. It was a lack of funding, not a lack of intent, that turned that into a partial-schedule situation.

Clearly, things were not good. Early in the season Ronnie qualified 14th at Daytona and fifth at Richmond, but after that he didn't start in the top 15 all year. He finished fifth in the Daytona 500 and ninth at Talladega, but that was all Ronnie.

He ran that handful of races with Hoss Ellington in 1987, and then he was gone. It surprised me when he left as abruptly as he did, but he was growing his automotive business, and, let's face it, once again the results on the track were not there. Ronnie ran five races with Hoss, and his average qualifying position was 23rd or 24th. Hoss's cars had won some races in the '70s with Donnie Allison, and he'd won in 1980 with David Pearson at Darlington, but that was no longer a top-tier team. In fact, Ronnie got Hoss his last top-ten finish, when he ran eighth at Darlington. So I could understand Ronnie leaving.

Naturally, I didn't see him nearly as much as I once had, but we never really lost touch. I even bought a car or two from Ronnie. I remember buying my mom an Accord, and helping my sister buy a car from him.

As for how he's remembered, I think that in every sport there's a tendency to judge athletes only by what they achieve at the very highest level. Nobody knows, or cares, how many minor-league home runs Babe Ruth had; the only number they associate with him is 714, which is how many he hit in the big leagues. The same is true in racing. Jimmy Means was a *great* Late Model Sportsman driver; he won track championships at Nashville and at Huntsville, Alabama, and Jimmy could go anywhere in the South and dust the field. But today, most people know him as a journeyman driver in the Cup series. That's just the way it goes.

And it's the same with Ronnie. When he had good enough equipment in the Cup series, you saw how talented he was. But, for one reason or another—most of them beyond his control—he could not put up the big numbers every week. I suppose when you reach the top level of your sport, you have to box up and put away all of your previous successes, at least until the time comes when somebody puts together a book like this.

But when I think of Ronnie, I'll always remember three things: First, in my opinion he was the greatest driver ever to run the outside groove at Stafford; second, he won the biggest upset in superspeedway history at Talladega; and third, his driving ability was exceeded only by his popularity with the fans.

I don't think for a minute that he was any less a race driver in 1987 than he'd ever been. But I think Ronnie realized that the opportunity for him to get into one of the really good cars had passed. And one thing that Ron Bouchard never could have been was a field-filler.

PART FIVE

Second Life

ROBIN HARTFORD

Bouchard hedged his bet when he walked away from Hoss Ellington's car in 1987. For the next year or two, he was quoted here and there as saying he had "not retired," that he was on more of a "leave of absence," and that if a well-sponsored, limited-schedule ride came along, he'd race "for a few more years." Keeping his racing options open, just in case.

Truth is, for quite some time he'd been hedging the same bet in the opposite direction, keeping his *non*-racing options open.

It all started in Ron's Race Hill Farm years, when a Carolina pal named Wayne Smith began sharing with Bouchard the finer points of his trade, which was the used-car game. It came down to what folks wanted, and what folks didn't want. And what folks up North seemed to want were vehicles fresh from Dixie, where mild winters meant little snow, where little snow meant no road salt, and where no road salt meant no rust.

And when Mr. Smith pointed out to Mr. Bouchard that a fellow might make a buck specializing in the sale of Southern iron to Northern buyers, Mr. Bouchard was intrigued. Soon he had Smith scouting vehicles, pickup trucks at first, that might prove attractive back in Fitchburg. Maximizing his opportunities, he started bringing them north two at a time. On Sunday evenings—"after Ronnie had run a 500-mile race," Paula points out—husband and wife would rendezvous with the trucks. She'd quickly clean the one they chose to drive, while he hooked a tow bar to the other.

"Then we'd grab a burger from McDonald's," says Paula, "and start driving home."

Thus was born Ron Bouchard's B&B Auto Sales, located on a corner of the Lunenburg Street property where father Bob still operated Red & White Movers. The low-mileage, low-rust inventory at B&B was constantly updated.

"Back then, the Winston Cup garage closed at five o'clock, no ifs, ands, or buts," says David Ifft, then Bouchard's crew chief. "They'd announce. 'Put your tools down, the garage is closed,' and you had to leave. Well, Ronnie used to get one of those autotrader magazines, and the two of us would drive around and find all the cars and pickups in the area. Some weeks he'd buy two or three."

Or more. That created a transport problem, which Bouchard solved by flying in buddies like Dave Rossbach—who'd retired from General Electric and set up shop at B&B, doing machine work and breathing new life into used cars—to serve as return-trip drivers. In time he decided that finding a car-hauler and a driver was more cost-effective than all those one-way plane tickets. Enter another reliable compadre, Bob Bergeron, making steady loops between Fitchburg and various Southern hamlets. While Bouchard was busy practicing and qualifying, "Bergie and I would drive around and load up the cars Ronnie had picked out," says Paula.

Ricky Rudd recalls pulling up beside Bouchard in a speedway parking lot. Ricky was in what he calls "a pretty car," a black and gold Buick Regal belonging to his wife, Linda.

The story still brings a chuckle from Rudd: "Ronnie said, 'That's a nice car.' Next thing you know, he bought it from me."

Crafty racer, crafty entrepreneur. Never cheap, but mindful that a dollar was a dollar, he made every trip count. Once, in late autumn, a pickup Bouchard brought home had its bed loaded with reclining chairs he'd bought for a song in North Carolina. "Ronnie knew some people might want to buy those chairs for Christmas presents," says Paula. "So he trucked 'em home."

The furniture department at B&B did a brisk holiday trade.

There was, Paula says, no long-term plan for this used-car thing beyond the secondary income it provided, and certainly no visions of a full-bore automobile dealership, "at least none that Ronnie ever mentioned."

Ah, but Bouchard had hit the big time in a period when the Winston Cup garage area had a distinct new-car smell. There was, at last, real money to be made driving stock cars; not to the level that Dale Earnhardt and Jeff Gordon would raise the bar a decade down the line, but real money nonetheless, and a handful of smart racers found ways to let their money make *more* money. Several, including Cale Yarborough, Dick Brooks, and Darrell Waltrip, were operating auto dealerships. Honda was the hot brand, and one driver or another—likely Brooks—pointed out to Bouchard that a towering man who'd popped up regularly at Winston Cup races was a Honda executive. His name was Jack Billmyer.

Next you had another example of the luck—or at least the fortunate timing—that had followed Ron Bouchard around since that afternoon at Brookline Speedway 20 years earlier, when neither Bob Bouchard nor Pete Salvatore was around to keep 14-year-old Ronnie out of a race car, and out of his first victory lane.

In February of 1984 at Daytona, aboard that temperamental Busch Series rocket fielded by John Dufour and Jack Beebe, Bouchard bounced in and out of the lead in the Goody's 300. If someone wanted to draft past him, that was fine; convinced he had the fastest car in the field, he'd calmly retake the lead a few laps later. Then his V-6 engine scattered its innards all over Volusia County, and Bouchard coasted deadstick into the garage area.

As he climbed from the car, dejected, a voice next to him said, "Man, you were flying out there."

"Yeah," came the driver's reflexive response. "Too bad the motor broke."

Then, recognizing the tall fellow who'd stopped to console him, Ronnie said, "Aren't you Mr. Billmyer?"

"Yes."

The conversation was short, and amounted to this:
BOUCHARD: "I'd sure like to have one of those Honda dealerships."
BILLMYER: "Where exactly do you live, Ron?"
BOUCHARD: "In Massachusetts. Near Worcester."

Second Life 193

Billmyer gave him a business card, and instructed Bouchard to call early in the week at such-and-such time.

Which Bouchard certainly did. Fittingly, the story of that phone call has a touch of used-car chaos attached. At Daytona, Ronnie had bought a van from Richard Petty, then traded the van for a Cadillac, which he and Paula were driving home. Predictably, temperatures dropped as they rode north. Unpredictably, the heater on the Caddy was kaput. Eventually things got so chilly that Paula dug into the laundry bag for extra layers of clothing, and slid close to her husband for heat. At the scheduled hour they peeled off I-95, found a payphone, and called Billmyer, but he was on another line. They headed up the highway for ten miles or so, took another exit, called again, and found Billmyer still unavailable. They spotted a Kmart, bought a blanket, draped it across both of them, and got back on the road. This pattern—drive, shiver, call, repeat—went on until they finally connected.

"It's yours," said Jack Billmyer. "You'll be getting our letter of intent soon."

The rest of the ride was upbeat, until they arrived home to discover that their furnace had failed during their absence. Paula said, "Everything was frozen. There was ice in the toilet."

But they had a Honda dealership. And that led to what was, in hindsight, a remarkable second life for a fellow whose first life had been pretty remarkable, too.

Conditioned to keep an eye on spending, Bouchard bought a chunk of his dad's property, essentially nudging Red & White Movers over a tad. He handled much of the contracting and site work himself; you can close your eyes and picture Bob Bouchard, feisty Pepe, and all other available hands pitching in. "I helped with some of the construction work," says son Gene.

The finished dealership was dubbed The Honda Store. It opened in 1986—a troubled racing year for Ron—with a ribbon-cutting attended by Honda's regional brass and a politician or two. Sales were immediately brisk, and the business pages soon told of the place topping this consumer-satisfaction index or picking up that dealer award. Not surprisingly, when Honda launched its upscale Acura brand, Bouchard was granted a franchise a half-hour down the highway in Auburn. Then a Mitsubishi dealership joined Honda on Lunenburg Street, and, well, you may sense a pattern. Before anyone knew it, the new-car stores had squashed B&B Auto Sales; Dave Rossbach bought the machine-shop inventory and moved it to Jean Michaud's old body-shop digs.

So if by May of '87 Bouchard's love for race cars had cooled, his business was hot, and his name still had weight with potential customers. Perfect timing for a transition. Says old friend Clyde McLeod, "If you're around racing a while, you see that some people make it, and some people—talented people—get used up and left behind. Ronnie wasn't going to let that happen to him."

He did his best to avoid race tracks altogether—"In his mind, it was like quitting cigarettes," says Paula—showing up only occasionally to watch son Robbie compete at familiar haunts like Monadnock and Stafford. That gave Ronnie a small taste of what he had put Bob and Lorraine Bouchard through.

Sister JoAnn says, "Watching Robbie made Ronnie nervous. He said, 'Jesus, I don't know how Mom and Dad ever did this.'"

And though he had run scores of Modified races and the odd Busch Series event against kid brother Ken, he was busy selling cars in Massachusetts while Kenny was picking up NASCAR's Winston Cup Rookie of the Year award in 1988. To this day, the Bouchards remain the only siblings to share that honor.

"It was great for us, but really great for our parents," Kenny reflects, "I know it's something my dad was proud of."

It is obvious now that whatever focus Ron Bouchard brought to racing—and you don't win like he did without focus—was simply redirected toward business as the 1980s melted away.

He watched the money: "Jack Beebe told my father something he never forgot," says son Rob. "Jack said, 'If I can buy a bolt cheaper than my parts guy is paying for the same bolt, that man is in trouble.'"

And he absolutely watched the competition: "You get reports from the manufacturers that tell you how you're doing compared to other dealerships in your region," says Paula. "Ronnie didn't want to be anywhere near the bottom of those lists. He was definitely as competitive in business as he was in racing."

This, she adds, "was somebody who a few years earlier knew nothing about the automotive business, and nothing about finance."

Bouchard's secret, always, was that he was smart enough to know what he didn't know. Just like he followed George Summers around Seekonk Speedway, and just like he sought Buddy Baker's counsel at Talladega, he knew who to listen to in the auto business. He found a friend in multi-brand dealer Jim Powers, whom he'd met through an industry group, and ultimately hired Marlin Knight, a Powers alum, to help run what across the '90s blossomed into Ron Bouchard's Auto Stores, adding Chrysler, Dodge, Kia, Nissan, and partial interest in a Tennessee Toyota outlet.

When he ran out of space in the new century, he found a plot of land just outside Fitchburg on Route 2 in Lancaster. Up went a string of sales-and-service buildings the likes of which the B&B-era Bouchard would never have dreamed.

"I was up there one day when he was putting up his new dealerships," says his friendly Modified rival Bugs Stevens. "I was stunned. He was showing me this and that, and all these people were coming in and out: bankers, lawyers, everybody."

His face was on billboards and in TV spots, amusing his brief promotional partner Russ Conway, who says, "This was the same guy who told me he didn't know anything about advertising!"

As business ticked upward, this second life of Bouchard's allowed him to back off a bit, and to find time—to *make* time—for things that in the past had slipped through the cracks. He clearly relished his second swing at fatherhood, spending time with son Chad and encouraging the young man's budding career as a golfer, at the same knowing firsthand how little room there is at the top of any professional sport.

Meanwhile, his older children and *their* children—The Kid from Fitchburg ended up a grandfather five times over—gave him reasons to throw weekend cookouts. Says Paula, "In the beginning of his racing career he missed out on a lot with the kids. I think he saw this as a good way to reconnect."

And also a way to exercise a growing, if surprising, culinary habit. "He'd flip through the TV channels and see these shows on Food Network," Paula grins. "I'd be in the kitchen, cooking, and Ronnie would walk by and say, 'Hey, put in a little of this,' or, 'Add a little of that.' I would joke around and say, 'If you want to make dinner, be my guest.'

"And that's just what started happening. He really got into it. He even started doing the grocery shopping. Anytime we had overnight guests, Ronnie loved to make them breakfast."

To widen the hosting possibilities, he bought what he called a boat, but was in fact a 72-foot yacht. Brother-in-law Ed Flemke Jr. recalls running a Saturday-night NASCAR Modified Tour race at Maine's Beech Ridge Motor Speedway, and spending Sunday with Ron and Paula on the boat in Kennebunkport.

"I hate boats," Eddie says. "But we're up on the third deck of this thing, and I'm sitting there with a glass of wine, thinking I could really get used to this. Ronnie said to me, 'There's no sense having something like this unless you can share it with people.'"

He made time, too, for old racing chums. New Hampshire International Speedway, as it was known then, gave Bouchard a chance to visit old cronies in the Cup garage. David Ifft says, "I'd fly into Manchester, and Ronnie and I would go to the track, and maybe have dinner with Richard Childress. I've known Richard forever, and he and Ronnie were real good friends."

And he'd never stopped going to Speedweeks, driving across Florida each February from his winter home near Naples and tying up with George Summers, who had a condo in Daytona Beach.

There was more: Ron and Paula started traveling, bringing home touristy photos of Paris, of Italian fishing villages, of African wildlife. You wonder what sorts of things went through their heads, these two racing brats, all grown up, seeing the City of Light and the wonders of the Dark Continent.

Always, the road led back to Greater Fitchburg, where, from the dust of a used-car sideline, Ron Bouchard's Auto Stores had become part of the landscape and part of the economy.

BY PAULA BOUCHARD

"I never saw him take on anything unless he knew what he was doing"

Growing a business ... and growing it, and growing it

MIKE ADASKAVEG

Though she knew she was marrying a racer, it's doubtful that Paula Bouchard foresaw what other adventures lay ahead. As their used-car sideline expanded into a Honda dealership and then a full-fledged multi-brand enterprise, at no step was Ron a hands-off operator. That meant she wasn't, either. She recalls that when blizzards necessitated overnight plowing runs, "Ronnie always wanted company, so I'd ride in the tractor with him." That same spirit of togetherness helped grow the business, says Tracey Bouchard DiNardo: "My dad was a risk-taker, yes, but he did enough planning to make those risks pay off. And, you know, Paula was right there saying, 'This is what you want to do, and you've thought it out. Let's do it.' They were a team." Paula Bouchard was interviewed at the dealership complex in Lancaster that stands as a monument to their teamwork.

When we opened The Honda Store in 1986, Marvin Rifchin was the first customer. As a matter of fact, he purchased the first *two* cars we sold, and he actually bought them before we were even open for business. We had a grand-opening reception before the public opening of the dealership, and Marvin said, "I want this one and that one."

That was so fitting, because he and Ronnie had such a great relationship. Ronnie thought of Marvin like a second father, and Marvin was just as fond of Ronnie. As the years went on, Marvin ended up buying several cars from us.

What I remember most from those early days is the work. It was nothing to be there 12 or 15 hours a day. After we closed, I'd clean the bathrooms. That was our dealership, and I was proud of it, so I wanted it to look good. It made me think back to when I was a girl, and my father had a gas station; my brother Eddie and I used to do whatever needed to be done—work the graveyard shift, clean toilets, anything—and it never bothered us, because we felt that pride of ownership. I'm sure Ronnie had the same feeling, going back to seeing his dad at the moving company.

In the beginning, we were closed on Sundays. Ronnie felt that if our people worked all week, they needed to have at least some time to spend with their families. But every other dealership in the area was open all weekend, which meant we were putting ourselves at a disadvantage, and he finally decided we needed to be open Sundays, too. So instead of asking our employees to come in when they didn't really want to, we'd work Sundays ourselves. We might bring in one or two salesmen, just in case it got busy, but I'd answer the phone and Ronnie would wait on customers.

He put a lot of effort into learning everything he could about the automobile business. Car dealers have what are called Twenty Groups; basically, you meet with a small handful of dealers from around the country, and because you aren't direct competitors you help one another by talking about your strengths and weaknesses. When Ronnie went to his first Twenty Group meeting, he decided that the best thing to do was to just sit and listen. Eventually a fellow named Jim Powers spoke, and Ronnie was impressed; he made up his mind that this was the brightest guy in the room, and he made a point of befriending Jim. Ronnie understood that when it comes to business, there's always someone who knows more than you do, and that's the guy you want to learn from.

After The Honda Store was up and running, we were able to get a franchise for Acura, Honda's luxury brand, which was still very new. We found a location in Auburn, right alongside the Massachusetts Turnpike, and starting building what became Acura of Auburn. Ronnie did as much of the contracting himself as he possibly could, just like he had done in Fitchburg, to keep the costs down. He spent hours and hours there on a bulldozer. Chad was just a baby, and I used to drive him down there, 35 miles each way, because that was the only way they could see each other.

The hardest thing to deal with, early on, was very simple: money. You've got to look at so many different ways of doing things. We built The Honda Store on property we bought from Ronnie's dad, and we paid that off in increments. That was simple enough. But we financed the building of our Acura dealership through a bank that also handled what is called floorplanning; basically, the bank pays the manufacturer for the cars in your showroom, and as you sell each car you pay back the bank. It's complicated to explain, but very common in the automobile business.

Well, after we were open, the bank we'd been dealing with changed hands. The new bank now held our mortgage, but they did not offer floorplanning, which meant that if we wanted cars, we had to pay for them ourselves up front. Ronnie and I borrowed money from some close friends just to be sure we kept enough cars in our inventory until we got everything straightened out. I'll never forget meeting one of these friends to pick up the money, and hurrying back to Fitchburg because we needed to get the money deposited that day. I actually got stopped for speeding. It was such a nerve-wracking time.

Even after you get past things like that, there are always issues to deal with when you own a business. The phone would ring in the middle of the night, and it would be the security company telling us that an alarm had gone off. Ronnie would get dressed and hurry down there to be sure everything was okay. For a while we had problems with kids breaking into cars, and that made him so angry. He took it personally. He was offended that someone would damage his property, or take something that belonged to him; he couldn't understand it. Some nights, he'd go down to the lot and sit there in his car, keeping an eye on things.

Then there were the winter nights when he'd get up at 3:00 a.m. to go and plow the lots. Again, if he did that himself, it was money saved. He'd plow the lot in Fitchburg, and then he'd go over to Marvin's factory—after he had moved M&H Tire from Watertown to Gardner, west of Fitchburg—and plow the parking lot so Marvin didn't have to worry about it. Once he got done there, he'd run down to Auburn and clear the Acura lot.

Not long after Acura of Auburn opened, we added a Mitsubishi dealership in Fitchburg, right beside The Honda Store. Then we bought a Nissan franchise from someone in the area who was getting out of the business, and a Dodge/Chrysler franchise from another person, and then Kia came the same way. It wasn't all planned; these opportunities came up, and they looked good, so that's the way we went.

We even ended up getting involved with a Toyota dealership in Gallatin, Tennessee. Jim Powers, Ronnie's friend from the Twenty Group, was interested in that franchise, but he was looking for a partner, and Ronnie decided it looked like another opportunity. We didn't have to actively manage it—I don't think Ronnie even went down there more than a few times—and it turned out to be a tremendous investment.

As time went on, we got to the point where things were stable enough, and we had enough good people in place, that we didn't need to be at the business every day for things to run smoothly. We started to take a little time here, and a little time there. We bought a house in Florida, and we started spending time there every winter: first a couple of weeks, then a month, and finally three months. Ronnie loved it there; he'd get together with friends and play golf. I think those trips to Florida taught him that it was okay to relax.

But, again, you're never totally off-duty. Our managers could handle just about anything that came up, so very seldom did they call us. Still, every week I'd get a FedEx box with any paperwork I had to take care of, and every night Ronnie would go through that day's numbers from each of the dealerships. He refused to do email; he used to say, "Ah, you don't need a computer." He was right: he didn't need a computer, because I had one! I'd get the reports emailed to me, and Ronnie would sit there with those sheets and a calculator. He was a numbers person; he had to see the numbers.

And then there was the boat. For the longest time, that was Ronnie's dream: He wanted to own a nice boat. I think that started because every February he'd drive over to Daytona, which to him was a great chance to see everybody, and he would always end up on Earnhardt's boat. Early in the week, before Teresa got down there, Dale would be at the boat by himself, so he and Ronnie would sit there, eat dinner, and just talk.

I think that to Ronnie, it seemed like having a home away from home. He'd say, "We can sell our house in Florida, and in the winter we'll just get on the boat and go from place to place."

I didn't particularly care for the idea, because that sounded like too slow a pace of life for me. But it was what he wanted, so we ended up getting a big boat, 72 feet, and somebody—I wish I could remember who—came up with the perfect name: *Dealership*.

Ronnie really enjoyed that boat. We'd park it at Marina Bay in Boston and drive over there from Fitchburg on the weekends, when the kids and some of our friends would come out and spend time with us. Then we started taking short vacations with it—we might leave for a week, and go to Maine—and Ronnie would get some of his buddies together for short trips. Eventually, he even took it all the way to Florida for Speedweeks.

After a while, though, the problems you have with a boat can drive you crazy. Every little problem becomes an ordeal, and when you have a big problem—like a blown engine, which happened to us—it can be a major headache. In the end, I think the novelty of the boating life just wore off for both of us, and we sold it.

We sort of replaced the adventure of the boat by traveling. Through the automotive business you can win these wonderful trips, but we had never really taken advantage of that. So we went to Paris, went to Italy, went to Africa on a photo safari; we saw so many beautiful places. I looked at it as a reward. We had worked really hard, and this was the return for that.

All this time, of course, Chad was growing up. He took an interest in golf when he was very young, and I think that was because it was something he could do with his father. Whenever Ronnie was around people, the talk always turned to racing, racing, racing; Chad wasn't even three years old when his dad retired, so he has no racing memories, and I'm sure he felt left out of those conversations. But with Ronnie playing more and more golf, I think Chad decided that if he learned how to play, this would be something they had in common. So he tried it, and loved it, and he was very good at it. In the summers I'd enroll him in a youth program at the local course, so he could play as often as he wanted.

He played golf in high school, and went on to play when he was in college in Florida. He did so well at every step of the way that he decided to play professionally. He stayed in Florida after he got out of school, and divided his time between tournaments and caddying part-time at a country club. When he wasn't doing that, he practiced non-stop, even if it was 100 degrees.

Chad tried so hard to get his PGA card, and he came very close. But golf is a lot like racing: It's hard enough to be good at the local level, but every time you take another step up, it gets even more difficult. He was living on the east coast of Florida, and our house was on the west coast, so every so often either Ronnie or I would say, "Road trip!" I'd pack some clothes, Ronnie would put together a picnic lunch for us to eat on the way, and we'd take a leisurely, three-hour drive over there. Then we'd watch Chad practice, and just make a fun day out of it. And, naturally, anytime he had a tournament, we tried to go and see him play.

At the end of the day, Ronnie would turn into that numbers person again: "Chad, you're missing on 30 percent of your par threes …"

Several years ago, we began moving most of our dealerships from the old Red & White property to a new location on Route 2 in Lancaster, just east of Fitchburg. We had outgrown our old space, and Route 2—which brings a lot of people in and out of Boston—offered a lot more visibility. We left the Chrysler, Dodge, and Ram Trucks stores in Fitchburg, and beginning in 2010 we moved Nissan, then Honda, and finally Kia to Lancaster.

That was a big step, between buying the property, preparing the site, and putting up the buildings. It was definitely something Ronnie put a lot of thought into. One day I was standing in line at the bank, and up ahead of me were two guys we knew. They didn't see me, and I heard one of them say to the other, "How about that Bouchard, moving his dealerships out to the highway? Can you imagine the loan he must be taking out to do that?"

But I trusted Ronnie's judgment. By then we had been selling cars for almost 25 years, and we had been together for more than 35. I never saw him take on anything unless he knew what he was doing, so when he started talking about this move, I never questioned it. I just figured, "Okay, this is what's next. This is what we're going to do."

And that was the right decision, because things have gone well. Of course, just because things are going well, that doesn't mean it's easy. There's always *something* that requires your attention. If everything is fantastic with one department, another department falters; you get that one fixed, and the next one has a problem. Each department is almost like a child, because you never stop looking after them and you never stop worrying.

Ronnie genuinely cared about the people who worked for him. Both of us were brought up Catholic, but when you spend your life racing on Sundays, it seems like you never get to church. Then when he retired from driving, we couldn't go very much because we were always at work. But when we started going to Florida during the winter, we began attending church services because we finally had time. Every Sunday, Ronnie would say a prayer for his employees; he wanted them to be healthy, and he wanted everything to go well in their lives, because he felt a responsibility to them. He *cared*. When the economy had its downturn in 2007 and '08 and people everywhere were losing their jobs, he was so relieved, and so proud, that he didn't have to lay anybody off.

Really, he was proud of what he had been able to build. He took great pride in how things looked, and how they were presented. If he stepped out of his car when he got here and saw a piece of paper on the ground, he picked it up. Part of that was because he always thought he should lead by example. But I really think it was mostly that pride; it was the pride of ownership that I mentioned earlier, and pride that all of his hard work had paid off.

BY CHAD BOUCHARD

"I'd play with a toy tractor in the dirt while he played on the big tractor"

Lessons in work, competition, and life: a son's view

Chad Bouchard grew up around plenty of racers, although to him they were more like family and friends. His dad, having hung up his helmet, was pouring all of his energy into the automobile business, and George Summers—whom Chad calls "another grandfather to me"—was now a smiling, easygoing golfer, not the tenacious wheelman of old. Golf was Chad's sport, too, although he took it well past the "easygoing" stage. These days, Chad is vice president of sales and marketing for Ron Bouchard's Auto Stores. Says his part-time grandpa, Mr. Summers, "Chad reminds me so much of Ronnie. When he was just a young kid, he'd come out and play golf with Ronnie and me and whoever else was with us, and he could fit right in just like Ronnie fit in when he first came to Seekonk Speedway. He's got that same personality."

BOUCHARD FAMILY COLLECTION

All my life I've had people tell me that I should have been a race driver, that I had the bloodlines for it. Everybody who knows me knows that my dad raced, and most of them know that his brother, Kenny, raced. Some of them know that my mom's brother, Eddie, raced. It's the older people who remember that my Grandfather Eddie, my mom's father, was also a great racer.

But it just wasn't something I wanted to do. When I was young, I messed around with go-karts, and I had fun doing it, but it wasn't as entertaining as the other sports I played. And I can't remember my dad racing; I was *there* for some of it, but my first memories are of the years after he retired, like 1990 or '91.

So what I remember most about him in my early years is the work ethic he had. When I was leaving for school at 7:30 or 8:00 a.m., he was going to work, and he didn't come home until I was already in bed. When he was building the Acura dealership, I'd play with a toy tractor in the dirt while he played on the big tractor. He took a lot of pride in working hard, and being successful.

When I was young, I played hockey, baseball, basketball, and soccer. By high school, it was hockey and golf. What originally got me into golf was that it was the first thing I could do that involved spending time with my dad. He was playing in tournaments here and there, and I guess I thought, "Hey, if I had my own clubs, I could play with him and Georgie Summers and the guys."

Early on I liked hockey more, but that changed as I became a better golfer. I wanted to play sports in college, and I just wasn't good enough in hockey. I had some breakthroughs in golf, and suddenly there were opportunities to play in college. When schools started reaching out, there was that realization: "Hey, if they want me, I must be all right." I ended up going to the University of Tampa, where I had the chance to play a lot.

The thing about golf is that when you do well, it's very gratifying. In team sports, there's one winning side and one losing side, so you end up winning half the time, and when your team does win, it may not have been *you* that made the difference. Golf is like racing: You have a team behind you—a pit crew in racing, or the caddy and swing coach in golf—but when it comes right down to it, it's on your shoulders. And, just like in racing, you lose a lot more than you win, so when you do win, it's really special.

I had a really good run in the Massachusetts Amateur Golf Championship in 2009, at The Country Club in Brookline. I reached match play by the skin of my teeth; I was ranked 32nd out of 32 who made the cut. That meant my first match was against the number one seed, but I won it, and then I kept winning. It went on for four days; my mom and dad were there every day, watching. I made it to the quarterfinals. That was when golf went from being fun to being something I really wanted to focus on. I wanted to get better. I wanted to *win*. I decided that I would try playing professionally as soon as I got out of college.

My first pro tournament was in Boca Raton, Florida, and it was a rough day. Golf is like any other sport: You can be the best player in your school, or the best player in your state, but once you get to the pros you realize that everybody there was the best where he came from.

I played once on the Web.com Tour, which is the equivalent of the Xfinity Series in NASCAR, and I went through what's called Q-School—qualifying school for the PGA Tour—four or five times, and also Q-School for the Canadian

Tour. You've got to go through those schools to earn your tour card, and there are multiple stages to each one. It's pretty intense, because everybody there has the same goal you do, and you know that one bad swing, one bad hole, one bad round, and it's time to start over.

Most people who watch golf on television know all the familiar names, but they don't see the work that went into getting those names where they are. Sure, some of the top stars were standouts as junior players, and at 14 years old they had people predicting they'd make millions of dollars playing golf. But there are also plenty of guys who don't get their PGA Tour cards until they're 28 or 30, who work at it for years before they start making big money, if they ever do. For most pro golfers, it's a struggle.

It was always great to have my parents there watching me, although in the beginning my mom screamed like she was at a race. It was like she was *trying* to embarrass me. When I tell people that, they say, "Could you really pick out her voice?" Trust me, *everybody* could pick it out.

When they couldn't be there, I'd always call later to tell them how I'd done. Of course, whenever I played poorly I didn't want to talk to my dad too soon. He was very competitive, and being competitive makes you more critical. As a golfer, you tend to make excuses—you blame this, you blame that—but my dad would say, "No, Chad, you played badly. It's on you."

At the same time, he made sure to tell me that it was okay, that I just needed to focus on it 100 percent. He'd say, "It's not going to be easy, but you're never going to reach a goal without putting the proper effort into it."

I'm definitely glad that I gave it a shot. Before I went away to college, my idea was that I'd just stay close to home and work. But when I look back now, I can definitely see that there was a growth in me thanks to continuing my education, doing my own thing, and really *pursuing* something like I did with golf. If I'd made it, that would have been great, but I met a lot of good people and I have the closure of knowing that I tried.

I was lucky, because I had the support of my parents when I was trying to make that work. I caddied to make extra money when I wasn't playing, but they definitely supported me. As a racer, my dad didn't have that option early on; he always had to work a full-time job, and race on the weekends.

I was also lucky that I got to spend a lot of time with my dad when he was getting all the dealerships going. My very first job in life was selling lemonade to the employees and customers at the store in Fitchburg. Later on, I worked a lot of different jobs for him when school was out. I never stayed in one department for long, but he made sure that I saw every department, even if it was just for a month or two in the summer.

If you haven't done every job around an operation this big—and there are a *lot* of jobs here—how can you relate to the people who do those jobs? How can you show compassion, or motivate them? That's something he instilled in me.

You know, one thing that always impressed me about my dad was that whenever we were out somewhere—whether it was a golf tournament or a bar in Daytona—sooner or later somebody would recognize him and stop to talk, and he would always take the time to chat with them. He would talk to them like they were friends.

They'd say, "Hey, do you remember me?"

He'd say, "Sure," and then they'd have a conversation.

Later I'd ask him, "Who was that?"

He'd shrug and say, "I don't know."

I always thought that was interesting, because although that conversation didn't change his day, he knew that to the other person it was probably a big deal. He knew it was important. I think that's a skill, to put yourself in the other person's shoes in that moment.

He did the same thing at work. If he was talking with a manager—or anybody here, really—he would try to look at things the way they looked at them. He believed in taking care of his employees, and doing right by the community.

I think he was that way with fans, friends, everybody. And I've tried to learn from that.

BY MICHELLE BOUCHARD

"He worked very hard, and he was one of those people who always gave his best"

A daughter's thoughts on her very driven dad

According to her sister Tracey, Michelle Bouchard is the member of the family who most remains "addicted to Cup racing." Well, Michelle—called Mimi by family and friends—is hardly to blame for that; virtually every weekend of her childhood and her young adult life, like those of her siblings, was spent watching Modifieds race at New England tracks and Cup cars race on television. Today, from an office at one of her dad's

BOUCHARD FAMILY COLLECTION

dealerships, she can see how his racing fame and business lives overlapped. "I'm sure we have sold cars to people from Connecticut or New Hampshire who watched him win Modified races there," she says. "I'm also sure there have been customers who just love watching NASCAR on TV, who didn't really know my dad but knew that he had raced in the Cup series. They bought from him because he was Ron Bouchard."

I've worked for my father's company for 25 years. That seems hard to believe sometimes, but it's true. My first job at The Honda Store was being that person who makes the follow-up calls to the service customers, and asks if everything went well for them. I liked working for him, but I did not like *that* job. I've always been shy, and I was even more shy back then, so making those calls was not an easy thing for me. But I got over that by thinking, "This is my father's business, and I'm going to do whatever I need to do to help him."

From there I moved over to being a receptionist, working six days a week. That still involved a lot of telephone work, obviously, but taking incoming calls was better than actually making calls. After that I spent some time as assistant to Marlin Knight, who has been our chief operating officer since 1996. Then at some point our office manager retired and I took that job, which is what I'm still doing today. There's a lot involved, and it's stressful sometimes, but I love it.

Robbie works here, too, and even though he's in a different building I usually see him every day, and there are times when I'll need to check with him on a business question, or vice versa. But it's nice, because it's more like calling my brother than just calling somebody in a different office.

As a boss, my father treated me no differently than he treated everybody else here, because that's the way you have to do it when there's family involved. The only bad part, and I say this with a smile, was that sometimes it was hard to get away from the job. Even if I was at his house, visiting, sooner or later he would bring up work.

When he decided that he wasn't going to race anymore, that was definitely a case of mixed emotions for me. From his side, he was doing what he felt was right for him; I understood that then, and I certainly understand it even better today. And it meant we would get to see him more—a lot more—which was good. I also recall that he seemed really excited to be running his own business, and it was nice to see him like that.

At the same time, I was disappointed a little bit. I loved watching the Cup races, and rooting for him. By the end of his time in that series, more and more of the races were televised, and it was fun being able to sit there and cheer him on. In fact, right to this day, because of him, I still look forward to the NASCAR races on television. I root for Jimmie Johnson, and I watch every week.

Anyway, if the race was televised, we watched, and if it wasn't on TV we'd listen to it on the radio. It was a regular thing. We'd all gather at my grandmother's house, and either sit around the radio or stare at the television.

At first it was hard for me to believe that this was really my father out there racing. There had always been races that we'd see a little bit of on television, like the Daytona 500, but to me those races involved a whole different group of people. To suddenly see him out there *with* those people, racing on TV, was strange when I was 12 years old. But once I got used to it, it was nice. It was incredible.

Before that, of course, all of his racing had been done a lot closer to home. I sort of remember going to my first race, and then going to more and being surprised by so many things. At first I didn't know anything about the sport, and I really didn't know anything about my father, either. You know, when you're that young, your dad is just your dad, right? But then I'd listen to people tell these stories about how he had won his first race when he was 14 years old, and to me that was amazing. It's hard enough just to picture your parents *being* 14 years old, and then to think that he actually drove a race car at that age.

One thing I've never forgotten is that whenever we rode to the track with my father, those were scary times for me. It wasn't because I was afraid of his driving; my main concern, every time, was, "Dad, do we have enough gas? Are we going to run out?" I remember looking over his shoulder at the gas gauge, and it seemed like it was *always* just about empty. He would cut it so close. Maybe that's just a guy thing.

The funny thing is, I remember riding *to* a lot of races, but I don't remember coming *home* from very many. I think I was usually asleep before we left the parking lot. That was especially true if we were riding with my father, because he would always hang around after the races, talking with people. When you're the ages we were back then—me, Tracey, Gene, and Robbie—that ends up being a long day and night. Luckily, I never had trouble sleeping in the car. The other good thing was that as long as I was asleep, I didn't have to worry about the gas anymore!

As a kid, it seemed to me like my father won most of the races he ran, although now I'm sure that other drivers won their share, too. I think maybe the wins were just so exciting that they blocked out the nights when he didn't win. He'd race every Friday night, Saturday night, and Sunday night, and even if he won just once it meant the whole weekend was good.

One of the really special things about him winning was that sometimes we'd get to go out on the track and have our picture taken with him. That happened at a lot of places: Stafford, Thompson, Westboro, Monadnock, just about everywhere. I loved doing that.

When he left to go racing in the Cup series, I really missed seeing my dad race in person. Like I said, I did enjoy watching him on television, but I really liked sitting in the grandstands with my family and *seeing* him race. But I was so proud to think that now my dad was in the big leagues, and I absolutely loved it when he would still drive the Modifieds, either on weekends when there wasn't a Cup race or maybe at a midweek event.

He was a great father. He was strict with us, but only when he had to be. I have to say, as kids we were pretty well behaved. As we grew up, we weren't hanging out around town on the weekends, getting into trouble. We were at the races, or watching the races on TV, with our family. That was our life.

My dad was very social. I wish I could be more like him in that way. I'm not a great talker, but he was able to stand there and have a conversation with anybody. It seemed to me that he was comfortable in any situation. No matter what was going on, there he was, always with that great smile. He liked people, and he liked entertaining; when he had people over at his house, he was the center of attention, the life of the party, even without trying to be.

He just *enjoyed* life, and he was able to do more in the short life that he had than most people ever imagine doing. Looking back, I think that anything he really wanted to do, he ended up doing. He wanted to race, and he did that; he wanted to be successful in business, and he was; later he decided that he wanted to travel, and he and Paula traveled the world.

He worked very hard, and he was one of those people who always gave his best. He was going to do whatever it took to succeed, and to make people happy. He was driven, and he wanted us to be driven, too. That must have rubbed off, because I still do the best job I can, for *him*.

I think part of that drive, when it came to business, was just the competitive nature that was left over from racing. He still wanted to be number one, only now he wanted to be the number one car dealer. But it wasn't *just* that; I also think he worked so hard because he wanted to be sure his family had a future in the car business. And that's exactly what's happened.

Sometimes if I'm riding along on Route 2, going to Boston or wherever, I'll be daydreaming and then suddenly I'll see the dealerships. And I'll think, "Wow. Look what he was able to build."

BY GEORGE SUMMERS

"Never did we do anything without having a good time"

Rivals, traveling buddies, and train-wreck survivors

SUMMERS FAMILY COLLECTION

Few drivers can boast of having won the last race they ever ran. George Summers was victorious in his final two, winning Modified features at Oxford, Maine, and Thompson, Connecticut, in the autumn of 1983. Later, with both his trucking business and Bouchard's auto empire doing well, the two friendly foes became inseparable knock-around chums. Their wives even laughed about their closeness. Maggie Summers recalls Ron explaining why he was playing in three golf tournaments in a single week: "Ronnie said, 'I've got this one Friday, and George has two more on Saturday and Sunday.' Paula said, 'But Ronnie, George is retired. You're not!'" Among George's prized possessions: a framed photo of Bouchard's three-wide Talladega win, a reminder of those early Seekonk nights when the pair of them always ran that way, scraping the wall. At the bottom, in Bouchard's handwriting, are the words, "Look, Georgie, no sparks!"

As race drivers, Ronnie and I were closer than most, to the point where we'd kid each other and hang around together a little bit after the races. But it was after we both got done racing that we really started to bond.

We saw each other at least once a week for I don't know how many years. If we didn't play golf, we went to lunch. If we didn't go to lunch, we ran off and took care of some errand one of us had to do.

The phone would ring, and Maggie would answer it. She'd hand it to me and say, "It's Ronnie."

He and I would talk a while, and Maggie would get back to whatever she'd been doing. But when I hung up, she'd always say, "All right, George, where are you going this time?"

We spent so much time together that people used to joke around about it. They'd say, "When you see Bouchard coming, you know Summers is right behind him," or vice versa.

Years ago the two of us stopped at Dale Earnhardt's shop, and after we visited with Dale for a while, he took us around the place. Bob Park—Steve's father, who was a Modified driver himself for a long time—was working for Dale then, and as Dale came around the corner he said to Bob, "Hey, I've got one of your buddies here."

Bob looked up, saw Ronnie standing there, and said, "Where's Summers?"

Then I came around the corner, and Bob said, "I knew it!"

We were very comfortable together. It was just a natural fit. Like, sometimes guys will talk about getting together to play golf, but then it all falls apart because they can't get a foursome together. We didn't care about things like that. Ronnie would call and say, "Hey, George, what are you doing this afternoon?"

I'd say, "Well, I'm not too busy. Why?"

He'd say, "Okay, let's meet at such-and-such course, and we'll play."

The two of us would go play a round of golf, by ourselves, and talk about all kinds of things. We just enjoyed each other's company. We didn't need a whole group. Just the two of us, that was enough.

It seemed like we played golf at every course in New England, sometimes in charity events and sometimes just getting together with friends. We used to play every year up in Loudon, New Hampshire, not far from the race track, in a tournament Ricky Craven was involved with. We also played down in Connecticut, when Randy LaJoie organized a charity tournament. And at least once a year, we'd go out toward Springfield and play with Bob Polverari.

As Ronnie's business got bigger, he ended up getting involved with various tournaments as a sponsor. Sometimes he might sponsor a hole, and in other cases he'd even put up a new car for anybody who got a hole-in-one. Well, that just meant more golf for us.

My phone would ring: "Hey, Georgie, I'm signed up to play in this tournament on Saturday, and they need a fill-in. Help me out here! Come on up!"

Anytime there was a tournament or an outing that had anything to do with the city of Fitchburg, he wanted to be part of it. His friend Charlie Tasca was an officer in the police department for years—actually, Charlie was the chief for a while—so anytime they held any kind of police benefit, we'd go.

Sometimes it went the other way, and Ronnie and I would drag Charlie to different places. Now, anyone who knew Ronnie would tell you that no matter where he was, he always had to be the last one to leave. The three of us were at one function or another, and at the end of the evening Bouchard was chit-chatting with everybody in the place.

Charlie said, "Geez, George, when are we going to get out of here?"

I said, "Charlie, you know better than to ask that question. When this place is finally cleaned out, then we can go."

Well, it got to the point where there were only three tables of people left, and then two, and finally just one.

I said, "It won't be long, now Charlie!"

Charlie stood there a minute, looking things over. Then he walked over to that table and said to all the people sitting there, "Hey, would you folks mind leaving, so we can get the hell out of here?"

It's funny, but with Ronnie and me, our golfing was a lot like our racing had been: In the beginning I had him covered, but the more he played, the better he got, and eventually there came a point where he was better than I was. And even though we were always playing just for fun, both of us were competitive. That was just like our racing, too.

Ronnie would even try to use a little psychology on me. If I put together three or four really good holes, he'd say, "Georgie, you're having a great game. Do you realize how good your score is going to be if you keep playing like this?"

I'd hear that for about two or three holes, and then I'd tell him, "Knock it off, Bouchard. You're just trying to screw with my brain."

He'd say, "Yeah, and I don't have much to work with!"

After we got done golfing, we'd always stop into the clubhouse for a beer, or maybe a few beers, and just shoot the breeze for a while. We'd get drinking and laughing, and sooner or later he'd say to me, "You know something, George? You're a train wreck!"

A lot of times we golfed on Sunday afternoons, and when we'd get to the clubhouse there would be a Cup race on television, so we'd sit and watch that. That was always fun until the broadcasters started talking about the "bump-and-run" passes that those guys get away with, where one guy just drives down into the corner and knocks the other guy's car out of the way. We both hated that, because in our day you just didn't race that way.

But I would get a lot more fired up about it than Ronnie did. I'd start hollering about those damn bump-and-runs, and Ronnie would try to calm me down by saying, "Aw, George, that's just the way they do it these days."

Well, that never made me feel any better about it. So one day after he said that, I took a big sip of my beer and I told him, "You know, Bouchard, it's too bad they didn't let us get away with that stuff years ago. Do you realize how many more wins I'd have had if I'd just knocked you out of the way at Seekonk and Westboro?"

He just laughed and said, one more time, "Georgie, you're a train wreck."

We went to quite a few races together, especially up at New Hampshire, because we liked watching the Modifieds there. That was almost like a social trip for us; we'd see a lot of people and talk to some old friends—both in the Modified pit area and in the Cup garage—and it would be just a nice, pleasant day.

Although, now that I think about it, we did have one day up there that was pretty interesting. Ronnie and I were going to go to Loudon on Thursday for the golf tournament and the lobster dinner they'd have at the track, and then come home. I had a small motorhome, and my son, Ricky, was going to stay in it for the weekend, but he couldn't leave until the next day. Ricky asked me if I'd take the motorhome up to the track and park it for him, so I drove that, and Ronnie drove his car. We got to the track and parked the motorhome on the side of a hill in one of the camping areas up there. I called Ricky to tell him where it was parked, and then Ronnie and I went on with the rest of our day.

The golf was fun, and the lobster dinner was great. The only problem was, they parked a truck full of Budweiser alongside the tent where they held the dinner, and I think Bouchard and I emptied out most of that truck ourselves while we hung around and talked with everybody.

So now it was getting toward the end of the evening, and Ronnie said, "I don't know about you, George, but there's no way I can drive home."

I said, "Me neither. But we can stay in my camper, if we can just find the damn thing!"

He thought that was a good idea, so off we went. We finally remembered where we'd parked it, and we pulled the car in right alongside. Next door there was a group of guys standing around, drinking beer, and they noticed that on the front of the car he had one of those plastic license plates that said "Ron Bouchard's Auto Stores."

Well, it turned out these guys were from Maine, and, naturally, they recognized that name. They were pointing at the plate and hollering, "Yeah, Ron Bouchard!"

I got out and said, "Really? You guys remember that sonofabitch?"

We started talking with them, and pretty soon they figured out that this guy standing with them actually *was* Ronnie Bouchard. We ended up having a few more beers with them before we gave up and went to bed.

I think that was a double train wreck.

In the morning, we got up and headed home. Ricky got to the track and found the camper. Like I said, it was parked on the side of a hill, so it sat at an angle. Ricky started talking with those guys from Maine, and he said, "I can't believe my father parked this thing like that, and that they slept in it that way."

They told him, "Well, it didn't look quite so bad last night. They must have both slept on the same side!"

Boy, we had some good times ...

When Ronnie had his boat, he'd call and say, "Come on, Georgie. Let's go to Florida." His captain lived in North Carolina, so that's where the boat stayed during the winter. He and I would drive down there, get on the boat, and head to Florida.

One year we had David Ifft with us, and David is a joker. We were sailing down the Intracoastal Waterway, and we were almost to Ormond Beach, just north of Daytona. Well, that's where Vic and Sandy Kangas live, so Ronnie called ahead and said, "Hey, Vic, we're going to be going past you guys in a few minutes."

Vic told him, "When you get to the Ormond Beach bridge, we'll be on it."

So we get to the bridge, and we can see Vic and Sandy standing there, waving. Ronnie and I are at the side of the boat, waving back, but not David. Instead, he drops his pants and moons 'em!

The last time Ronnie I went to Florida together was in the fall of 2014. We never had trouble carrying on a conversation, and I don't think there was a quiet minute in that car from the time we left Massachusetts. We made a detour through Charlotte, because the NASCAR Hall of Fame wanted some of his stuff, and we visited a bunch of friends in that area. We stopped to see Clyde McLeod, who both of us had known forever, and checked out Ray Evernham's shop and all the cars he's collected, and we drove over to Richard Childress's place. Then we headed down to David Ifft's house, where we had a little party and stayed the night.

It was just an enjoyable trip, like so many others we had taken.

We were together as friends, good friends, for 50 years. It's amazing how fast it all went.

In 2013, Seekonk Speedway started what they call their Wall of Fame, and the first three drivers they honored were Bugsy Stevens, Ronnie, and me. It was a beautiful night, and they rode us around the track on golf carts, with all the people waving. That was just so fitting, because to all three of us, that track was home. And I think about that now, because for Ronnie and me that's where it all started, with him showing up there for the first time and chasing me around in warm-ups.

Over the years, our families grew to be so close. You know, Ronnie had a beautiful '36 Ford, perfectly restored, and when our daughter Kathie was about to get married, Ronnie said, "Why don't I come down with that car, and I'll drive you guys to the church and the reception."

I told him that would be really nice. When he showed up, he was all dressed up like a chauffeur, wearing a big top hat.

To Maggie and me, his kids were like our own kids, and I know he and Paula felt the same way about our family. When Mary, our oldest daughter, got married, Chad was just a little boy, and he was in the wedding party.

We raced together, we golfed together, and we did a lot of traveling, and never did we do anything without having a good time.

You know, there was a 14-year difference in our ages, so early on our relationship was almost like father and son. But as you get older, things change, and you don't look at somebody's age the same way you used to. So, as time went by, it was like the gap between our ages closed up, and we became more like brothers.

That's how it was, really. We were like a couple of brothers.

God, what memories I've got. I'll never forget the guy. I'll never, ever forget him.

PART SIX

Checkered Flag

DICK BERGGREN

On a lousy Thursday morning in December of 2015, word shot around Motorsports America that Ron Bouchard was gone. The news hit like a thud, anywhere and everywhere. What was it Mike Joy had said? That Ronnie never met a stranger? Well, when everybody is a friend, grief has real weight.

His old Winston Cup crew chief, David Ifft, had just come in from fiddling around at his South Carolina shop. "I sat down in front of the TV, and turned on one of the sports channels," he says. "You know that little news-update deal that scrolls across the bottom of the screen? I thought I saw something that said 'Bouchard,' but I missed it. So I watched until it came around again, and there it was. I could not believe it."

Geoff Bodine, whose relationship was Bouchard was occasionally frosty but never frozen—says, "My brother Brett called me. Someone called him—I believe it was George or Maggie Summers—and Brett immediately called me. It was a shock."

As for George Summers, as close a pal as Bouchard had, being the bearer of this bad news took on a whole new dimension.

"There's a bunch of us old racers from the Northeast who either live in the Daytona area, or spend time there in the winter," George says. "Every year, once we all get down there, we meet up for breakfast. It's always such a happy thing. This year it just so happened that it was on the morning Ronnie died.

"To walk in there and see those guys—Bugsy Stevens, Leo Cleary, Billy Harman, Greg Sacks, Bobby Judkins, and several others—was the hardest thing for me, because they didn't know yet."

Stevens, just inside the restaurant, saw bad news coming, but had no idea what it was.

"George had tears in his eyes, standing outside the door," Bugsy remembers. "I said, 'What's the matter?' He said that Ronnie had just passed away.

"I couldn't believe it. *Ronnie Bouchard*. Jesus."

There was a common thread to almost everyone's surprise, best summed up by Ricky Rudd: "I did not realize his health was declining. I guess a lot of people didn't."

Oh, there had been hints, but none for a while. Several years earlier, Bouchard had suffered a collapsed lung, no small matter. But he bounced back from that; though occasionally short of breath, he was as robust as any 60-something ex-racer had a right to be. Every now and again folks might ask around if Ronnie didn't turn up for this function or that one, but the general conclusion was always the same: that he was busy, not ailing.

"Anytime I saw him," said Pete Salvatore, his old mentor, "he looked good. He was always smiling."

Behind the grin, though, there was real trouble this time. Bouchard had a lung cancer scare in 2010, though few knew about the diagnosis or the subsequent surgery. Now, after years of clean checkups, his cancer had roared back, aggressively. There might have been signs at the end of 2014, when he and Summers made their near-annual drive to Florida. Maggie Summers recalls her husband telling her then, "I think Ronnie might be in a little more trouble than we realized. He's hurting more than he's letting on." But the official diagnosis didn't come until May of 2015, and the outlook was not bright.

Ron Bouchard, as you'll read, chose to keep this news to himself. Dignity over sympathy, he figured, and who among us wouldn't wish to be that stoic, that tough?

"You know how people say somebody is like an open book?" asks Ed Flemke Jr., friend and brother-in-law. "Ronnie was probably the most open-book person I ever knew, unless he had something he wanted to keep to himself. In that case, he just would not speak."

So if you heard anything at all about the Kid from Fitchburg across the 2015 race season, it was not about his uncertain future, but instead his glorious past. He was preparing to open what he called the RB Racing Museum in his hometown, on the same patch of ground where his father's moving business and race cars had gotten this whole thing started. He had several people—Flemke, Chuck Grime, and Maine fabricating whiz Bobby Turner, among others—working on restorations and recreations of cars that had been central to his short-track career. Others driven through the years by Summers, brother Ken Bouchard, and the late Steady Eddie Flemke were also being readied. And David Ifft had done some remarkable sleuthing to track down Bouchard's Talladega 500 winner, which had been sold off, raced anonymously in ARCA, parked in garages in Georgia and Alabama, and ultimately discovered in Mooresville, North Carolina, "with a tree growing up through the engine bay."

The museum opened with an invitation-only reception in September, with a couple hundred of Bouchard's closest friends digging the old cars, digging the memorabilia, digging one another's company, and mostly digging this wonderful vibe that Ronnie had created. There had never been any disputing that he was Fitchburg's favorite racing son. On this night, he was New England's.

Promoter Dick Williams recalls, "A group of us were standing there—Greg Sacks, Bobby Turner, just a bunch of guys—and you couldn't help but look at all the trophies. It really drove home how many of my races Ronnie had won. At one point I said, 'Geez, I bought *that* trophy, and *that* one, and *that* one …'

"Sacks said, 'Ronnie, you owe this poor guy. He paid for all those trophies, and you took 'em all home!' And we laughed, just like we all used to at the races."

Among those traveling in for the occasion were Bob and Gussie Johnson. Seeing them, says Flemke, "was one of my highlights from that night, because Bob was beaming. He knew he was a big part of Ronnie getting where he got."

Johnson says, "That whole night was pretty awesome. I saw a lot of people I hadn't seen in years."

Days later, over the weekend, came the public opening, with something like a thousand people filing in and the New England Antique Racers club ringing the lot with grand old cars.

"When that museum opened," says George Summers, "Ronnie was just so proud."

He was also dying.

The sorrow in that realization is tempered—not much, but, yes, a little bit—by the secondary realization that he was the only person there who, in his own way, was able to say goodbye.

"Ronnie got to go to his own wake," says Flemke.

After her husband's death, Paula Bouchard created the RB Racing Charity, with the stated aim of fighting lung cancer and preserving "Ron Bouchard's legacy of helping to improve the local community and the lives of children." Among her first initiatives: a fundraising drive to purchase a pair of vans to transport cancer patients from Worcester's Hope Lodge to their treatment sessions in Boston.

"Cancer touches everybody's lives," she says. "It's a horrific disease."

A few months removed from Bouchard's passing, the sting of that December thud still remains. It is masked at times by the laughter brought on by old racing stories, or by warm smiles touched off by certain photographs. But it's there.

"I remember telling Ronnie at his museum opening that I wanted to come back when it wasn't so busy," says Bob Johnson, "so I could check out the rest of his operation and spend some time with him. And that ain't going to happen."

Clyde McLeod says, "In life, you lose touch sometimes. It happens when you're busy. Ronnie used to say every year, 'You and Annie have to come see us in Florida this winter.' But I was working, and we always had stuff going on. This was the year we were finally going to go."

Listen to David Ifft: "I've got a picture of Ronnie at home. I get up every morning and see that thing, and I get pissed off. I just ask why. Why?"

And Chuck Grime: "It's tough for me to even think about him being gone. I'm sure I'm not the only person in this boat, but there were so many things I wish I had said to him."

But what would be the right thing? Is there one at all?

Ed Flemke Jr., fumbling for words the last time he visited Ron Bouchard, came about as close as you could hope to under the circumstances.

"It was time for me to go," Eddie recalls, "and he said, 'I guess this is one race I'm not going to win.'

"I told him, 'Well, Ronnie, you led the most laps.'"

Didn't he, though?

BY PAULA BOUCHARD

"God only knows what was going through his mind..."

Private pain, and a courageous, dignified struggle

Grit surfaces in the most unlikely places. Such is the case with Paula Bouchard, who over 40 years at Ron's side had seen a life filled with terrific highs only to have it all crash down around them when cancer took her husband at age 67. In their time together she had been a babysitter, a wife, a stepmom, a mother, a traveling companion, a business partner, and a best friend, which is certainly all anyone could want in a mate. She speaks in the following paragraphs about Ronnie's strength and courage; he'd have no doubt been proud of hers, too. An old philosopher a world away from Fitchburg—and Talladega and Stafford Springs and all the places where Ron and Paula had their best moments—said, "Being deeply loved by someone gives you strength, while loving someone deeply gives you courage." Amen to that, and for that.

DICK BERGGREN

Ronnie was such a strong person, and so courageous. In the last ten years of his life, he had a lot go wrong, in terms of his health. But he kept things to himself, and he dealt with everything day by day.

Four times, he had what is called a spontaneous pneumothorax, which is basically a collapsed lung. The first time he was in the air, flying to an auto show in Las Vegas. His flight made a scheduled stop in Cincinnati, and when he called me he was so out of breath that for a minute I thought the plane had crash-landed. He had terrible pain in his chest, but it was on his right side so he knew it wasn't a heart problem. They brought him by ambulance to a hospital, and I flew out that same day.

He had to go through a procedure where they insert a tube through your ribs to help the lung re-inflate. We ended up staying there for a couple of days, because it takes time for the doctors to be sure that the lung is healing. He was not allowed to fly, so we rented a car and drove home to Massachusetts. He actually felt good enough on the trip that he helped me drive.

Some time later he was misdiagnosed with an enlarged prostate, which turned out to be diverticulitis, so he had to have surgery for that.

Early in 2010, he was diagnosed with Stage 2 lung cancer. Ronnie's way of dealing with that was to say, "Doc, do whatever you have to do to get me another 20 years. Give me all you got," meaning chemo, radiation, whatever it took.

He never wanted to know the specifics. I read everything I could to learn about the prognosis, and I printed it out for him. But he kept his distance; he didn't want to talk about it.

"Just give me another 20 years," he'd say.

They removed a portion of his left lung, and then we made daily trips to the Dana-Farber/Brigham and Women's Cancer Center in Boston for treatments. Every day, back and forth, through the snow, with Ronnie driving both ways. Then he developed an infection after the surgery, which meant another short hospital stay. After they sent him home, he had to receive antibiotics intravenously for a month; every day, I'd clean out the connecting tube and hook him up to a new bag of antibiotics. Through it all, his spirits were incredibly strong.

We kept all of this to ourselves, partly because he believed it was a private thing and partly because we had 200 people working at the dealerships, and he didn't want to worry them. We told the kids and a couple of key employees, and that was it.

For the next five years, we walked on eggshells. You're always concerned about the next checkup, the next round of tests. Every time they say things look good, you're so relieved, and for a while life seems normal. Then two weeks prior to the next checkup, you're on eggshells again.

In the meantime, we still had a business to run. Our dealerships in Lancaster were new at that time, and one of the manufacturer reps had stopped by. He said, "You know, Ronnie, you really should put up some photos from your racing career."

That was something we hadn't done to any extent, either at work or at home. Ronnie had accomplished so much, but we never really had anything on display, other than a few racing photos in his office. So we did that in the Honda dealership, and a funny thing happened: Customers would walk over from the Nissan and Kia buildings because someone there had mentioned these photos. So I got together some more photos, and did the same thing there. I think seeing all that, and thinking about all the history, is what got Ronnie thinking about a museum.

We had the Talladega-winning car, and had lots of other items that were significant in Ronnie's career. A museum would be an ideal way to have it all in one place. And with most of the dealerships having moved from their original location in Fitchburg, we had a perfect spot for it, because that very site had been the home to his father's first race cars. So, over a period of time, that museum became our project; I did the design work along with our good friend Mary Summers, and we had so much help from Bob Bergeron in gathering everything and figuring out where it was going to go. Ronnie would come by to check out how things were going, and he was happy to see it all coming together.

We went to Florida for the winter of 2014–15 knowing that the following spring, in May, Ronnie had another test scheduled. If it went well, that would mark five years since he'd been declared cancer-free after his lung surgery, and that five-year point is a big milestone. But toward the end of our stay in Florida, Ronnie wasn't feeling well; in fact, we had some Honda meetings to attend and he was unable to go, so Chad and I went in his place.

When we got back to Massachusetts, we went for Ronnie's checkup, and they told us his cancer had returned. We broke the news to the kids. Gene, Robbie, Michelle, and Tracey all live close by, and Chad had said, "Anytime you want me to come home, Dad, I'll be there." Now he made plans to move back from Florida.

Our hospital schedule at that point was a week of radiation visits, then some time off, and then a regimen of chemotherapy.

The museum had been coming along well, and we decided to have a private opening for invited guests. We picked September 24, a Thursday night, because it coincided with a NASCAR weekend at New Hampshire Motor Speedway, and this way some of those people would be able to come. There was pressure to get everything done on time, so in the weeks before the opening I spent a lot of time there with Mary and Bergie. I could tell Ronnie was pleased with it; by then we had several cars in place, as well as trophy collections, old suits and helmets, and hundreds of photos. I'm sure it had to bring back all kinds of memories for him.

Sometimes at the museum I'd see him standing in the doorway, looking out. I'd say to myself, "I wonder what he's thinking..."

He insisted that we had to stay quiet about his illness, especially with this private event coming up. The last thing he wanted was a pity party, with people asking how he was feeling. He wanted that night to be a celebration.

And that's exactly what it turned out to be. The opening of the RB Racing Museum had a wonderful turnout, over 200 people. There were car owners Ronnie had driven for, drivers he had raced against, lots of people who had worked with him on different teams, and so many familiar faces.

It was a proud evening for him. I could see that on his face. It was also a big relief for me; I was so glad that he was able to see it happen, and that he got to spend that time with so many of his friends. And everyone who came went home with great memories of that night, instead of thinking, "Wow, this could be the end."

Which, of course, it was. There were eleven weeks between the opening of the museum and Ronnie's passing, and in that time things only got worse. The cancer went from his lung to his brain to his sacrum, and then it ravaged his whole body.

The Monday after the opening, we were back in the real world, back to our schedule—work and doctors—and trying to keep everything together.

One evening we had to go to a wake, and we went straight there from a chemotherapy session.

We drove down to Connecticut twice to visit Jack Beebe, who was very ill with cancer himself. Jack was at home; he knew that he was near the end of his life. He passed away in October, and his wife, Chris, asked if Ronnie would say something at Jack's funeral. Here was Ronnie, dying of his own cancer, but he got up in front of everybody and spoke.

All along, the treatments were taking more and more out of him. He developed neuropathy, nerve damage in his feet; he said it was like walking in golf shoes that had the spikes on the inside. And he was finding it harder to breathe. At the dealership we'd come in through a side door, but that meant coming up two flights of stairs and he got to the point where he couldn't do that anymore.

He was in constant pain, excruciating pain. Sometimes when we went into Boston for a chemo treatment, I'd pack an overnight bag because he'd hurt so bad that the doctors would insist that he just spend the night. And he'd always want me to stay; he'd ask the nurse, "Can you provide a bed or a chair for my wife? I'd like her to be with me."

We had these little routines we got into. He had to be sure we had a five-dollar bill handy, so he could tip the man who met us at the hospital door with the wheelchair. That was Ronnie; this man was doing something nice for him, so he wanted to do something nice in return.

Throughout all of this, his courage never wavered. By now I was the one driving back and forth to Boston, and it was so hard looking over at him in the passenger seat, sometimes sleeping and sometimes resting, again just gazing into the distance.

God only knows what was going through his mind.

He didn't want to have dinner with anybody, didn't want to socialize at all, which was unusual for him. He was slowly disconnecting, I think, from the world.

And yet every day, whenever possible, he would come into this office and sit at his desk. He spent a lot of time tightening things up at the business, making sure everything was in order. Sometimes I'd look up and catch him staring at me. Sometimes, if things were slow, he'd turn on the TV. If he had to walk out of the office, where someone might see him, he'd just put on his game face and never let on how badly he was feeling.

To watch somebody who'd had so much strength and power get weaker ... to have to help him get out of bed every day ... to lift his leg over the side of the tub while he held onto the showerhead ... to dress him ...

But we got through it. We did it together.

On what turned out to be our final regular trip to Boston—it was November 23, Ronnie's birthday—he received Opdivo, a new type of chemotherapy that is meant to prolong your life. It was a few days before Thanksgiving, and one of the doctors said, "Just go home, Ronnie, and enjoy the holidays."

He was being polite, but I remember thinking that something about that phrase didn't sound right. I think that's just how you react in these situations: You find yourself always reading between the lines.

We were on our way home, and I was driving, and Ronnie said, "I think maybe now I'd better tell my friend George ..."

He meant George Summers, his best buddy. So he called George, and they talked.

That night at 10:00 p.m., I gave him his nightly painkillers, and then we both fell asleep. Because of everything we'd been through, every time I woke up I'd listen carefully to his breathing. Well, on this night, it sounded not quite normal, so right away I called Boston. The doctor I spoke with looked up Ronnie's chart from that day, and didn't see anything alarming. It was 2:30 a.m., but I said, "Maybe I should bring him there."

She suggested that the best thing would be to bring him to the local emergency room, so we went to a hospital in Leominster. The doctor there called Dana-Farber/Brigham and Women's, and Ronnie's oncologist happened to be on call. The oncologist told the ER doctor to start Ronnie on some antibiotics, which they did. I asked if we could bring him to Boston, because that's where his doctors were. They said, sure, we could have him transferred. At 8:00 a.m., they put him in an ambulance and took him there.

That ride to Boston was the last time he was outside a hospital.

When we got him to there, Ronnie said, "I know I'm dying. You'd better call the kids."

I said, "Hon, you're not dying ..."

But I thought to myself that if, God forbid, something happened and I hadn't called the kids ...

So at about 10:30, I called Chad. I told him, "Dad wants to see you guys. Please get everybody together, and come here."

By then they had Ronnie on a lot of medication, and I think he was starting to get foggy. I told him the kids were on their way, and he said, "Oh, they don't need to come. I'm all right."

You know, earlier I mentioned the pain he was in. When he was in the hospital this final time, they discovered that he had a fractured hip, and we never even knew it. He had been living with a fractured hip. When I heard that, my heart fell to my feet. Think how much pain you'd have to be feeling in the rest of your body to not complain about a *fractured hip*.

To watch a loved one die of cancer … there are no words to describe that.

He was in the hospital for a little over two weeks. I wanted to bring Ronnie home at the end, but we couldn't do that because he needed constant oxygen.

He died on December 10.

A lot of people were shocked, and some were even upset that we hadn't told them how ill Ronnie was. I understood that, but this was Ronnie's idea. It just wasn't in his nature to want anyone feeling sorry for him. And it's comforting to me to know that they never had to see him sick, never had to see him fading away. The last image they had of Ron Bouchard—at a race, or at the museum opening, or wherever—was of him smiling, looking happy.

He did it his way.

Ronnie had an amazing life.

I was privileged to have loved him, and to have cared for him.

Afterword

Ron Bouchard's life wasn't long, by modern standards. He was only 67. But, boy, if you were lucky enough to watch it play out, you know that it was a big life, by *any* standards.

The real shame of his career is that casual fans who knew him only through what he'd done on NASCAR's biggest stages—his Winston Cup triumph at Talladega, and those two Busch Series victories at Darlington—never understood what a prolific winner he had been.

But all who ever went up against Bouchard knew what they were dealing with. George Summers tells a story about Ronnie introducing him to Dale Earnhardt at Daytona way back when, and saying, "George is the guy who taught me how to turn left." They were standing in a group, and when Bouchard turned to talk with someone else, Earnhardt—in that low, conspiratorial voice he'd employ when he wanted to make a serious point—told Summers, "Buddy, if you really taught him, you did a damn good job, because that guy could drive a race car."

Back home in the Northeast, they'd never forgotten that. For his funeral, hundreds packed the huge St. Joseph Church in Fitchburg. The cortege was headed by brother Ken, wheeling that Talladega-winning Buick: white flanks, yellow top, a vivid blue #47 on its doors. The previous evening, three or four times as many folks—locals, auto-industry reps, and a Who's Who of area racing—stood in the rain for hours to pay their respects.

The weather was appropriate: tears for the Kid.

But come morning, when the procession carried him home, the clouds parted just enough to reveal a sky as blue as the numbers on that Buick, and the sun beamed down like Bouchard's wide, bright smile.

INDEX

Airborne Park Speedway, Plattsburgh, NY, 56
Albany-Saratoga Speedway, Malta, NY, 43, 56
Alkas, Dave, 110
Allard, Lee, 91, 119, 123, 129
Allison, Bobby, 26, 76, 89, 138, 139, 140, 168, 170 and throughout
Allison, Donnie, 76, 140, 189
Anderson, M.C., 166
Armstrong, Carol, 104, 119
Armstrong, Dick, 6, 16, 22, 23, 29–31, 37, 40, 42 and throughout
Armstrong, Kim, 117
Arute Jr., Jack "Jackie," 49–52, 61–66, 86, 123, 124, 185, 186
Arute, Jack, 41, 44, 45, 49–52, 83, 86–87, 89 and throughout
Astle, Deke, 20, 34
Astle, Fred, 20
Astle, Jon, 20
Atlanta Motor Speedway, Hampton, GA, 135, 142, 149, 155, 179, 189
Atlantic Racing Association, 2
Bahre, Bob, 186
Baker, Buddy, 137, 139, 143, 166, 178–181, 183–184, 195
Barbeau, Red, 20, 34
Barrett, Stan, 136
Barry, Art, 42
Bateman, Jack, 118
Baumgardner, Wayne, 139
Beam, Mike, 140
Becker, Al, 68, 69
Beebe, Chris, 224
Beebe, Jack, 104, 105, 114, 120, 130, 134–136, 138–140 and throughout
Beebe, Mike, 134
Beech Ridge Speedway, Scarborough, ME, 196
Benson, Johnny, 153
Bergeron, Bob "Bergie," 13, 17, 27, 69, 76, 139, 192, 223

Bergeron, JoAnn Bouchard, 2, 4, 5, 13–18, 45, 75, 88, 92 and throughout
Berggren, Dick, 44
Berghman, Debbie, 117
Bergin, Gene, 25, 41, 42, 56, 62, 65, 88, 93 and throughout
Billmyer, Jack, 188, 193, 194
Bird, Amos, 4
Bird, Steve, 4, 150, 153–158, 167, 168, 186
Blaisdell, Calvin, 19, 20, 26, 27, 34, 76, 90, 96
Bodine, Brett, 107, 186, 218
Bodine, Geoff, 6, 23, 31, 42, 45, 46, 65, 76 and throughout
Bodine, Todd, 107
Boehler, Len, 41, 49, 56, 71, 87, 90–92, 96, 108 and throughout
Bonneau, Alice, 121, 123
Bonneau, Paul, 119, 121–123
Bonneau, Rich, 121–126
Bosco, Jimmy, 29, 47
Bouchard, Bob, 2–4, 7, 8, 10, 13–17, 20, 21, 23, 24 and throughout
Bouchard, Chad, 139, 151, 164, 196, 198, 201, 203–206, 216 and throughout
Bouchard, Gene, 5, 73–78, 116, 117, 135, 194
Bouchard, Joshua, 73
Bouchard, Katie, 73
Bouchard, Ken, 2, 13, 14, 17, 19, 23, 25, 40, and throughout
Bouchard, Lorraine, 2, 4, 11, 13–15, 75, 116, 123, 138 and throughout
Bouchard, Michelle, 5, 74, 150, 172, 207–210, 223
Bouchard, Paula Flemke, 45, 79, 81, 82, 89, 109–111, 119 and throughout
Bouchard, Regi, 5, 6, 36

Bouchard, Rob, 5, 74–76, 115–120, 123, 138, 139, 194 and throughout
Bourget, Tommy, 23
Boyd, Lew, 180
Boyer, Paul, 44, 45
Brady, Anne, 117
Brady, Brian, 116
Brady, Joe, 42, 71, 96, 97, 116, 123, 165, 166 and throughout
Bristol Motor Speedway, Bristol, TN, 136, 142, 150, 156
Brookline Speedway, Brookline, NH, 2, 3, 4, 7, 8, 11, 14, 15, 18, 25 and throughout
Brooks, Dick, 132, 193
Bubbico, Joe, 80
Byrnes, Steve, 180
Caraway Speedway, Sophia, NC, 91
Carlson, Teddy, 21
Carroll, Ed, 185
Caruso, Mario "Fats", 7, 9, 93
Catamount Stadium, Milton, VT, 56
Cerease, Angie, 71
Champion, Bill, 159
Charland, Rene, 40
Charlotte Motor Speedway, Concord, NC, 61, 160, 168, 170, 189
Cherenzia, Sam, 128
Childress, Richard, 157, 163, 215
Cleary, Leo, 22, 42, 49, 56, 61, 91, 101, 108 and throughout
Colson, Fran, 178
Colwell, George, 179
Connecticut Dragway, Colchester, CT, 19
Conway, Russ, 4, 139, 177–184, 185, 195
Cook, Jerry, 42, 43, 45, 46, 88, 89, 90, 91 and throughout
Corazzo, Billy, 71, 88, 107, 109, 110
Craven, Ricky, 212

229

Curb, Mike, 140, 188, 189
Curley, Ken, 27, 34
Dana-Farber/Brigham and Women's Cancer Center., 222, 225
Danbury Racearena, Danbury, CT, 86
Danville Bee, 44
Darlington Raceway, Darlington, SC, 139, 168, 170, 188, 189, 227
Davis, Bill, 130
Daytona International Speedway, Daytona Beach, FL, 45, 46, 61, 71, 89, 91, 101, 135 and throughout
DeSarro, Bryan, 90
DeSarro, Fred, 22, 41, 46, 56, 57, 62, 65, 70 and throughout
DeSarro, Gary, 90
DeSarro, Linda, 90
Dias, Dave, 34
DiNardo, Al, 171
DiNardo, Anthony, 171
DiNardo, Tracey Bouchard, 5, 74, 150, 171–176, 197, 207, 209, 223
Dingman, Billy, 25, 139
Dodge, Ben, 124, 125
Dodge, Herb, 2, 5, 6
Dorton, Randy, 160
Dostie, Jerry, 23, 40, 63
Dover International Speedway, Dover, DE, 135, 151, 168, 169, 172
Dowd, Russ, 125
Drezek, Rick, 83
Dufour, John, 139, 168, 193
Earles, Clay, 64
Earnhardt Jr., Dale, 184
Earnhardt, Dale, 115, 136, 138, 139, 150, 170, 171, 183, 184 and throughout
Earnhardt, Teresa, 150, 184, 200
Echo, Bob, 137
Echo, Jared, 137
Eggleston, Homer, 3
Elder, Jake, 139, 161
Ellington, Hoss, 140, 189, 192
Elliott, Bill, 157
Elliott, Charlie, 177, 178

Ellis, Bobby, 124
Ellis, Lenny, 124, 125
Evans, Richie, 6, 42, 43–47, 89, 90, 92, 96, 97 and throughout
Evernham, Ray, 215
Farone, Butch, 65
Federici, Frank, 126
Felton, Freddy, 118
Fenway Park, Boston, MA, 5
Fiandaca, Pete, 3, 23, 153, 154, 158, 179
Fierson, Chuck, 43
Flemke Jr., Ed, 79–84, 89, 134, 136, 138, 147, 196, 198 and throughout
Flemke, Ed, 22, 41, 42, 43, 45, 46, 56, 57 and throughout
Flynn, Bill, 71
Foyt, A.J., 42
France Jr., Bill, 57, 144, 183
France Sr., Bill, 112, 113
Frederick, Brian, 126
Fuller, Bobby, 183
Fuller, Jeff, 183
Fuller, Rick, 183
Gahan, Ernie, 6, 29
Gant, Harry, 42, 96, 105, 136, 141–143, 151, 154, 155 and throughout
Garbarino, Bob, 42
Garde, Cheech, 167, 168
Gardner, Bill, 160, 161
Garuti Family, 110
Gazaway, Joe, 144, 145
Giroux, Denis, 23, 31, 42, 43
Gordon, Jeff, 62, 193
Grant, Earl, 61
Greger, Stan, 80, 93, 108, 110
Griffith, Andy, 136
Grime, Chuck, 87, 88, 89, 91, 98, 118, 124, 134, 219–220 and throughout
Hagwood, Steve, 2
Hall, Barney, 186
Hamilton, Pete, 42
Hanley, Junior, 89, 186
Harbach, Fred, 108
Harman, Billy, 218
Harrington, Hop, 6, 22, 23, 30, 40, 89, 97, 101 and throughout

Harris, Phil, 122
Hartman, Jimmy, 2
Hartung, Kenny, 137
Harty, Marty, 3, 25, 26
Hathaway, Randy, 104
Hendrick, Ray, 6, 22, 29, 43, 44, 57, 100, 101 and throughout
Hendrick, Rick, 160, 186
Hewitt, Moose, 53
Hoenig, Don, 90, 179, 180
Hood, Bill, 87, 94
Howard, Joe, 123
Hoyle, Eddie, 20, 34, 121
Hudson Speedway, Hudson, NH, 4, 26, 33, 68, 153, 177, 178, 180, 183–184
Humphrey, Sen. Gordon, 180, 181
Huntsville Speedway, Huntsville, AL, 189
Hyde, Harry, 160
Ifft, David, 139, 157, 165–170, 192, 196, 215, 218–220
Indianapolis Motor Speedway, Indianapolis, IN, 61
Irvan, Ernie, 141
Jackson, Wally, 112, 150
Janisaitis, John, 124
Jarzombek, Charlie, 89, 108, 116
Jeffries, Chuck, 124
Johnson, Bob, 23, 40–54, 56, 58, 59, 62, 63, 70 and throughout
Johnson, Gussie, 40, 47, 51, 62, 74, 136, 150, 219
Johnson, Jimmie, 208
Johnson, Junior, 154, 157, 161
Johnson, Tommy, 160
Joy, Mike, 61, 123, 124, 163, 183, 185–190, 218
Judkins, Bob, 41, 42, 53, 81, 87–89, 91, 93–98 and throughout
Kalkowski, Steve, 88, 89, 119, 124, 137
Kangas, Sandy, 215
Kangas, Vic, 5, 6, 19, 21–23, 25–32, 34, 40 and throughout
Keene Fairgrounds Speedway, Keene, NH, 9, 10
Kent, George, 45, 108

Kingsport Speedway, Kingsport, TN, 89, 90, 96, 98
Knight, Marlin, 195, 208
Koivu, Dick, 21
Koszela, Sonny, 41, 50, 56, 64, 71, 97
Krebs, Art, 144, 145
Labonte, Kim, 150
Labonte, Terry, 137, 139, 142, 156, 162, 166, 187
LaJoie, Don, 53
LaJoie, Randy, 141, 146, 153, 212
Laughlin, Mike, 168
Lee USA Speedway, Lee, NH, 177, 183
LeSieur, Val, 122
Levesque, Tiny, 21
Libbey, Jim, 181
Lind, Dave, 181
Lindblad, Rollie, 88, 94, 97
Lukasavage, John, 70, 71
Lund, Tiny, 26
Lussier, Annette, 73
Makar, Jimmy, 160
Mantle, Mickey, 41
Marquis, Jerry, 93
Marsh, Teddy, 71
Martinsville Speedway, Ridgeway, VA, 42–48, 52, 55, 58, 59, 64, 76, 91 and throughout
Marvel, Bob, 29
Mays, Willie, 41
McClure, Al, 100
McDuffie, J.D., 154
McLaughlin, Mike, 107
McLean, T.K., 100
McLeod, Ann Marie, 110, 138, 148, 149, 151, 152, 220
McLeod, Clyde, 107–114, 136, 138, 148, 149, 151, 194, 215, 220 and throughout
Means, Jimmy, 189
Melling, Harry, 157
Membrino, Jap, 110
Metrolina Speedway, Charlotte, NC, 100
Michaud, Jean, 71, 150, 194
Michaud, Julie, 117
Michaud, Kathie, 117

Michigan International Speedway, Brooklyn, MI, 138, 144, 157, 169, 187, 188
Miller, Ray, 42, 108
Mitchell, Clayton, 6, 29
Monadnock Speedway, Winchester, NH, 18, 19, 44, 45, 52, 59, 67, 88 and throughout
Moore, Bud, 157, 163, 165
Mordino, Tony, 93
Moroso, Rob, 153
Motor Racing Network, 65, 86, 185
Murphy, Mike, 178, 179
Murray, George, 123
Murray, Jim, 167
Nacewicz, Billy, 113
Nashville Superspeedway, Nashville, TN, 167, 168, 169, 188, 189
National Speed Sport News, 159
Needham, Hal, 136, 142, 186
Nemechek, Joe, 25
New England Auto Racers (NEAR), 3, 42, 220
New Hampshire Motor Speedway, Loudon, NH, 163, 186, 214, 223
New Smyrna Speedway, New Smyrna Beach, FL, 89, 91, 96, 111–113, 134, 151
Newman, Paul, 140
North Wilkesboro Speedway, North Wilkesboro, NC, 156, 187
Norwood Arena, Norwood, MA, 33, 41, 56, 80
Onners, Mike, 3
Orange Dragway, Orange, MA, 19
Orsini, Mario, 21
Osgood, Bryan, 43, 48
Oswego Speedway, Oswego, NY, 43, 45, 49, 118, 119, 137
Oxford Plains Speedway, Oxford, ME, 69, 76, 211
Park, Bob, 212
Park, Steve, 212
Parsons, Benny, 165, 167, 170
Parsons, Marcia, 150

Pearson, David, 42, 140, 154, 157, 189
Peterson, Pete, 166
Petty, Kyle, 139
Petty, Lynda, 140, 150
Petty, Richard, 42, 137, 139, 140, 154, 157, 179–185, 194
Pines Speedway, Groveland, MA, 4, 11, 15, 33, 154
Plainville Stadium, Plainville, CT, 67, 80, 86, 88, 108, 110
Pocono Raceway, Long Pond, PA, 6, 16, 22, 23, 29–32, 37, 43, 47 and throughout
Pocono Record, 43
Polverari, Bob, 136, 212
Powers, Jim, 195, 198, 199
Progin, Tinker, 15, 26
ProSpeed Revue, 122
Radewick, Marty, 118
Radford, Paul, 42, 96
Ramstrom, Bob, 71
Randolph, Dunk, 118
Ranier, Harry, 157
RB Racing Museum, Fitchburg, MA, 13, 219, 220, 222–224
Red & White Movers, 2, 3, 10, 11, 13, 16, 17, 21, 23 and throughout
Reynolds, Burt, 136, 186
Richardson, Paul, 179
Richmond, Tim, 139, 182–185
Richmond International Raceway, Richmond, VA, 136, 142, 189
Rifchin, Marvin, 28, 45, 81, 87–91, 93–97, 103, 108 and throughout
Riverside International Raceway, Riverside, CA, 148, 160, 167, 168, 189
Riverside Park, Agawam, MA, 67, 81, 86, 104, 108, 185
Rocco, Ronnie, 110
Rockingham Speedway, Rockingham, NC, 135, 138, 142, 160
Rosati, John, 86, 107
Rosenfield, Joe, 34, 35

Ross, Billy "Hooks", 20, 26
Ross, Brian, 116
Ross, Chris, 116
Rossbach, Dave, 5, 6, 19–24, 27, 34, 40, 45, 68 and throughout
Roy, Louie "Bugsy", 16, 21, 138
Rudd, A.J., 160
Rudd, Linda, 150, 160, 161, 163, 164, 192
Rudd, Ricky, 137, 139, 150, 156, 159–164, 192–193
Ruggiero, Reggie, 110, 125, 182
Ruth, Babe, 189
Sacks, Greg, 119, 123, 129, 218, 219
Saleeba, Wally, 5, 16, 64
Salvatore, Pete, 2–4, 7–12, 13–15, 17, 68, 137, 153, 193, 218
San Bernardino County Sun, 44
Sanborn, Sammy, 4
Sanford Dragway, Sanford, ME, 19
Santos, Bob, 42, 56, 62
Savitsky, Barbara, 89, 90, 139
Schlaefer, Richie, 116, 117
Schrader, Ken, 141
Schulz, Fred, 42
Seekonk Speedway, Seekonk, MA, 4, 5, 11, 15, 16, 18, 19–21, 24 and throughout
Seymour the Clown, 65, 75
Shangri-La Speedway, Owego, NY, 45, 181
Slater, Bill, 64, 89
Sleeper, Wes, 45, 76
Smart, Don "Max" 138, 149, 151
Smart, Terry, 138, 149, 151
Smith, Ken, 139, 177, 178, 180, 185
Smith, Phil, 86, 88
Smith, Wayne, 192
Solhem, Ralph, 71
Speedway Scene, 34, 91, 92, 122, 136
Spencer, Jimmy, 186
Sprague, Bobby, 20, 21
Squier, Ken, 86, 175
St. Angelo, Ed, 117
Stacy, J.D., 144, 157

Stafford Motor Speedway, Stafford Springs, CT, 5, 11, 16, 18, 22, 23, 28, 29, 30 and throughout
Star Speedway, Epping, NH, 89, 96, 102, 177
Stearns, Bob, 71
Stevens, Bugs, 6, 22, 25, 29, 35, 38, 40–46, 55–60 and throughout
Stock Car Racing, 6, 44
Sturdevant, Bruce, 124
Sturdevant, Kathy, 124
Summers Jr., George, 5
Summers, Bill, 5
Summers, George, 5, 15, 20, 25, 27, 31, 33–38, 40 and throughout
Summers, Kathie, 5, 36, 37, 216
Summers, Maggie, 5, 33, 36, 37, 138, 151, 211, 212, 218, 219
Summers, Mary, 5, 216, 223
Summers, Rick, 5, 214, 215
Talladega Superspeedway, Talladega, AL, 4, 11, 137–140, 142–144, 147, 148, 153 and throughout
Tant, Jack, 6, 29
Tasca, Charlie, 212, 213
Tattersall Jr., Harvey, 69, 128
Taylor, Billy, 104
Taylor, Gomer, 123
Thompson Speedway, Thompson, CT, 6, 11, 18, 29, 33, 41, 45, 46 and throughout
Thompson, Dick, 44
Thompson, Lucky, 3
Thornton, Bill, 44
Tourigny, Dave, 41
Trenton Speedway, Trenton, NJ, 6, 7, 16, 23, 31, 32, 37, 42 and throughout
Trevis, Floyd, 165
Trickle, Dick, 113
Tripp, Johnny, 117
Troyer, Maynard, 42, 43, 46, 49, 76, 90, 108, 115 and throughout
Turner, Bobby, 52, 219
Utica-Rome Speedway, Vernon, NY, 41, 56

Vanesse, Ron, 80
Venditti, D. Anthony, 4, 5, 22, 28, 34, 36, 57, 68–69 and throughout
Venditti, Irene, 68, 117
Waltrip, Darrell, 137, 138, 139, 143, 156, 161, 162, 165 and throughout
Warren, Bentley, 15, 182
Waterford Speedbowl, Waterford, CT, 59, 67, 81, 86, 88, 89, 96, 102 and throughout
Welch, Bill, 61
West Peabody Speedway, West Peabody, MA, 11, 20
Westboro Speedway, Westboro, MA, 3, 4, 7, 9–11, 13–15, 17, 18, 20 and throughout
White, Ben, 140
Williams, Dick, 91, 127–132, 219
Williams, Ted, 5
Wood Brothers Racing, 154, 157, 178
Worley, Satch, 42, 53, 89, 96, 104, 134, 154
Wyckoff, Ron, 108, 109
Yarborough, Cale, 42, 139, 154, 165, 166, 183, 184, 185, 193 and throughout
Yates, Robert, 161
Yerrington, Ed, 86
Young, Lucky, 180
Zalenski, Beebe, 81
Zanardi, Pete, 57, 64
Zenobi, Billy, 108